CC Certified in Cybersecurity Cert Guide

Companion Website and Pearson Test Prep Access Code

Access interactive study tools on this book's companion website, including practice test software, review exercises, the Key Term flash card application, a study planner, and more!

To access the companion website, simply follow these steps:

1. Go to www.pearsonITcertification.com/register.

2. Enter the **print book ISBN**: 9780138200381.

3. Answer the security question to validate your purchase.

4. Go to your account page.

5. Click on the **Registered Products** tab.

6. Under the book listing, click on the **Access Bonus Content** link.

When you register your book, your Pearson Test Prep practice test access code will automatically be populated with the book listing under the Registered Products tab. You will need this code to access the practice test that comes with this book. You can redeem the code at **PearsonTestPrep.com**. Simply choose Pearson IT Certification as your product group and log into the site with the same credentials you used to register your book. Click the **Activate New Product** button and enter the access code. More detailed instructions on how to redeem your access code for both the online and desktop versions can be found on the companion website.

If you have any issues accessing the companion website or obtaining your Pearson Test Prep practice test access code, you can contact our support team by going to **pearsonitp.echelp.org**.

CC Certified in Cybersecurity Cert Guide

Mari Galloway
Amena Jamali

CC Certified in Cybersecurity Cert Guide

ISBN-13: 978-0-13-820038-1
ISBN-10: 0-13-820038-6

Library of Congress Cataloging-in-Publication Data Is on File.

1 2024

Trademarks

Warning and Disclaimer

Special Sales

For information about buying this title in bulk quantities, or for special sales opportunities (which may include electronic versions; custom cover designs; and content particular to your business, training goals, marketing focus, or branding interests), please contact our corporate sales department at corpsales@pearsoned.com or (800) 382-3419.

For government sales inquiries, please contact governmentsales@pearsoned.com.

For questions about sales outside the U.S., please contact intlcs@pearson.com.

GM K12, Early Career and Professional Learning
Soo Kang

Executive Editor
James Manly

Development Editor
Christopher A. Cleveland

Managing Editor
Sandra Schroeder

Senior Project Editor
Tonya Simpson

Copy Editor
Bill McManus

Indexer
Timothy Wright

Proofreader
Barbara Mack

Technical Editor
Dominique West

Publishing Coordinator
Cindy Teeters

Cover Designer
Chuti Prasertsith

Compositor
codeMantra

Contents at a Glance

Introduction   xviii

CHAPTER 1   Cybersecurity Principles   3

CHAPTER 2   Risk Management   13

CHAPTER 3   Threats to Security   33

CHAPTER 4   Physical Access Controls   53

CHAPTER 5   Logical Access Controls   71

CHAPTER 6   Computer Networking Fundamentals   85

CHAPTER 7   Network Security Infrastructure   111

CHAPTER 8   Data and the System   139

CHAPTER 9   Security in the Life   157

CHAPTER 10   Security in Emergencies   175

CHAPTER 11   Tying It All Together   199

CHAPTER 12   After the Certification   205

CHAPTER 13   Final Preparation   209

APPENDIX A   Answers to the "Do I Know This Already?" Quizzes and Q&A   211

APPENDIX B   *CC Certified in Cybersecurity Cert Guide* Exam Updates   223

Glossary of Key Terms   225

Index   239

Online Elements:

Glossary of Key Terms

APPENDIX A   Answers to the "Do I Know This Already?" Quizzes and Q&A

APPENDIX B   *CC Certified in Cybersecurity Cert Guide* Exam Updates

APPENDIX C   Study Planner

Table of Contents

Introduction   xviii

Chapter 1   **Cybersecurity Principles   3**

"Do I Know This Already?" Quiz   3

Foundation Topics   6

Information Assurance   6

The CIA Triad   7

Confidentiality   7

Integrity   8

Availability   8

Privacy   9

ISC2 Code of Ethics   9

Exam Preparation Tasks   10

Review All Key Topics   10

Define Key Terms   11

Q&A   11

References   11

Chapter 2   **Risk Management   13**

"Do I Know This Already" Quiz   13

Foundation Topics   18

Risk Management   18

Risks, Threats, and Vulnerabilities   18

The Scope of Risk Management   21

The Risk Management Process   22

Risk Identification   23

Risk Assessment   24

Risk Treatment   26

Security Controls and Governance   28

Exam Preparation Tasks   30

Review All Key Topics   30

Define Key Terms   31

Q&A   31

References   31

Chapter 3   Threats to Security   33

"Do I Know This Already?" Quiz   33

Foundation Topics   38

Threats to Security   38

Common Threat Categories   39

Malware   39

Viruses   39

Worms   40

Trojans   41

Ransomware   41

Advanced Persistent Threats   43

Network Attacks   43

Distributed Denial-of-Service Attack   43

Man-in-the-Middle Attack   44

Side-Channel Attack   44

Detection and Mitigation Techniques   44

Detection Tools   45

Scanning and Penetration Testing   48

Exam Preparation Tasks   48

Review All Key Topics   48

Define Key Terms   49

Q&A   49

References   50

Chapter 4   Physical Access Controls   53

"Do I Know This Already?" Quiz   53

Foundation Topics   56

Physical Security Controls   56

Badge Systems   56

Gates for Physical Protection   59

Types of Gate Entry Systems   59

Access Control   62

Environmental Design   62

Monitoring for Physical Security   63

Security Guards   63

Closed-Circuit Television   64

Alarm Systems   65

Logs and Documentation   65

Authorized Versus Unauthorized Personnel   66

Exam Preparation Tasks   66

Review All Key Topics   66

Define Key Terms   67

Q&A   67

References   67

Chapter 5   Logical Access Controls   71

"Do I Know This Already?" Quiz   71

Foundation Topics   74

Need to Know and Least Privilege   74

Segregation of Duties   75

Security Models   76

Discretionary Access Control   76

Mandatory Access Control   77

Role-Based Access Control   79

IAM and Automation   81

Exam Preparation Tasks   81

Review All Key Topics   81

Define Key Terms   82

Q&A   82

References   82

Chapter 6   Computer Networking Fundamentals   85

"Do I Know This Already" Quiz   85

Foundation Topics   89

Understanding Computer Networking   89

Ports and Protocols   93

OSI Model   94

Application Layer (Layer 7)   95

Presentation Layer (Layer 6)   96

Session Layer (Layer 5)   96

Transport Layer (Layer 4)   97

Network Layer (Layer 3)   98

Internet Protocol   98

Data Link Layer (Layer 2)   102

Protocols   103

Wireless   104

Physical Layer (Layer 1)   106

TCP/IP Model   106

Exam Preparation Tasks   107

Review All Key Topics   107

Define Key Terms   108

Q&A   108

References   109

Chapter 7   Network Security Infrastructure   111

"Do I Know This Already" Quiz   111

Foundation Topics   115

On-Premises Network Security Infrastructure   115

Environmental Controls   115

Fire Suppression Systems   116

Redundancy and High Availability   117

Memorandum of Understanding and Memorandum of Agreement   117

Designing Secure Networks   118

Demilitarized Zones   121

Virtual Local Area Networks   121

Virtual Private Networks   122

Network Access Control   123

Embedded Systems   124

Cloud Network Security Infrastructure   125

Cloud Deployment Models   125

Public   125

Private   126

Community   127

Hybrid   128

Cloud Service Models   129

Infrastructure as a Service   130

Platform as a Service   130

Software as a Service   131

Service-Level Agreement   132

Managed Service Provider   133

Cloud Challenges   134

Exam Preparation Tasks   135

Review All Key Topics   135

Define Key Terms   135

Q&A   136

References   136

Chapter 8   **Data and the System   139**

"Do I Know This Already?" Quiz   139

Foundation Topics   143

Data Security   143

Encryption   143

Hashing   144

Non-Repudiation   145

Authentication   146

One-Time Passwords   147

Password Policy   147

Data Handling   149

Data Classification   149

Data Labeling   150

Data Retention   151

Data Destruction   152

Data Handling Policy   153

Exam Preparation Tasks   153

Review All Key Topics   153

Define Key Terms   154

Q&A   154

References   154

Chapter 9   Security in the Life   157

"Do I Know This Already?" Quiz   158

Foundation Topics   162

System Hardening   162

    Baselines   162

    Patch Management   164

    Vulnerability Management   165

    System Updates and Upgrades   165

Logging and Monitoring   166

Security Policies   167

    Acceptable Use Policy   167

    Bring Your Own Device Policy   167

    Change Management Policy   168

    Privacy Policy   169

Security Awareness Training   170

    Social Engineering   170

    Password Protection   171

Exam Preparation Tasks   172

Review All Key Topics   172

Define Key Terms   172

Q&A   172

Reference   173

Chapter 10   Security in Emergencies   175

"Do I Know This Already?" Quiz   176

Foundation Topics   180

Incident Response   180

    Detection   181

    Classification   181

    Containment   182

    Response   183

    Recovery   183

    Reflection   183

    Testing   183

Business Continuity   184

Business Impact Analysis   184

Testing   185

Backup and Recovery   185

Disaster Recovery   188

Recovery Time Objective   189

Recovery Point Objective   189

Maximum Tolerable Downtime   190

Replication, Hot Sites, Warm Sites, and Cold Sites   190

Failover Testing   191

Governance Processes   191

Policies   193

Standards   193

Procedures   193

Guidelines   194

Regulations and Laws   194

Exam Preparation Tasks   195

Review All Key Topics   195

Define Key Terms   196

Q&A   196

References   197

Chapter 11   Tying It All Together   199

Security as a Whole   199

Defense-in-Depth   199

The Castle Analogy   200

The Whole of Information Assurance   202

Summary   202

Chapter 12   After the Certification   205

Take a Breather and Reflect   205

Update Your Professional Profiles   205

Showcase Your Passion and Knowledge   205

Seek Mentorship and Sponsorship   206

Stay Informed About Emerging Threats and Technologies   206

Contribute to the Community Through Thought Leadership   206

Explore Further Education Opportunities   207

Evaluate Career Progress and Set New Goals   207

Summary   207

Chapter 13   Final Preparation   209

Suggested Plan for Final Review and Study   209

Summary   210

Appendix A   Answers to the "Do I Know This Already?" Quizzes and Q&A   211

Appendix B   *CC Certified in Cybersecurity Cert Guide* Exam Updates   223

Glossary of Key Terms   225

Index   239

Online Elements:

Glossary of Key Terms

Appendix A   Answers to the "Do I Know This Already?" Quizzes and Q&A

Appendix B   *CC Certified in Cybersecurity Cert Guide* Exam Updates

Appendix C   Study Planner

About the Authors

Mari Galloway, a best-selling author of *Securing Our Future* and cyber professional, is the CEO and a founding board member for the Women's Society of Cyberjutsu (WSC), one of the fastest growing 501(c)3 nonprofit cybersecurity communities dedicated to bringing more women and girls to cyber. WSC provides its members with the resources and support required to enter and advance as cybersecurity professionals.

Mari began her career with Accenture, where she excelled as a network engineer. Mari is also a 2023 Presidential Lifetime Award winner and the inaugural ISC2 Diversity Award winner for 2019. With over 15 years in IT and cybersecurity, her experience spans network design, security architecture, risk assessments, vulnerability management, incident response, and policy development across government and commercial industries.

Mari holds a variety of technical and management certifications (CISSP, GIAC, CCNA, etc.) as well as a Bachelor of Business Administration in Computer Information Systems from Columbus State University and a Master of Science in Information Systems from Strayer University.

Mari is currently a resident of Las Vegas and is the CEO of a cybersecurity consulting company. She regularly contributes content to security blogs and training companies across the country as well as an adjunct professor for the University of Maryland Global Campus (UMGC). She also lends her time to various organizations as an award judge, mentor, and advisor. Outside of being a geek, Mari enjoys arts, puzzles, and Lego!

Amena Jamali is a person with multiple facets. With her rational mind, she is a cybersecurity auditor and an aspiring scholar in the field of disinformation research and cyber psychology. With her creative mind, she is an epic fantasy author with four books published so far in the *The Lord of Freedom* series and many more coming. Her pursuit of truth has been shaped by an eclectic mixture of education: a Bachelor of Arts in Politics and a Master of Science in Cybersecurity from the University of Dallas, which is located in her home state of Texas. In various forums, she speaks and writes about political philosophy, information ethics, governance, risk, compliance, and data privacy, and she is equally passionate about diversity, equity, and inclusion and about the representation of powerful women in literature. A firm believer in the supportive power of community, Amena is an active member of and leader in the Women's Society of Cyberjutsu and has in 2023 won that organization's Cyber Rising Star Award. When she is not working, writing, or theorizing, she reads, learns languages, watches superhero movies, embroiders, and bakes delicious pies.

Dedication

From Mari:

To my mom and sister, thank you for always supporting any and every decision I have made, including writing this book. To the rest of my family and friends, your support on this journey does not go unnoticed. Thank you for always believing in me and motivating me to keep dreaming big.

From Amena:

To my mother and my father, who introduced me to technology and taught me its value in building a better and more equitable world, and to the Divine for Whose praise I offer all of my creative efforts. Thank you for being with me on every journey.

Acknowledgments

Mari and Amena together offer our thanks to the women and allies of the Women's Society of Cyberjutsu. Their encouragement, amplification, and support have kept us going even on the most difficult days, and without them we would not have been able to write this book. We hope our work here will contribute to WSC's mission of empowering women to succeed in cybersecurity.

About the Technical Reviewer

Dominique West is a seasoned security leader with more than a decade of experience in the information technology industry. Specializing in digital cloud transformation, information security governance, risk, and compliance management, as well as cloud and cybersecurity strategy, Dominique has made significant contributions across various industries.

At Datadog, Dominique leads the Governance, Risk, and Compliance division, leveraging her extensive experience to align compliance initiatives with strategic business objectives. Her leadership is instrumental in maintaining and executing a robust compliance roadmap crucial to supporting Datadog's growth and revenue targets while upholding established security standards. Dominique takes pride in cultivating teams that not only excel but also embody a proactive and constructive security mindset. Her multifaceted expertise, spanning cloud security, risk management, compliance, and overall cybersecurity, drives excellence within Datadog and beyond.

Dominique holds a Bachelor of Business Administration in Computer Information Systems from Baruch College, as well as a Master of Science in Cybersecurity from the University of Dallas. Her expertise is further underscored by her CISSP certification. Beyond her professional accomplishments, Dominique is deeply committed to fostering diversity and inclusion in the cybersecurity field. She is the founder of Security in Color, a platform dedicated to providing education and career resources in cybersecurity to underrepresented groups. Additionally, Dominique serves as the NYC Chapter lead for the Women's Society of Cyberjutsu, a nonprofit organization focused on empowering women and allies in cybersecurity.

Dominique's dedication to education extends beyond her advocacy work. She has developed several courses, in partnership with LinkedIn and Pluralsight, aimed at educating users about cloud security, cybersecurity, as well as governance, risk, and compliance (GRC). Additionally, Dominique has lent her expertise as a technical editor, co-contributor for various cybersecurity professional books, and is the co-author for the Google Cloud Professional Cloud Security Engineer exam.

We Want to Hear from You!

As the reader of this book, *you* are our most important critic and commentator. We value your opinion and want to know what we're doing right, what we could do better, what areas you'd like to see us publish in, and any other words of wisdom you're willing to pass our way.

We welcome your comments. You can email or write to let us know what you did or didn't like about this book—as well as what we can do to make our books better.

Please note that we cannot help you with technical problems related to the topic of this book.

When you write, please be sure to include this book's title and author as well as your name and email address. We will carefully review your comments and share them with the author and editors who worked on the book.

Email: community@informit.com

Reader Services

Register your copy of *CC Certified in Cybersecurity Cert Guide* for convenient access to downloads, updates, and corrections as they become available. To start the registration process, go to www.pearsonitcertification.com/register and log in or create an account*. Enter the product ISBN 9780138200381 and click Submit. When the process is complete, you will find any available bonus content under Registered Products.

*Be sure to check the box that you would like to hear from us to receive exclusive discounts on future editions of this product.

Introduction

Welcome to the *CC Certified in Cybersecurity Cert Guide*. Certified in Cybersecurity is a new certification by ISC2 that enables new entrants to cybersecurity to demonstrate their comprehension of essential technical concepts to employers as they begin their cybersecurity career. The Certified in Cybersecurity exam is designed to be vendor-neutral and measures your knowledge of industry-standard technologies and methodologies. It acts as a great stepping stone to other vendor-specific certifications and careers. We developed this book to be a resource that you can use to study for the exam and then keep on your bookshelf for later use as a cybersecurity practitioner.

We'd like to note that covering all security concepts in depth in a single book is not feasible. However, you aren't expected to have that level of knowledge for the Certified in Cybersecurity exam, which is intended to assess a basic level of technical and governance-related security knowledge. Keep this in mind while reading through this text, and remember that the main goal of this book is to help you pass the Certified in Cybersecurity exam, not to be the master of all security. Not just yet at least!

Good luck as you prepare to take the Certified in Cybersecurity exam. As you read through this book, you will be building an impenetrable castle of knowledge (rather like security itself!), which will culminate in the know-how to pass the exam.

Goals and Methods

The number one goal of this book is to help you pass the ISC2 Certified in Cybersecurity exam. To that effect, we have filled this book and practice exams with more than 200 questions/answers and explanations. The exams are located in Pearson Test Prep practice test software in a custom test environment. These tests are geared to check your knowledge and ready you for the real exam.

The ISC2 Certified in Cybersecurity exam involves familiarity with computer security theory and hands-on know-how. To aid you in mastering and understanding the Certified in Cybersecurity objectives, this book uses the following methods:

- **Opening topics list:** This defines the topics to be covered in the chapter.

- **Foundation Topics:** The heart of the chapter. The text explains the topics from a theory-based standpoint, as well as from a hands-on perspective. This includes in-depth descriptions, tables, and figures that are geared to build your knowledge so that you can pass the exam. The chapters are broken down into two or more Foundation Topics sections each.

- **Key Topics:** The Key Topic icons indicate important sections, paragraphs, figures, tables, and lists of information that you should know for the exam. They are interspersed throughout the chapter and are listed in table format at the end of the chapter.

- **Key Terms:** Key terms are *emphasized* in each chapter and are listed without definitions at the end of each chapter. See whether you can define them after you have read the chapter, and then check your work against the complete key term definitions in the glossary.

- **Q&A:** These quizzes, and answers with explanations, are meant to gauge your knowledge of the subjects. If an answer to a question doesn't come readily to you, be sure to review that portion of the chapter.

- **Practice Exams:** There are 200 exams included in the Pearson Test Prep practice test software. These exams test your knowledge and skills in a realistic testing environment. Take these after you have read through the entire book. Master one, then move on to the next. Take any available bonus exams last.

Who Should Read This Book?

This book is intended for anyone who wants to enter the field of cybersecurity or to cement their knowledge of the basics. We recommend this book to a variety of readers, including those who are preparing for the Certified in Cybersecurity exam and those who want a reminder of the principles and foundations of cybersecurity.

This book is also written for those people who intend to study for additional cybersecurity certifications after passing the Certified in Cybersecurity exam. Where possible, we have elaborated on topics such that these readers would be able to transition to future studies and expand their comprehension of the subject material.

Because the Certified in Cybersecurity exam is intended for new entrants to the field who might not have IT experience, the authors recommend only that you have an elementary grasp of networking and computer operations (e.g., understand the basics of operating systems, networks, and password setup) before you begin Chapter 1. For a deeper exploration of any topic in this book, the authors recommend further study. The focus of this book is to show how the elements of cybersecurity weave together into a cohesive whole and to provide a hint of what to expect upon entrance into the field.

Certified in Cybersecurity Exam Topics

If you haven't bookmarked or reviewed the Certified in Cybersecurity exam objectives, do it now from the ISC2 website: https://www.isc2.org/certifications/cc/cc-certification-exam-outline. Use the exam objectives list to aid in your studies while you use this book.

The following two tables are excerpts from the exam objectives document. Table I-1 lists the Certified in Cybersecurity domains and each domain's percentage of the exam.

Table I-1   Certified in Cybersecurity Exam Domains

Domain	Exam Topic	% of Exam
1	Security Principles	26%
2	Business Continuity (BC), Disaster Recovery (DR) & Incident Response Concepts	10%
3	Access Controls Concepts	22%
4	Network Security	24%
5	Security Operations	18%

The Certified in Cybersecurity domains are then further broken down into individual objectives.

Table I-2 lists the Certified in Cybersecurity exam objectives and their related chapters in this book. It does not include the topics listed for each objective, but you will find those topics listed at the beginning of the corresponding chapter.

Table I-2   Certified in Cybersecurity Exam Objectives

Objective	Chapter(s)
Domain 1: Security Principles	
1.1 Understand the security concepts of information assurance	1, 8
1.2 Understand the risk management process	2
1.3 Understand security controls	2
1.4 Understand ISC2 Code of Ethics	1
1.5 Understand governance processes	2, 10

Objective	Chapter(s)
Domain 2: Business Continuity (BC), Disaster Recovery (DR) & Incidence Response Concepts	
2.1 Understand business continuity (BC)	10
2.2 Understand disaster recovery (DR)	10
2.3 Understand incident response	10
Domain 3: Access Controls Concepts	
3.1 Understand physical access controls	4
3.2 Understand logical access controls	5
Domain 4: Network Security	
4.1 Understand computer networking	6
4.2 Understand network threats and attacks	3
4.3 Understand network security infrastructure	7
Domain 5: Security Operations	
5.1 Understand data security	8, 9
5.2 Understand system hardening	9
5.3 Understand best practice security policies	8, 9
5.4 Understand security awareness training	9

How to Access the Pearson Test Prep (PTP) App

You have two options for installing and using the Pearson Test Prep application: a web app and a desktop app. To use the Pearson Test Prep application, start by accessing the registration code that comes with the book. You can access the code in these ways:

- You can get your access code by registering the print ISBN 9780138200381 on https://www.pearsonitcertification.com/register. Make sure to use the print book ISBN, regardless of whether you purchased an eBook or the print book. After you register the book, your access code will be populated on your account page under the Registered Products tab. Instructions for how to redeem the code are available on the book's companion website by clicking the **Access Bonus Content** link.

- If you purchase the Premium Edition eBook and Practice Test directly from the Pearson IT Certification website, the code will be populated on your account page after purchase. Just log in at https://www.pearsonitcertification.com, click **Account** to see details of your account, and click the **Digital Purchases** tab.

NOTE   After you register your book, your code can always be found in your account under the Registered Products tab.

Once you have the access code, to find instructions about both the PTP web app and the desktop app, follow these steps:

Step 1.   Open this book's companion website as shown on the first page of the book.

Step 2.   Click the **Practice Exams** button.

Step 3.   Follow the instructions listed there for both installing the desktop app and using the web app.

Note that if you want to use the web app only at this point, just navigate to https://www.pearsontestprep.com, log in using the same credentials used to register your book or purchase the Premium Edition, and register for this book's practice tests using the registration code you just found. The process should take only a couple of minutes.

Customizing Your Exams

Once you are in the exam settings screen, you can choose to take exams in one of three modes:

- **Study mode:** Allows you to fully customize your exams and review answers as you are taking the exam. This is typically the mode you would use first to assess your knowledge and identify information gaps.

- **Practice Exam mode:** Locks certain customization options, as it is presenting a realistic exam experience. Use this mode when you are preparing to test your exam readiness.

- **Flash Card mode:** Strips out the answers and presents you with only the question stem. This mode is great for late-stage preparation when you really want to challenge yourself to provide answers without the benefit of seeing multiple-choice options. This mode will not provide the detailed score reports that the other two modes will, so you should not use it if you are trying to identify knowledge gaps.

In addition to these three modes, you will be able to select the source of your questions. You can choose to take exams that cover all of the chapters or you can narrow your selection to just a single chapter or the chapters that make up specific parts in the book. All chapters are selected by default. If you want to narrow your focus to individual chapters, simply deselect all the chapters and then select only those on which you wish to focus in the Objectives area.

You can also select the exam banks on which to focus. Each exam bank comes complete with a full exam of questions that cover topics in every chapter. You can have the test engine serve up exams from all banks or just from one individual bank by selecting the desired banks in the exam bank area.

There are several other customizations you can make to your exam from the exam settings screen, such as the time of the exam, the number of questions served up, whether to randomize questions and answers, whether to show the number of correct answers for multiple-answer questions, or whether to serve up only specific types of questions. You can also create custom test banks by selecting only questions that you have marked or questions on which you have added notes.

Updating Your Exams

If you are using the online version of the Pearson Test Prep software, you should always have access to the latest version of the software as well as the exam data. If you are using the Windows desktop version, every time you launch the software, it will check to see if there are any updates to your exam data and automatically download any changes that were made since the last time you used the software. This requires that you are connected to the Internet at the time you launch the software.

Sometimes, due to many factors, the exam data might not fully download when you activate your exam. If you find that figures or exhibits are missing, you might need to manually update your exams.

To update a particular exam you have already activated and downloaded, simply select the Tools tab and click the Update Products button. Again, this is only an issue with the desktop Windows application.

If you wish to check for updates to the Pearson Test Prep exam engine software, Windows desktop version, simply select the Tools tab and click the Update Application button. This will ensure you are running the latest version of the software engine.

Figure Credits

Cover image: Photon photo/Shutterstock

Figure 3.1: Nicescene/Shutterstock

Figure 4.2: Serjio74/Shutterstock

Figure 4.3: Fedor Selivanov/Shutterstock

Figure 4.4: Ratchat/Shutterstock

Figure 7.1: Ohmega1982/Shutterstock

Figure 7.2b: yyang/Shutterstock

Figure 7.4: vschlichting/123RF

This chapter covers the following topics and corresponding proficiencies:

- **Information assurance:** Describe the principles of securing information assets and information systems.

- **Confidentiality, integrity, and availability:** Describe the differences between the concepts of confidentiality, integrity, and availability, also known as the CIA triad, and the importance of each as a measure of information assurance.

- **Privacy:** Describe the concept of protecting sensitive information and understand the difference between privacy and confidentiality.

- **ISC2 Code of Ethics:** Understand the code of ethics to which those who attain the Certified in Cybersecurity certification are expected to adhere.

CHAPTER 1

Cybersecurity Principles

Welcome to cybersecurity! As you begin your journey to learn about the field, get your initial certification, and find your first role, there is a lot to learn about the basics. So, let's get started. In this chapter, you will learn about the principles of information assurance—the CIA triad, authentication, non-repudiation, and privacy—and the ISC2 Code of Ethics. The definitions given in this chapter will build your knowledge and understanding for digesting material in the chapters to come, as well as give you the terminology needed to get your start in cyber-security. The chapter will conclude with an overview of how the principles of information assurance are implemented.

This chapter covers the following Certified in Cybersecurity exam objectives:

- 1.1 Understand the security concepts of information assurance

  - 1.1a Confidentiality

  - 1.1b Integrity

  - 1.1c Availability

  - 1.1f Privacy

- 1.4 Understand ISC2 Code of Ethics

  - 1.4a Professional code of conduct

"Do I Know This Already?" Quiz

The "Do I Know This Already?" quiz allows you to decide whether you need to read this entire chapter or skip to the "Exam Preparation Tasks" section. If you doubt your selection of answers to these questions or your own assessment of your knowledge of these topics, you may want to read the entire chapter. Table 1-1 lists the major headings in this chapter and their corresponding "Do I Know This Already?" Quiz questions. You can find the answers in Appendix A, "Answers to the 'Do I Know This Already?' Quizzes and Q&A Sections." Good luck!

Table 1-1 "Do I Know This Already?" Section-to-Question Mapping

Foundation Topics Section	Questions
Information Assurance	1–2
The CIA Triad	3–5
Privacy	6
ISC2 Code of Ethics	7

CAUTION   The goal of self-assessment is to gauge your mastery of the topics in this chapter. If you do not know the answer to a question or are only partially sure of the answer, you should mark that question as wrong for purposes of the self-assessment. Giving yourself credit for an answer you correctly guess skews your self-assessment results and might provide you with a false sense of security.

1. What is information assurance?

    a. A law

    b. An objective

    c. Confidentiality

    d. A technical control

2. Information assurance is to provide which of the following?

    a. A guarantee of availability only

    b. Risk assessment

    c. A guarantee of data security

    d. None of these answers are correct.

3. What is confidentiality?

    a. Data secrecy

    b. Restricting access to data

    c. Preventing unauthorized disclosures

    d. All of these answers are correct.

4. What is integrity?

    a. Preventing data from being corrupted

    b. Not allowing unauthorized changes

    c. Tracking and logging file access

    d. All of these answers are correct.

5. What is availability?

    a. Timely access to data

    b. Reliable functionality of information systems

    c. Uninterrupted data flows

    d. All of these answers are correct.

6. Privacy is _____.

    a. A fancy name for confidentiality

    b. The control, possession, and secrecy of a person's or group's data

    c. A purely technical control

    d. Something made up by lawyers and politicians

7. Which of these isn't part of one of the four canons of the ISC2 Code of Ethics?

    a. Maintaining a perfect track record of preventing security incidents

    b. Protecting society and the common good

    c. Protecting the profession

    d. Acting with honor and honesty

Foundation Topics

We live in an interconnected world where both individual and collective actions have the potential to result in inspiring goodness or tragic harm. The mission of cybersecurity is to protect each of us, our community, our critical infrastructure, our economies, and our nations from the harm that can result from inadvertent or intentional misuse, compromise, or destruction of information and information systems. The pursuit of that mission is accomplished through the implementation of various types of security and IT controls—the most important of which will be discussed in this guide. But, first, a few principles.

Information Assurance

We discussed mission and implementation. But what is the link between the two? When we implement controls in order to fulfill our mission, what task are we actually seeking to accomplish? That task is information assurance.

Information assurance is, essentially, about ensuring data is where it is supposed to be, in the form it is supposed to be, and accessible only to the intended people to whom it is supposed to be accessible. Information assurance is intended to provide a guarantee of data security, and that is the crux of cybersecurity, because data is the lifeblood of the Information Age.

Data comprises the systems and the applications we use—it is what makes them valuable. Imagine a computer system without data. Would we expend resources to protect an empty system? Sure, the computers, servers, routers, and cables have financial value, but we wouldn't even assemble the system unless it was intended to contain data. So, data is what we aim to protect, and that is why the objective of cybersecurity, information assurance, is about data in all of its various forms. Consequently, when we think about that objective, we also consider the systems that protect the data, the applications that process or generate the data, and the people who use the data or who are the subjects of the data. We must analyze all the ways the data is tied to the lives of human beings and arrange our assessment of threats and efforts of protection accordingly. These elements together lead us to the definition of *cybersecurity*: the protection of data, systems, and networks from unauthorized access, criminal use, and other threats.

With this understanding, we grasp the mission and the objective of cybersecurity. Now, let's dive deeper into the principles.

The CIA Triad

There are six components to information assurance: the pillars of confidentiality, integrity, and availability, and the concepts of privacy, *authentication*, and *non-repudiation*. Because these last two concepts require knowledge of access controls and cryptography, we have elected to discuss them in Chapter 9, "Security in the Life." However, their definitions are included at the end of this chapter.

 ### Confidentiality

Let's discuss confidentiality first. According to the National Institute of Standards and Technology (NIST) publication *Minimum Security Requirements for Federal Information and Information Systems* (FIPS Pub. 200), *confidentiality* is "preserving authorized restrictions on information access and disclosure, including means for protecting personal privacy and proprietary information." What this means, in practice, is understanding the nature of the data and implementing appropriate protections—understanding whether the data is secret and, if so, how secret the data is; ensuring that the data is treated with the level of care required; and ensuring that the data is accessed only by users who are supposed to have access.

To further elaborate on this concept, let's consider an example: protected health information (PHI), a category of data that encompasses medical records as defined under the U.S. Health Insurance Portability and Accountability Act (HIPAA) (see Chapter 8, "Data and the System," and Chapter 10, "Security in Emergencies," for more information about PHI). HIPAA requires PHI to be considered confidential in every organization that deals with it. Broadly, PHI is sensitive data about a person's mental and physical health and could include, among other information, the results of doctor visits, surgeries, and exams. Disclosure of a person's PHI could be a source of great harm to that person.

Now consider a different example: a company's business secrets, such as proprietary algorithms, designs, and strategies. If that information were no longer confidential, it could be a source of great harm to that company and potentially destroy its business. Keeping the information secret and preventing unauthorized disclosure of it ensures that it retains its value.

These are some of the types of data that we in cybersecurity are tasked to protect. The more harm that the unauthorized disclosure of a certain set of data would cause, the greater the level of confidentiality and thus the greater the level of control required to protect it. This is why many organizations have multiple tiers of confidentiality, such as public, internal, and confidential, or public, confidential, secret, and top secret. Multiple types of controls are used to ensure confidentiality in an organization, including access control and encryption. We'll discuss these in depth later.

So, if we now know what confidentiality means, we also understand why controls have to be designed in a way that ensures this pillar of the CIA triad remains inviolate.

Integrity

Integrity is the next pillar of the CIA triad. Referring again to FIPS Pub. 200, NIST defines *integrity* as "guarding against improper information modification or destruction, and includes ensuring information non-repudiation and authenticity." Essentially, integrity means ensuring the data isn't changed or deleted without authorization and being able to prove that.

Consider what would happen if the data we were trying to protect was secret but corrupted. It wouldn't be of much use then. With our examples of PHI and business secrets, if the letters or the numbers were jumbled or the files wouldn't open, the data would lose all value, and there would be no point to our having kept it secret. And what if that data was information stored in an official system of record, such as one for birth certificates or public benefit information? That could have an impact on people's lives. So, ensuring that information isn't changed or destroyed without proper authorization is essential to the value of the data. Controls used to ensure integrity include file integrity monitoring (as the name suggests), logging access and change attempts, and access control.

Availability

Availability is the final pillar of the CIA triad. FIPS Pub. 200 defines *availability* as "ensuring timely and reliable access to and use of information." Essentially, availability means ensuring the data is accessible when and how it's needed.

Having data that is secret and uncorrupted is all well and good, but what's the point if we can't use the data? Data does not (usually, at least) exist in systems only as a record of the world on a cold hard drive that's never, ever supposed to be accessed—data is meant to be accessed for specific purposes, used in various ways by applications, and those applications provide certain services to individuals and organizations. If the data isn't available to those applications at the time that they need it, users wouldn't be able to accomplish their tasks.

Taking our earlier examples a little further, imagine a medical device that delivers medication. A certain type of data is required for the use of that device, so, if the device doesn't get that data, or doesn't get the data at the time it is supposed to, how would that impact the patient? Alternatively, imagine a business application that processes critical business records and compiles a certain kind of report. If the data flow to that application is interrupted, the user wouldn't be able to generate the expected report. The data must be usable at the correct time. Controls to ensure availability include network redundancy, capacity management, and service-level agreement (SLA) monitoring.

NOTE   For the Certified in Cybersecurity exam, understand how the three pillars of the CIA triad are distinct and why each is important—the pillars will show up in exam questions, and subsequent concepts and categorizations build upon them.

Privacy

Let's move on to another integral concept of information assurance: *privacy*. There are multiple definitions of privacy, as this is a topic of great importance in the field today; however, to begin our discussion, let's consider this definition of *privacy* from NIST Special Publication 800-130: "Assurance that the confidentiality of, and access to, certain information about an entity is protected." Essentially, privacy is proof that sensitive data is secret, will remain so, and won't be accessed without permission.

As we can see from that definition, privacy is related to confidentiality. But, while confidentiality is primarily a cybersecurity concept, or a legal or a business one, privacy is a political and a philosophical idea as well as a cybersecurity term, a question of rights beyond only the uses in technology. Confidentiality is restricted to the controls necessary to keeping the information secret, while privacy is, as NIST IR 4734 states (in an older definition maintained in the organization's online glossary), "the right of a party to maintain control over and confidentiality of information about itself." To simplify it in order to understand the difference, confidentiality is about the technical secrecy of data, whereas privacy is the control and possession of data, as well as its secrecy.

Remember our earlier example about health information? What would happen to the people who are the subjects of that data if it was posted on the Internet?

This difference between confidentiality and privacy is an important distinction, especially as more and more states pass privacy laws in the United States and more and more nations pass such laws around the world. As the world grows increasingly more connected, with increasingly larger amounts of information about individuals becoming digitized, collectors and processors of data have a great responsibility to ensure that data remains private. As cybersecurity professionals, we are at the forefront of ensuring data privacy is managed responsibly. Yet that responsibly is not only legal but ethical as well. Which brings us to our final topic for this first chapter.

ISC2 Code of Ethics

The governing body for the Certified in Cybersecurity certification, ISC2, has published a code of ethics on its website that all professionals who are certified by the organization must follow. The *ISC2 Code of Ethics* offers very general guidance in order to give direction while also not becoming a replacement for ethical judgment. So that you know what you will be agreeing to as you proceed on this journey, that code has been copied in the text that follows:

Code of Ethics Preamble:

- The safety and welfare of society and the common good, duty to our principals, and to each other, requires that we adhere, and be seen to adhere, to the highest ethical standards of behavior.

- Therefore, strict adherence to this Code is a condition of certification.

Code of Ethics Canons:

- Protect society, the common good, necessary public trust and confidence, and the infrastructure.

- Act honorably, honestly, justly, responsibly, and legally.

- Provide diligent and competent service to principals.

- Advance and protect the profession.

In the authors' opinion, we believe these words say plenty about the mission of cyber-security, the ethical principles we are all called upon to uphold, the responsibilities we have to our organizations, our societies, and our nations, and the duty of community we owe to each other as we go about our roles, no matter what they might be.

Exam Preparation Tasks

As mentioned in the Introduction, you have a couple of choices for exam preparation: the exercises here, Chapter 13, "Final Preparation," and the exam simulation questions in the Pearson Test Prep Software Online.

Review All Key Topics

Review the most important topics in this chapter, noted with the Key Topics icon in the outer margin of the page. Table 1-2 lists a reference of these key topics and the page numbers on which each is found.

Table 1-2 Key Topics for Chapter 1

Key Topic Element	Description	Page Number
Section	Information Assurance	6
Section	Confidentiality	7
Section	Integrity	8

Key Topic Element	Description	Page Number
Section	Availability	8
Section	Privacy	9
Section	ISC2 Code of Ethics	9

Define Key Terms

Define the following key terms from this chapter and check your answers in the glossary:

information assurance, authentication, non-repudiation, confidentiality, integrity, availability, privacy, ISC2 Code of Ethics

Q&A

The answers to these questions appear in Appendix A. For practice with the multiple-choice format of the Certified in Cybersecurity exam questions, use the Pearson Test Prep Software Online.

1. What is the objective of information assurance and why is it important?

2. What are the three pillars of information assurance? What do they each stand for?

3. What is privacy, what is its relationship to confidentiality, and why is it important?

4. What is the ISC2 Code of Ethics?

References

CISA, "What Is Cybersecurity?": https://www.cisa.gov/news-events/news/what-cybersecurity#:~:text=Cybersecurity%20is%20the%20art%20of,integrity%2C%20and%20availability%20of%20information

NIST FIPS Pub. 200, *Minimum Security Requirements for Federal Information and Information Systems* (Appendix A): https://nvlpubs.nist.gov/nistpubs/FIPS/NIST.FIPS.200.pdf

NIST SP 800-130, *A Framework for Designing Cryptographic Key Management Systems*: https://nvlpubs.nist.gov/nistpubs/SpecialPublications/NIST.SP.800-130.pdf

NIST IR 4734, *Foundations of a Security Policy for Use of the National Research and Educational Network*: https://nvlpubs.nist.gov/nistpubs/Legacy/IR/nistir4734.pdf

ISC2 Code of Ethics: https://www.isc2.org/Ethics

This chapter covers the following topics:

- **Risk management:** Understand the process of managing risk such that future emergencies are adequately prepared for.

- **Threats and vulnerabilities:** Differentiate between threats and vulnerabilities and the roles each play in risk management.

- **Likelihood and impact:** Differentiate between likelihood and impact and the roles each play in a risk assessment.

- **Risk priorities:** Describe the concept of assigning priorities to risks so that the organization can judge which ones are more important and in which order they must be remediated.

- **Risk identification:** Describe the process of considering a variety of areas, including technological, business, and regulatory, and deciding which risks are applicable to an organization.

- **Risk assessment:** Describe the process of scoring risk and deciding responses to risks based on the organization's risk tolerance.

- **Risk tolerance:** Understand the concept of risk appetite, as well as what factors decide an organization's risk appetite.

- **Risk treatment:** Describe the process of mapping out plans for risk, monitoring the implementation of those plans, and regularly reviewing them to ensure risks are addressed per the organization's requirements.

- **Security controls:** Understand the concept of administrative, technical, and physical safeguards designed to address risk.

- **Governance processes:** Understand the importance of governance documentation in establishing security controls.

Risk Management

Now that you've learned about the cybersecurity principles introduced in Chapter 1, this chapter discusses another foundational area: risk management. By understanding risk management and the related terminology, you will have the foundational knowledge to understand why certain security controls are implemented in certain ways and in certain situations. You will gain a better understanding of the big picture as you start to put together the parts—which will help you understand the method behind the madness, to paraphrase Shakespeare. The chapter will conclude with an overview on security controls and introduce the technical areas covered in the chapters to come.

This chapter covers the following Certified in Cybersecurity exam objectives:

- 1.2 Understand the risk management process
  - 1.2a Risk management (e.g., risk priorities, risk tolerance)
  - 1.2b Risk identification, assessment and treatment
- 1.3 Understand security controls
  - 1.3a Technical controls
  - 1.3b Administrative controls
  - 1.3c Physical controls
- 1.5 Understand governance processes
  - 1.5a Policies
  - 1.5b Procedures
  - 1.5c Standards
  - 1.5d Regulations and laws

"Do I Know This Already" Quiz

The "Do I Know This Already?" quiz allows you to decide whether you need to read this entire chapter or skip to the "Exam Preparation Tasks" section.

If you doubt your selection of answers to these questions or your own assessment of your knowledge of these topics, you may want to read the entire chapter. Table 2-1 lists the major headings in this chapter and their corresponding "Do I Know This Already?" Quiz questions. You can find the answers in Appendix A, "Answers to the 'Do I Know This Already?' Quizzes and Q&A Sections." Good luck!

Table 2-1 "Do I Know This Already?" Section-to-Question Mapping

Foundation Topics Section	Questions
Risk Management	1
Risks, Threats, and Vulnerabilities	2–5
The Scope of Risk Management	6
The Risk Management Process	7–14
Security Controls and Governance	15–17

CAUTION The goal of self-assessment is to gauge your mastery of the topics in this chapter. If you do not know the answer to a question or are only partially sure of the answer, you should mark that question as wrong for purposes of the self-assessment. Giving yourself credit for an answer you correctly guess skews your self-assessment results and might provide you with a false sense of security.

1. What is risk management?
   a. The source of rationale behind cybersecurity controls
   b. Planning for future emergencies
   c. A lot of administrative work
   d. All of these answers are correct.

2. Which of the following is a source of danger to information systems?
   a. Risk
   b. Threat
   c. Vulnerability
   d. All of these answers are correct.

3. Which of the following is a weakness in information systems?
   a. Risk
   b. Threat

  c. Vulnerability

  d. All of these answers are correct.

4. Which of the following are two components to risk?

  a. Threat and vulnerability

  b. Treatment and assessment

  c. Priorities and tolerance

  d. Likelihood and impact

5. How are risk priorities determined?

  a. Through the calculation of likelihood and impact

  b. Based on the analyst's whim

  c. Based on what an organization can afford to address

  d. All risks are given equal priority

6. What does it mean to determine the scope of a risk assessment?

  a. Looking at the company offices through a telescope

  b. Determining what the risk analyst has time to assess

  c. Determining whether the assessment covers one system, multiple systems, or the whole organization

  d. Risk assessments should cover every part of the organization.

7. How many steps are there in risk management?

  a. Three

  b. Five

  c. Six

  d. There are various models, so all these answers are correct.

8. What types of risks should be considered in a risk assessment?

  a. Only technical risks

  b. Only business risks

  c. Only legal and regulatory risks

  d. All of these answers are correct.

9. How should risks be identified?

   a. By reading industry articles, journals, and reports

   b. By evaluating the current state of the organization's systems

   c. Using professional experience and judgment

   d. All of these answers are correct.

10. What happens in a risk assessment?

   a. Based on risk identification and prioritization, scoring risks, evaluating scores, and choosing a response

   b. Treating risks based on what's best for the organization

   c. Brainstorming possible emergencies

   d. Creating large and annoying matrices

11. What are the four types of responses to risks?

   a. Mitigate, remediate, ameliorate, reduce

   b. Avoid, accept, reduce, transfer

   c. Deny, transfer, reduce, ignore

   d. Tolerate, treat, transfer, accept

12. What is risk tolerance?

   a. How risk-averse an organization is

   b. The measuring stick by which we choose our risk responses

   c. The result of a variety of factors, such as organization type and leadership

   d. All of these answers are correct.

13. Which of the following is the risk that will remain after a treatment plan is implemented?

   a. Mitigated risk

   b. Risk tolerance

   c. Business risk

   d. Residual risk

14. What are the three parts to risk treatment?

   a. Mapping out a plan, assigning a control owner, and regular monitoring and review

   b. Assigning ratings, assessing the organization, and regular monitoring and review

   c. Mapping out a plan, planning a meeting, and holding said meeting

   d. One part: deciding how risk will be treated

15. How are security controls related to risk management?

   a. They are not related.

   b. Each control addresses a risk, whether directly defined or not.

   c. They are a type of risk management.

   d. They are the defined and documented risk treatment plans.

16. What are the three types of security controls?

   a. Written, technical, and managerial

   b. Penetrating testing, vulnerability scanning, and cryptography

   c. Administrative, technical, and physical

   d. Risk management, access control, and network security

17. What is governance documentation? (Choose all that apply.)

   a. Unnecessary, boring things to read

   b. Documentation based on regulations and laws

   c. Part of every control in a well-developed information security program

   d. Documentation used only by the human resources department

Foundation Topics

Risk Management

What is risk management? It is, at its core, a simple idea: planning for future emergencies and engaging in activities to lessen the impact of, or even prevent, those emergencies. It's sort of like installing fire alarms, replacing their batteries every six months to a year, and making an escape plan in case of a fire (hopefully at least some of us do that!). Risk management is a way to prevent catastrophe through preparation, and it's a critical part of cybersecurity. It explains *why* certain security controls are implemented and configured in certain ways. Without risk management, we would be directionless and unable to fulfill our mission of protection.

So, then, why do we have a whole chapter for this simple idea? Why do we have a list of terms to memorize and procedures to follow? Well, although risk management is simple, it is also incredibly complex—both because of the need to foresee multiple types of threats and vulnerabilities and because it is not always given priority. Risk management feels a lot like administrative overhead and bureaucratic red tape, with its requirements for documentation, planning, monitoring, and review. Not every organization invests time and resources into managing all the risks that need to be addressed, deeming it unnecessary. However, that feeling of frustration belies the domain's importance: each component of the risk management process provides a measure of reassurance that an organization is undertaking adequate preparation for future needs and that there isn't anything being overlooked or omitted.

In this world of increasing cyber risk, where attacks can target even small organizations, being well prepared for the future is no unnecessary reassurance.

Risks, Threats, and Vulnerabilities

Before we proceed, let's take a look at the definitions of three important risk management terms.

First, *risk*: NIST's *Risk Management Framework for Information Systems and Organizations* (Special Publication 800-37, Revision 2) states that risk is "[a] measure of the extent to which an entity is threatened by a potential circumstance or event, and typically is a function of: (i) the adverse impact, or magnitude of harm, that would arise if the circumstance or event occurs; and (ii) the likelihood of occurrence." Essentially, risk is a measure of how dangerous something is. Note the two components, impact and likelihood.

Second, *threat*: NIST SP 800-37 Rev. 2 states that a threat is "[a]ny circumstance or event with the potential to adversely impact organizational operations, organizational assets, individuals, other organizations, or the Nation through a system via unauthorized access, destruction, disclosure, modification of information, and/or denial of service." Essentially, a threat is the source of the danger. You could consider a threat to be, in a sense, the source of risk.

Third, *vulnerability*: NIST SP 800-37 Rev 2 states that a vulnerability is "[w]eakness in an information system, system security procedures, internal controls, or implementation that could be exploited or triggered by a threat source." Essentially, a vulnerability is a weakness that a threat can take advantage of. You could consider a vulnerability to be the weakness that lets a risk become reality.

Now that we have definitions for these terms, let's consider how they go together. When identifying the risks that we need to remediate, we must consider the following:

- What sorts of threats exist

- Whether we have weaknesses in our systems that those threats could exploit

- The potential impact of each threat (how much destruction that threat could cause if it exploited our vulnerability) and its likelihood (the possibility of this disaster occurring)

Risk is calculated as impact × likelihood. Both impact and likelihood can be rated as low, medium, or high (a quantitative calculation) or, alternatively, using a numerical rating system (a quantitative calculation). These calculations help set up a risk rating table.

For an example, Table 2-2 provides a basic risk matrix (or rating table). The Explanation column states the reasoning behind each calculation. Note that this table provides only an approximation of a real-world scenario. Specific organizations may have different calculations depending on their infrastructure and environments. The highest rating between likelihood and impact is used for the total risk rating here.

Table 2-2 Basic Risk Matrix

Risk	Impact	Likelihood	Total Risk	Explanation
Computer virus infection	Medium	Low	Medium	The system has updated antivirus and has firewalls between it and the Internet.
Ransomware attack	Low	High	High	System data is backed up daily, and we can lose some data without suffering a loss. However, organizations like ours are a target.

Risk	Impact	Likelihood	Total Risk	Explanation
Staff falling prey to phishing emails	Medium	Medium	Medium	Personnel have access to some sensitive data, and we do receive some phishing emails.
Malicious insider leaking documents on social media	High	Medium	High	Personnel have access to some sensitive data, and exposure would result in serious reputation harm.
Payment card data being stolen	High	Medium	High	We process a high volume of payment card data, and there is significant risk of being found in noncompliance with industry regulations.
Aliens stealing data	Low	Low	Low	Our data wouldn't be interesting enough to those not of Earth.

As you review this table, please remember that some organizations may use a scale to calculate risk ratings in accordance with the framework that they are required to comply with. In such cases, the use of the scale could result in the final total risk rating being different from the higher rating between likelihood and impact that is used here.

Although each of the items in this table may sound frightening, each does not necessarily apply equally to the system or organization being assessed. To determine risk, we need to consider the system or organization, the type of data, and any existing settings, configurations, or processes that address the threat. For example, although malware poses a great threat (see Chapter 11, "Tying It All Together"), there are ways to mitigate, or reduce, the risk of malware, such as using antivirus software to prevent computer viruses entering and spreading through our systems. The risk of a ransomware attack, phishing emails, or a malicious insider can also be mitigated with the right controls (as discussed later in this chapter). Finally, with these overall risk ratings, we can decide what to prioritize in our risk remediation efforts—although we might be worried about aliens, that's not necessarily a threat we need to prepare for! What we do decide to prioritize, the more severe risks to which we need to commit our budget and efforts first, become our *risk priorities*.

As a last tip for this section, Figure 2-1 illustrates how likelihood and impact work in determining risk ratings.

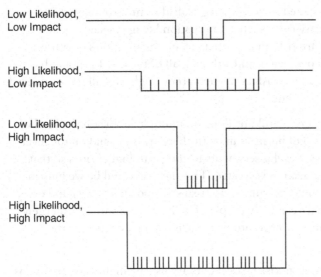

Figure 2-1 Determining Risk Ratings Through Likelihood and Impact

For the first diagram, imagine crossing the gap. When the gap is shallow and narrow, it is relatively easy to avoid falling into the gap when crossing it. In contrast, in the second diagram, the gap is shallow but wide, so the danger of falling is greater but the possible damage is not as great. In the third diagram, the gap is narrow but deep, so it might be easy to avoid falling but the possible damage is great. Finally, in the fourth diagram, which has a gap that is both wide and deep, avoiding falling in seems relatively impossible without some sort of safety mechanism.

The Scope of Risk Management

In the previous section, we used "system" and "organization" to describe the subject of a risk assessment. However, it is important to remember the distinction between the terms—in cybersecurity. Systems usually refer to IT systems, such as an application and supporting business and technical processes, while organizations refer to, in a sense, human systems, such as companies or government agencies. Depending on the size of an organization, a system might be one of many in an organization or its only one. In the case of the latter, the system might include all the business and technical processes of the organization, encompassing everything from physical spaces to networks (such as in a small business). Usually, however, the organization, with multiple systems and departments, is the one with a larger scope of risk.

Why do we draw this distinction? The answer is that risk is multifold. There are technical risks, like application updates causing crashes or wireless access failing; there are financial risks, like equipment being stolen or credit being revoked; there are business risks, like copyrighted material being leaked or massive personnel turnover; and there are security risks, such as encryption being cracked or data being stolen. In short, there are risks in every part of an organization's operations, including the behavior of its personnel, and although all of these risks should be considered in an organization-wide risk assessment, they might not all be considered in an assessment of a specific system.

In an ideal setup, risk assessments would be done on multiple levels: on the level of individual systems, on the level of business units (if there are any), and on the level of the organization, with lower-level assessments feeding into higher ones so that an overall picture of the organization is created. This picture would be we humans' best equivalent to a crystal ball: gathering every (realistic!) possible threat and every existing vulnerability so that we can truly prepare for the various sorts of emergencies that might hit us. An ounce of prevention is worth a pound of cure, as the proverb goes.

However, as the authors have seen, risk assessments are usually highly compartmentalized, focusing on a specific system, or undertaken like a checklist, a document completed as quickly as possible and not really used as a guide in organizational planning. Yet, as the sections that follow will show, a well-conducted and thorough risk assessment ensures that that organizational planning is more efficient and more effective, especially when it comes to cybersecurity.

The Risk Management Process

Now, how does *risk management* work? There are various models for the risk management process. NIST SP 800-37 Rev. 2 discusses six steps, while other models, such as several we authors have studied, describe four or five steps. These steps are also given different names depending on the organization. So, taking into account several ideas, multiple real risk assessment reports, and the Certified in Cybersecurity exam objectives, we are presenting three steps, as illustrated in Figure 2-2: risk identification, risk assessment, and risk treatment.

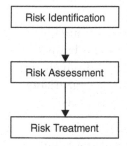

Figure 2-2 Risk Management Steps

Risk Identification

As indicated in the basic risk matrix example shown earlier in Table 2-2, the first step of a risk assessment is *risk identification*, the process of identifying which risks an organization faces. This is where an understanding of both cybersecurity and the organization's big picture first shows its value: threats emerge and recede, and not every threat is applicable to every organization.

To understand the concept better, let's first look at some threats that are a risk for most organizations:

- **Malware:** One of the most obvious threats is malware—viruses, worms, and Trojans can affect multiple types of information systems, and most organizations need to be wary of them (see Chapter 7, "Network Security Infrastructure").

- **Technological obsolescence:** This is a fancy term for software and hardware becoming old and out of date. Organizations certainly need to worry about laptops and servers aging (ever used an old device that has a memory problem?), as well as delivering software updates and patches in a timely fashion (see Chapter 9, "Security in the Life"), and this problem is not entirely deflected through the use of cloud services. Even virtual machines need to be updated and reevaluated for functionality.

- **Ransomware:** Most organizations need to consider the possibility of a ransomware attack, as the ten-year trend shows that these attacks are impacting more and more types of organizations, including small ones.

- **Malicious insiders:** Every organization faces the risk of malicious insiders (described in the following list of business risks).

In contrast, there are some threats that an organization might not need to worry about. For example, the idea of an Advanced Persistent Threat (APT), a highly skilled operation involving multiple steps, a lengthy timeline, and usually a foreign nation-state actor, might sound terrifying, but not every organization possesses the sort of data that renders it a target. Similarly, a distributed denial-of-service (DDoS) attack, an attack designed to overwhelm a network such that it can't handle legitimate traffic, might cause a lot of concern, but not every organization is a target. Not every organization is the likely target of an attacker with resources and skill aplenty, and that's something that should be taken into consideration when identifying risks. At the same time, though, the authors caution that organizations can become targets unexpectedly—that is why risk assessments are an annual process, to try and capture these changes.

Now that we've discussed some examples of cybersecurity risk, let's turn to business risks. Here are four examples of risks that show up on many comprehensive risk assessments:

- **Regulation Risk:** Every organization exists under a framework of laws and regulations, some more than most (for example, a bank faces many more regulations than, say, a marketing agency). The requirements imposed by those laws and regulations shape many organizational decisions, including the use of certain controls and the implementation of specific programs.

- **Fraud Risk:** Most organizations must address the risk of fraud, whether that is a customer that uses products or services without paying, a vendor that doesn't deliver or delivers faulty goods, or other ways in which they might face financial difficulties due to dishonest behavior.

- **Reputation Risk:** Most organizations have to consider the risks posed to their reputations, whether as a result of defamatory comments or posts on social media, bad publicity, or malicious rumors, as their reputations are what enable them to land client contracts and negotiate business arrangements. Other organizations don't usually want to do business with one that is regarded poorly, whether the infamy is deserved or not.

- **Malicious Insider Risk:** Overlapping with our discussion of cybersecurity risks is the malicious insider. This particular risk refers to the threat posed by a disgruntled member of an organization, an employee who feels mistreated or has become aligned with a rival, who may, depending on motivations and circumstances, exfiltrate data, install malware, sabotage devices, steal financial records, or leak certain information that results in reputation harm. Because the threat of a malicious insider could result in more than one type of risk, a robust risk assessment does not ignore these possibilities.

The previous list provides a few examples, but there are many sources of risk. So, how do you, a budding cybersecurity professional, find out more about them and identify which ones you need to consider in your assessments? This is where your knowledge and experience as cybersecurity practitioners comes into play. With your understanding of cybersecurity, you would read industry articles and publications, attend conferences, and follow reputable news sites and are able to use that information to gain an idea of the threat landscape and existing vulnerabilities, determine what would target your organizations, and identify what risks you face.

Risk Assessment

With our risks identified, let's move on to the next step of the risk management process: *risk assessment*. This is where the risk matrix comes into play. Revisiting the example risk matrix in Table 2-2, to begin the risk assessment, we list all the risks that make sense for our organization. Then, with our knowledge of our organization's vulnerabilities (such as unpatched systems or infrastructure exposed to the Internet) and already existing cybersecurity controls (such as antivirus software and daily backups), we determine the likelihood and the impact of each risk and, based on those determinations, prioritize the risks.

The risk matrix in Table 2-2 presents a qualitative approach that judgmentally rates both impact and likelihood as *low*, *medium*, or *high* and then gives an overall score based on the higher between the two. However, this scoring can also be done quantitatively, with numerical ratings, based on calculations of annualized loss expectancy. Alternatively, the assessment might include evaluating each potential risk based on the categories of confidentiality, integrity, and availability (see Chapter 1, "Cybersecurity Principles").

To put it simply, the risk assessment method of choice depends on the organization's needs and what works best for judging and prioritizing risk. For example, a large organization with many risks may need something quantitative so that it can sort out the most critical priority items to address first. A smaller organization, by contrast, or one with fewer risks, might be fine with a qualitative approach. The objective here is that the risk assessment should be as accurate as possible so that risks can be accurately prioritized, evaluated, and treated.

Now, merely researching and evaluating risks doesn't really do much beyond creating paperwork, and you may be wondering what the point of this process is. Well, here is the point: based on that matrix of risks and likelihood and impact, we determine what we need to do to mitigate them.

First, sorting the risks based on the priorities we've established, we evaluate each risk.

This evaluation is based on our organization's ***risk tolerance***. Risk tolerance refers to an organization's appetite for risk—how risk-averse it is or isn't. For example, an organization that processes sensitive healthcare data may be very risk-averse and unwilling to let any vulnerability go unaddressed because of the laws and regulations controlling the organization's industry. By contrast, a marketing agency, aware that the data it possesses is not highly regulated, may have more of a risk appetite. Some of this appetite is also based on the type of controls the organization already has in place, as well as individual leaders, so, as someone who may conduct a risk assessment someday, it will be up to you to know the tolerance of your organization.

Based on our organization's risk tolerance, we have four choices with which to address each risk:

- **Reduction or mitigation:** Implement administrative and technical controls through which the likelihood or the impact, or both, of the risk is decreased.

- **Transference:** Give the risk to another organization. For example, risk can be transferred by using a third-party service or buying insurance so that the impact of the risk is distributed among organizations.

■ **Acceptance:** Decide to take on the risk. For example, an organization may know that a particular system is unpatched but decide to keep using it because replacing that system would be more costly and bring on greater risks.

■ **Avoidance:** Choose to not engage in the activity that is the source of the risk. For example, an organization could decide not to expose a particular server to the Internet or use an application with a known vulnerability. In doing so, there would be no risk for that particular threat.

Table 2-3 provides an updated version of the risk matrix in Table 2-2 to give you an example of how all of this would look.

Table 2-3   Updated Risk Matrix for Risk Assessment

Risk	Total Risk	Explanation	Response
Computer virus infection	Medium	The system has updated antivirus and has firewalls between it and the Internet.	Avoid
Ransomware attack	High	System data is backed up daily, and we can lose some data without suffering a loss. However, organizations like ours are a target.	Mitigate
Staff falling prey to phishing emails	Medium	Personnel have access to some sensitive data, and we do receive some phishing emails.	Mitigate
Malicious insider leaking documents on social media	High	Personnel have access to some sensitive data, and exposure would result in serious reputation harm.	Mitigate
Payment card data being stolen	High	We process a high volume of payment card data, and there is significant risk of being found in noncompliance with industry regulations.	Transfer
Aliens stealing data	Low	Our data wouldn't be interesting enough to those not of Earth.	Accept

With these choices made, ideally documented in spreadsheets or with forms, we complete the actual assessment portion of the risk management process and move on to the final step.

Risk Treatment

In the final step of the risk management process, *risk treatment*, we design concrete steps to implement our response. Taking each risk and its response, let's begin to map out a plan.

Based on our prioritizations and responses, we would update our risk matrix to include the columns Treatment Plan, Residual Risk, and Control Owner, as outlined in Table 2-4.

Table 2-4   Updated Risk Matrix for Risk Treatment

Risk	Total Risk	Explanation	Response	Treatment Plan	Residual Risk	Control Owner
Computer virus infection	Medium	The system has updated antivirus and has firewalls between it and the Internet.	Avoid	Remove Internet access for the system.	Low	System Administrators
Ransomware attack	High	System data is backed up daily, and we can lose some data without suffering a loss. However, organizations like ours are a target.	Mitigate	Implement antivirus software on system endpoints that specifically scans for ransomware.	Low	System Administrators
Staff falling prey to phishing emails	Medium	Personnel have access to some sensitive data, and we do receive some phishing emails.	Mitigate	Implement a security awareness training program that includes phishing simulations.	Low	Information Security Team
Malicious insider leaking documents on social media	High	Personnel have access to some sensitive data, and exposure would result in serious reputation harm.	Mitigate	Implement role-based access control (RBAC) and limit access based on the principle of least privilege.	Low	Information Security Team, System Administrators
Payment card data being stolen	High	We process a high volume of payment card data, and there is significant risk of being found in noncompliance with industry regulations.	Transfer	Engage a third-party service to receive, process, and store payment card data.	Low	Chief Technical Officer
Aliens stealing data	Low	Our data wouldn't be interesting enough to those not of Earth.	Accept	Not implementing any controls here!	Low	Chief Technical Officer

In the matrix, notice how each treatment plan is aligned with the response, the current system status (see the Explanation column), and the level of priority. These treatment plans can be as elaborate or as simple as suits the organization's needs, and there are certainly other options for addressing each of the risk items listed in the matrix. The key point is that the plans should address each risk such that the *residual risk*, the risk that remains of the total risk once the plan is implemented, is negated or almost entirely negated.

You might have noticed that the Residual Risk column uses the same qualitative "high, medium, low" terminology to describe risk. Like total risk, residual risk can be described either qualitatively or quantitatively. As discussed in the "Risk Assessment" section, the approach for judging residual risk should be selected based on the organization and its requirements.

Now, let's move on to the last column: Control Owner. Obviously, after doing all the work to identify risk treatment plans, we need to ensure that they are actually implemented. In risk management, the method we use to ensure that risks are treated is twofold. First, in the document itself, or in an accompanying spreadsheet of some sort, we designate a *control owner*, someone whose job it is to put these plans in motion and check up on them. Usually, this control owner is a specific person or group of persons rather than the generic role names used in the example matrix in Table 2-4—those role names are intended to give you an idea of where to start looking for your perfect control owner!

The second part of ensuring risks are being treated is to implement a regular review process. In many cases, the authors have seen this review process integrated into quarterly corporate security meetings, in which upper management meet and review security concerns and requirements, including risk management documents and action items. These meetings, or some form of them, do tend to be recommended in the industry, as they ensure management buy-in and knowledge of information security needs and developments. The objective, however, isn't the meeting form or cadence—it's to ensure that risk assessment is regularly reviewed and risk treatment plan implementation is regularly monitored so that risks actually get addressed.

Security Controls and Governance

Now, if you've checked out the table of contents for this book or skimmed through later chapters, or if you already have some knowledge of IT and cybersecurity, you might have found the treatment plans rather familiar.

Everything we do in cybersecurity is intended, whether directly prescribed through a risk assessment or not, to address some sort of risk. We really do mean everything here: encryption, access control, physical security, network security, security operations, incident response, business continuity—even risk management (can you guess what risk is addressed by risk management itself?). Each of these areas, from risk management to disaster recovery, are *security controls*.

According to NIST SP 800-53 Rev. 5, *Security and Privacy Controls for Information Systems and Organizations*, security controls are "[t]he safeguards or countermeasures prescribed for an information system or an organization to protect the confidentiality, integrity, and availability of the system and its information." Essentially, security controls are the defenses of our metaphorical castle, and they come in a variety of forms: administrative, technical, and physical.

To better understand these forms, let's consider an example: access to a server room. As you will learn in the coming chapters, the ideal setup here is a document defining who is allowed to request access (administrative control), systems inside the room being protected by login requirements and multi-factor authentication (technical controls), and ID card readers configured to unlock the door for specific IDs (physical control).

You won't find all three forms of security control represented in every situation. Some areas require only technical safeguards, while others require only physical ones (though keep in mind that even a fully remote, cloud-based organization will always have the physical element of laptops and that the servers they're using do exist somewhere). But, in an organization with a well-established information security program, you will always find the administrative: governance documents that define organizational behavior such as policy, a procedure, a standard, or a set of guidelines. These governance documents and the oversight they establish in ensuring risks are being properly addressed and all controls are being implemented are referred to as *governance processes* (see Chapter 10, "Security in Emergencies").

In addition to the classification of controls as administrative, technical, or physical, security controls can be categorized based on their objective as preventive, detective, corrective, deterrent, and compensating. See Table 2-5 for definitions and examples.

Table 2-5 Classification of Controls Based on Their Objective

Control Type	Definition	Example
Preventive	A control that reduces the possibility of a threat	System hardening, security awareness training
Detective	A control that gathers information to discover the possibility of a threat	Logging and monitoring
Corrective	A control that takes action to stop threats when they are detected	Intrusion prevention system
Deterrent	A control that reduces the likelihood of a threat	Locked doors, security guards
Compensating	An alternate control put in place when controls that more immediately meet security requirements cannot be implemented	Restricting access to databases that cannot be encrypted

One final thing to note before we wrap up this chapter: many of these security controls are based upon regulations and laws. As we're seeing today, an ever-increasing number of countries are passing cybersecurity and data privacy laws, new industry standards are coming to the forefront, and many existing cybersecurity frameworks (such as the NIST and PCI frameworks) are becoming increasingly comprehensive. Depending on your organization's industry and activities, you might need to consider any number of these regulations and laws as you manage risks, create governance documentation, and design and implement security controls.

Exam Preparation Tasks

As mentioned in the Introduction, you have a couple of choices for exam preparation: the exercises here, Chapter 13, "Final Preparation," and the exam simulation questions in the Pearson Test Prep Software Online.

Review All Key Topics

Review the most important topics in this chapter, noted with the Key Topics icon in the outer margin of the page. Table 2-6 lists a reference of these key topics and the page numbers on which each is found.

Table 2-6 Key Topics for Chapter 2

Key Topic Element	Description	Page Number
Paragraph	Definition of risks	18
Paragraph	Definition of threats	19
Paragraph	Definition of vulnerabilities	19
Paragraph	Definition of risk priorities	20
Paragraph	Description of risk management	22
Paragraph	Description of risk identification	23
Paragraph	Description of risk assessment	24
Paragraph	Description of risk tolerance	25
Paragraph	Description of risk treatment	26
Paragraph	Description of security controls	29
Paragraph	Definition of governance processes	30

Define Key Terms

Define the following key terms from this chapter and check your answers in the glossary:

risk, threat, vulnerability, risk priorities, risk management, risk identification, risk assessment, risk tolerance, risk treatment, security controls, governance processes

Q&A

The answers to these questions appear in Appendix A. For more practice with exam format questions, use the Pearson Test Prep Software Online.

1. What are risks, threats, and vulnerabilities?

2. What is risk management?

3. What is the scope of a risk assessment?

4. How is a risk assessment conducted?

5. What are the options for risk response?

6. What are the types of security controls?

7. How are security controls related to risk management?

8. How is governance documentation related to security controls?

9. What is the relationship between security controls and laws and regulations?

References

NIST SP 800-37, Rev. 2, *Risk Management Framework for Information Systems and Organizations*: https://nvlpubs.nist.gov/nistpubs/SpecialPublications/NIST.SP.800-37r2.pdf

NIST SP 800-53, Rev. 5, *Security and Privacy Controls for Information Systems and Organizations*, https://nvlpubs.nist.gov/nistpubs/SpecialPublications/NIST.SP.800-53r5.pdf

Swanagan, Michael. "The 3 Types Of Security Controls (Expert Explains). *PurpleSec*, Dec. 7, 2023: Types Of Security Controls Explained (purplesec.us)

This chapter covers the following topics:

- **Threats to security:** Describe network threats and attacks and their impact on security.

- **Common threat categories:** Describe different types of threats that can impact organizations.

- **Security best practices and risk management:** Understand the identification and prevention of threats and the management of risks.

Threats to Security

Understanding the various types of threats to security will aid you in understanding the need for security controls and help you implement more effective protection measures and mitigation techniques as you enter the cybersecurity field and land your first role. In this chapter, we will look at the various types of threats to security and why it's essential to understand them, common threat types and mitigations, advanced techniques used by threat actors, and ways to discover and mitigate vulnerabilities.

This chapter covers the following Certified in Cybersecurity exam objectives:

- 4.2 Understand network threats and attacks

  - 4.2a Types of threats (e.g., distributed denial-of-service (DDoS), virus, worm, Trojan, on-path attack, side-channel)

  - 4.2b Identification (e.g., intrusion detection system (IDS), host-based intrusion detection system (HIDS), network intrusion detection system (NIDS))

  - 4.2c Prevention (e.g., antivirus, scans, firewalls, intrusion prevention system (IPS))

"Do I Know This Already?" Quiz

The "Do I Know This Already?" quiz allows you to decide whether you need to read this entire chapter or skip to the "Exam Preparation Tasks" section. If you doubt your selection of answers to these questions or your own assessment of your knowledge of these topics, you may want to read the entire chapter. Table 3-1 lists the major headings in this chapter and their corresponding "Do I Know This Already?" Quiz questions. You can find the answers in Appendix A, "Answers to the 'Do I Know This Already?' Quizzes and Q&A Sections." Good luck!

Table 3-1 "Do I Know This Already?" Section-to-Question Mapping

Foundation Topics Section	Questions
Threats to Security	1–3
Common Threat Categories	4, 5
Network Attacks	6–8
Detection and Mitigation Techniques	9, 10
Scanning and Penetration Testing	11, 12

CAUTION The goal of self-assessment is to gauge your mastery of the topics in this chapter. If you do not know the answer to a question or are only partially sure of the answer, you should mark that question as wrong for purposes of the self-assessment. Giving yourself credit for an answer you correctly guess skews your self-assessment results and might provide you with a false sense of security.

1. What is a threat in cybersecurity?

   a. A strategy to prevent data theft

   b. An event that leads to data destruction only

   c. Any circumstance or event with the potential to impact operations, assets, or individuals through unauthorized access, destruction, disclosure, or modification of information

   d. A way to reduce the time that it takes to investigate security issues

2. How can cybersecurity professionals prepare to defend against threats?

   a. By ignoring the latest news in the cybersecurity world

   b. By sharing information with peer organizations

   c. By ensuring all systems and devices have no vulnerabilities

   d. By allowing unauthorized access to information and systems

3. What is the purpose of threat intelligence?

   a. To encourage data theft and destruction

   b. To help cybersecurity professionals and executives make decisions about potential threats

   c. To slow down the investigation of security issues

   d. To keep emerging technology concerns around IoT, AI, and some aspects of the cloud a secret

4. What is ransomware?

    a. Code that runs on computer systems without the user's knowledge

    b. Malicious software designed to disrupt, damage, or gain unauthorized access to a computer system

    c. Standalone, self-replicating malware that causes damage to systems

    d. Malicious software that encrypts your data to block access in exchange for a ransom payment

5. What is the main difference between viruses and worms?

    a. Viruses can self-replicate, while worms need a human to execute them on a system.

    b. Viruses spread through the Internet, while worms spread through LANs.

    c. Viruses are malware that slows down systems, while worms cause extensive damage to systems.

    d. Viruses need human interaction to be successful, while worms can self-replicate and spread without human interaction.

6. What is the main difference between a DDoS attack and a regular DoS attack?

    a. A DDoS attack floods a system with traffic to multiple compromised devices, while a regular DoS attack floods one system with traffic to exhaust resources.

    b. A DDoS attack targets routers, switches, and servers, while a regular DoS attack targets individual devices.

    c. A DDoS attack alters data between communicating parties, while a regular DoS attack intercepts data between communicating parties.

    d. A DDoS attack requires physical access to a system, while a DoS attack is executed remotely.

7. Where are man-in-the-middle (MITM) attacks typically executed?

    a. Secure and encrypted networks

    b. Government organizations and military networks

    c. In places with insecure Wi-Fi, such as coffee shops or hotels

    d. Internal networks within an organization

8. How do side-channel attacks exploit system vulnerabilities?

    a. By intercepting and altering data between communicating parties

    b. By flooding a system with traffic through coordinated efforts

    c. By analyzing unintended information leaked by a system's physical implementation

    d. By gaining physical access to a system's hardware components

9. What are the two categories of firewalls?

    a. Stateful and stateless

    b. Network-based and host-based

    c. Proxy and packet filtering

    d. Next-generation and web application

10. What is the main difference between packet filtering firewalls and web application firewalls?

    a. Packet filtering firewalls inspect data packets based on payload content, while web application firewalls monitor IP information.

    b. Packet filtering firewalls authenticate clients and forward requests to servers, while web application firewalls authenticate servers and forward requests to clients.

    c. Packet filtering firewalls analyze surface-level data such as IP addresses and ports, while web application firewalls inspect HTTP traffic and protect against web-based attacks.

    d. Packet filtering firewalls utilize machine learning and behavior analytics, while web application firewalls conduct deep packet inspection.

11. What is the purpose of vulnerability scanning in cybersecurity?

    a. To exploit vulnerabilities found in an organization's environment

    b. To analyze behaviors on specific endpoints and respond to issues

    c. To determine what vulnerabilities an organization has, to prioritize remediation efforts, and to track progress

    d. To apply patches to software to fix vulnerabilities

12. What is the difference between vulnerability scanning and pentesting?

    a. Vulnerability scanning is used to exploit vulnerabilities, while pentesting analyzes behaviors on specific endpoints.

    b. Vulnerability scanning doesn't exploit the vulnerabilities, while pentesting aims to find and exploit vulnerabilities.

    c. Vulnerability scanning allows teams to test incident response and detection processes, while pentesting prioritizes remediation efforts.

    d. Vulnerability scanning gives a continuous look at what is going on in an organization, while pentesting is conducted with open-source tools.

13. What is the purpose of regularly updating and patching systems in cybersecurity?

    a. To analyze behaviors on specific endpoints and respond to issues

    b. To detect and protect against threats using predictive analytics

    c. To gain unauthorized access to systems and data

    d. To apply security fixes for vulnerabilities found in the software

Foundation Topics

Threats to Security

Chapter 2, "Risk Management," quotes the NIST SP 80-37 Rev. 2 definition of a *threat*. NIST provides an alternative but similar definition of *threat* in SP 1800-15:

> *Any circumstance or event with the potential to adversely impact organizational operations (including mission, functions, image, or reputation), organizational assets, or individuals through an information system via unauthorized access, destruction, disclosure, modification of information, and denial of service. Also, the potential for a threat source to successfully exploit a particular information system vulnerability.*

Understanding the threats that could impact an organization enables cybersecurity professionals to develop and implement strategies to help prevent unauthorized access and harm to data. With cyber threats evolving constantly, professionals need to be aware of any new tactics and techniques attackers may use to exploit vulnerabilities in an organization's environment.

Staying updated with the latest news in the cybersecurity world enables professionals to stay one step ahead of threat actors by proactively implementing effective mitigation and protection measures before these malicious actors exploit any vulnerabilities, thereby safeguarding their systems and data.

Security breaches occur when threat actors exploit vulnerabilities and gain unauthorized access to information, systems, and devices. A breach can significantly impact organizations and individuals in a variety of ways, such as the destruction of systems, changes to data, or, even worse, data theft. Understanding how threats impact an organization helps cybersecurity professionals to better defend their environments.

Threat intelligence is meant to help cybersecurity professionals and executives make decisions about threats that may affect them. Threat intelligence companies collect, process, and analyze information about a threat actor's *tactics, techniques, and procedures (TTPs)*. This analysis is then disseminated to customers and partners for use within their threat management programs. This data is shared via Information Sharing and Analysis Centers (ISACs) and Information Sharing and Analysis Organizations (ISAOs), government agencies such as the U.S. Cybersecurity and Infrastructure Security Agency (CISA), security vendors such as Unit 42 and Recorded Future, and open-source intelligence tools such as MISP (which formerly stood for the Malware Information Sharing Project).

Sharing threat intelligence with peer organizations is vital to protecting the infrastructure. This information allows security teams to reduce the time it takes to investigate issues and incidents discovered in their environments. This is also an excellent way to stay abreast of emerging technology concerns regarding the Internet of Things (IoT), artificial intelligence (AI), and some aspects of the cloud. While information sharing is essential for collective security, it also presents specific challenges. For example, organizations might be reluctant to share data from a breach due to concerns about reputational damage, fearing that disclosing such incidents could tarnish their image. Additionally, there is a risk of data becoming stale and no longer relevant over time, which can hinder the effectiveness of shared threat intelligence. However, the more we share, the better prepared we are for a security breach.

Common Threat Categories

Many threats can affect an organization. In this section, we discuss various types of threats that could potentially and probably have affected an organization you have engaged with in the past. These include *malware* and advanced persistent threat (APT). Let's dig in!

Malware

NIST SP 800-83 Rev. 1 states that "*Malware*, also known as *malicious code*, refers to a program that is covertly inserted into another program with the intent to destroy data, run destructive or intrusive programs, or otherwise compromise the confidentiality, integrity, or availability of the victim's data, applications, or operating system." Attackers use malware to gain unauthorized access to system files and other data. Typically, if your system is infected with malware, you will see an increase in system crashes, slow response times, and files not opening. There are a variety of different types of malware, including viruses, worms, Trojans, and ransomware.

Malware is designed specifically to disrupt, damage, or gain unauthorized access to a computer system. Malware can be downloaded on your system via email, from URLs you click, or from additional websites you visit. In each case, malware can damage your entire system, causing you to work overtime to fix the issue.

Viruses

Viruses are some of the most notorious malware variants out there. A *virus* is a program that runs on computer systems without the users' knowledge. If a user or system executes a compromised file, the virus can spread copies of itself throughout the network. Viruses utilize system resources to replicate and spread quickly through a network, which can impact performance and slow systems down.

NOTE   Viruses need some sort of delivery method and human interaction to be successful. This is different from worms, which can self-replicate.

One of the most dangerous viruses of the Internet era was the Melissa virus, which provided free credentials to adult websites in 1999 through email and forums. This virus was spread via Microsoft macros through Word email attachments. When a user opened an email with a Word attachment, the virus would send copies of itself to the first 50 contacts in their address book, causing widespread disruption affecting more than 300 organizations that year. Melissa was able to exploit the trust associated with opening email attachments proliferating and overwhelming email servers. Microsoft permanently blocked Internet access to Office macros in 2022.

Worms

Worms are standalone, self-replicating malware that causes significant damage to an organization's environment. Worms are typically spread through the Internet or a local area network (LAN). They will use the resources on the first compromised system(s) to start reconnaissance on the rest of the network.

Worms can be spread in a variety of ways:

- *Phishing* emails that are designed to trick the recipient into clicking a link can spread worms. Typically, phishing, as a form of social engineering, plays on human behavior. A subtype is *spear phishing*, which is a more targeted phishing campaign that usually targets executives or other employees higher in the organizational hierarchy. Phishing emails are regularly used to manipulate people into divulging information.

- *Network access* via shared network drives allows worms to spread through those areas quickly.

- Worms may use *security holes and misconfigurations* to spread throughout your organization.

- *External devices* such as USB drives and CDs can contain a worm that then spreads to other systems to cause havoc. To mitigate this risk, organizations employ data loss prevention (DLP) tools to monitor device use.

The Stuxnet worm, first detected in 2010, spread via USB drives and was mostly used for cyber warfare. This worm targeted critical industrial control system (ICS) infrastructure used to control nuclear power plants. This worm was the first of its kind worldwide, thus changing how we look at security for systems that were not built with security in mind.

Trojans

In Greek mythology, the Greeks defeated the city of Troy during the Trojan War by hiding soldiers in a giant wooden horse left outside the city gates, waiting for the Trojans to bring the horse inside to celebrate their apparent victory after the Greeks had pretended to retreat. The Greek soldiers then emerged from the horse's belly and sacked the city. Aptly named for that horse, Trojans operate in the same manner. *Trojans* are malicious programs or software disguised as harmless, useful tools to trick users into downloading them, after which they exfiltrate data from the system on which they are installed. Additionally, Trojans are stealthy, can be executed without permission or the user's knowledge, and serve a specific purpose such as data theft, remote control, facilitating other attacks, or persistence in the system.

The Trojan named Zeus, first detected in 2007, was designed to steal personal and financial data from compromised systems. What was unique at the time was that the hackers used Zeus to rope other systems into a botnet to steal money from major corporations, causing over $70 million in damages.

Ransomware

Ransomware has been a major threat in the tech space in the past few years, affecting government agencies, healthcare systems, and school systems and causing massive financial losses to organizations. *Ransomware* is malicious software that encrypts your data or systems to block access in exchange for some form of payment to regain access and decrypt that information, as illustrated in Figure 3-1. Threat actors use ransomware to access high-value data such as financial and intellectual property.

Ransomware can be delivered through various means, such as phishing emails or software vulnerabilities. It's important to note that ransomware typically has three main factors: encryption capabilities, a time limit to pay the ransom, and the ability to spread across networks.

Let's discuss two notable ransomware attacks that had very different impacts on organizations. WannaCry was discovered in 2010 and affected more than 200,000 systems across the globe by spreading through phishing emails and network scanning. WannaCry was able to spread quickly due to vulnerabilities in older versions of Microsoft software. The motive behind WannaCry was financial gain. Organizations impacted by WannaCry had to pay the attackers in Bitcoin to have their data decrypted.

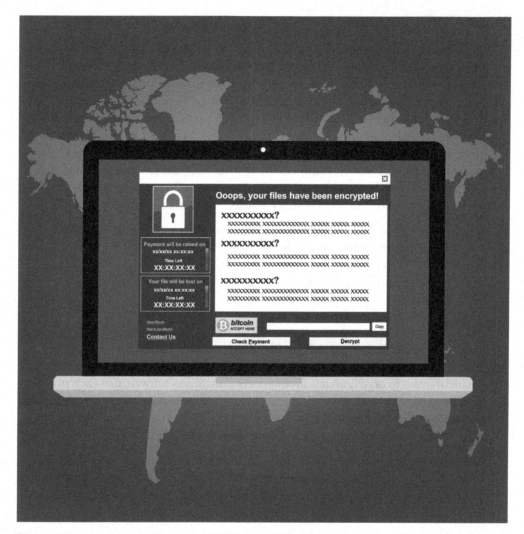

Figure 3-1   Ransomware (Image Credit: Nicescene/Shutterstock)

While WannaCry was for financial gain, the incident at Colonial Pipeline in 2021 caused a disruption of operations up and down the East Coast. This pipeline supplies 45% of the East Coast with fuel. This attack was attributed to the threat group DarkSide, which demanded that Colonial Pipeline Company pay 75 Bitcoin (worth approximately $5 million at the time) to access its systems again. The company paid the ransom and was able to resume operations. The Colonial Pipeline incident caused gas shortages for almost a week, leading to panic buying, price spikes in gas, and concerns for national security because the pipeline is considered critical infrastructure.

Advanced Persistent Threats

An *advanced persistent threat (APT)* is a highly sophisticated and targeted attack conducted by skilled threat actors, typically state-sponsored groups, looking to gain access to sensitive data or cause a disruption in operations. These threat actors utilize the malware techniques previously described to gain access to systems and wait. APTs have multiple stages of execution and can go undetected for long periods. Data exfiltration, intelligence gathering, or other malicious activities can occur during this time. Initial access for these actors typically is gained either through phishing or zero-day exploits. Network segmentation and a defense-in-depth strategy are great ways to protect against APT attacks. Additional detection and protection measures are discussed throughout this chapter.

Network Attacks

Network attacks pose a significant threat to the security of an organization's computer network. Threat actors will use various attacks that typically target systems such as routers, switches, servers, and other devices that data moves through. Let's look at three types of attacks that can impact an organization. This is not an exhaustive list of attacks.

Distributed Denial-of-Service Attack

A *distributed denial-of-service (DDoS)* attack is a malicious and coordinated effort by a threat actor to overwhelm a system's resources. This is achieved by flooding the system with a high volume of traffic. Unlike a typical denial-of-service (DoS) attack that only affects one system, a DDoS attack involves multiple systems within a computer network that are leveraged by the attacker. The main objective of a DDoS attack is to deny access to legitimate users, causing service disruptions and potentially damaging the reputation of the owner of the targeted system.

One common method employed in DDoS attacks is a *botnet*, consisting of a network of Internet-connected devices remotely controlled by the threat actor. These compromised devices enable the attacker to distribute the attack traffic across multiple sources, making mitigating and defending against the attack much more challenging. The following are common examples of DDoS attacks.

A *synchronization (SYN) flood* occurs when SYN requests are sent to a system but not responded to, creating half-open connections. SYN requests are the first part of the three-way handshake used to establish a connection with a system. By sending a large number of requests, resources are consumed while waiting for a response, preventing legitimate users from accessing that resource. We discuss the three-way handshake in Chapter 6, "Computer Networking Fundamentals."

A *User Datagram Protocol (UDP) flood* is similar to a SYN flood but uses UDP packets to flood a system and exhaust the resources. UDP is a connectionless protocol that offers faster delivery but sacrifices reliability because it doesn't require delivery confirmation. We discuss UDP in Chapter 6.

A *Hypertext Transfer Protocol (HTTP) flood* attacks web servers by sending HTTP Get and Post requests to the system to exhaust its resources. This application-based attack targets those systems at Layer 7 of the Open Systems Interconnection (OSI) model. We discuss the OSI model in Chapter 6.

Man-in-the-Middle Attack

A *man-in-the-middle (MITM) attack* occurs when a threat actor gains access to the communication channel between communicating parties and intercepts or alters the data, tricking victims into thinking they are communicating with each other. The attacker can now eavesdrop on sensitive information such as passwords, usernames, or financial data. MITM attacks are typically executed in places with insecure Wi-Fi, such as in coffee shops or hotels, and through spoofed websites. As a note, the phrase man-in-the-middle is now being replaced by "on path attack."

Side-Channel Attack

A *side-channel attack* exploits information leaked unintentionally by a system's physical implementation rather than a vulnerability in the software or an algorithm. By analyzing factors like power consumption or electromagnetic radiation, attackers can deduce sensitive data, such as passwords, without direct access, potentially compromising security measures. Side-channel attacks can occur in various contexts, including networks, and target specific devices or protocols. Protection against this type of attack can include limiting information in error and debugging log messages or using hardware-based security measures. For example, an attacker can intercept electromagnetic radiation emitted by a device during the process of entering a password. By analyzing variations in electromagnetic signals, such as those generated by keystrokes on a keyboard, the attacker can infer the sequence of characters being entered. This method allows the attacker to derive the password without directly accessing the device or obtaining it through traditional means.

Detection and Mitigation Techniques

While 100% prevention of cyberattacks isn't possible unless a system is isolated from Internet access, there are measures that organizations can take to help reduce the likelihood of a successful attack. One of the first documented signature-based antivirus programs, created in 1987 by Bernd Robert Fix, was used to remove the

Vienna virus. This virus infected .com files on DOS-based systems. The antivirus would then only alert on things that it had already seen. As malware and viruses evolved, antivirus software evolved. Next-generation antivirus (NGAV) protects against a group of behaviors, using predictive analytics driven by machine learning (ML) and AI to detect and protect against threats.

Endpoint detection and response (EDR) solutions emerged around 2013, creating a new category for responding to threats. EDR merged legacy AV capabilities with AI and ML. This allowed teams to analyze behaviors on specific endpoints (such as laptops or mobile phones) and respond to issues at any given time.

As the attack surface for organizations expanded and more data was being collected and processed, extended detection and response (XDR) was born. XDR gives organizations a look at threats across their entire technology ecosystem, including endpoint, network, and cloud. Organizations now have the ability to respond to threats and issues in near real time. With XDR sensors on all devices from the perimeter to the endpoint, security teams can get the full picture of what happened in one location.

In addition to implementing antivirus software, regularly updating and patching systems is critical to protecting data. The patches supplied by vendors typically include security fixes for vulnerabilities found in the software. Not applying patches leaves systems vulnerable to attacks. Threat actors can use these holes to gain unauthorized access to systems and data, take over all the systems, or launch attacks on other systems.

Detection Tools

There are many ways to detect and mitigate network-based attacks. One way to do this is to use an ***intrusion detection system (IDS)***. An IDS (hardware or software) monitors computer network traffic and sends alerts when it detects malicious activity or unauthorized access to systems as data enters and exits the network, in real time. An IDS analyzes network traffic, log files, and other data sources to detect suspicious activity associated with known threats. This is considered a ***network intrusion detection system IDS (NIDS)***. Whereas ***host-based intrusion detection system (HIDS)*** are directly on the host system or endpoint and monitor the traffic for that specific host vs. the entire network.

To boost security, organizations can deploy an *intrusion prevention system (IPS)* within their network traffic flow. An IPS, whether in hardware or software form, actively monitors for suspicious activity and blocks it as necessary. When a threat is detected and blocked, an alert is immediately sent to the system administration for further investigation.

These detection and prevention systems add an additional layer of protection when used along with firewalls.

Firewalls are network security devices that sit at the edge of a network, monitoring incoming and outgoing traffic to identify and block potential cyber threats based on predetermined security policies. Hardware or software firewalls act as a barrier between the internal network and the public Internet. The original firewalls were designed to inspect data packets as they traversed the network. Over time, firewalls improved, addressing application vulnerabilities and utilizing machine learning for advanced detection and prevention.

As illustrated in Figure 3-2, firewalls can be broken up into two categories:

- **Host-based firewall:** Firewall on the endpoint that protects that specific device

- **Network-based firewall:** Firewall on the network that protects the entire network

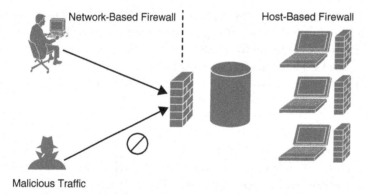

Figure 3-2   Host-Based Versus Network-Based Firewalls

Firewalls come in various types, each with distinct capabilities. Some of these types include

- Packet filtering firewalls

- Proxy, application-aware firewalls

- Web application firewalls

- Next-generation firewalls (NGFW)

Packet filtering firewalls inspect data packets as they traverse the network based on a predefined set of rules. These firewalls inspect the surface-level data, such as source and destination IP addresses and ports, to decide whether to allow or drop a packet. Any packet that fails inspection is dropped. Inspections are based on security policies and firewall rules similar to the example rule presented in Table 3-2.

Table 3-2 Sample Firewall Rule

Direction	Protocol	Source Address	Destination Address	Source Port	Destination Port	Action
Inbound	TCP	Any	22.34.145.6	Any	80	Allow
Inbound	TCP	Any	Any	Any	Any	Deny

With most firewalls, the order of the rules matters. Each rule inspects packets until one proves true. Once an action is taken, no other inspections are done on that packet. The rule outlined in Table 3-2 will allow incoming traffic to 22.34.145.6 over port 80 while denying all other traffic.

Because packet filtering firewalls inspect only surface-level data, they provide only basic levels of protection and are easier to bypass.

Packet filtering firewalls can be either of the following types:

- **Stateless:** Inspect each packet individually

- **Stateful:** Track connections and use previous data packets to make a final decision

A *proxy, application-aware firewall* operates at the application layer of the OSI model. These devices monitor application traffic between a client and server for malicious activity based on the content or payload of the packet in addition to the source and destination IP information.

When a client wants to establish a connection with a server, the proxy firewall first authenticates the client and then forwards the request to the server on behalf of the client. This allows the firewall to inspect and filter all traffic between the client and server, reducing the risk of malicious traffic reaching the server or client.

Web application firewalls (WAFs) are similar to proxy firewalls but are specific to protecting against web-based server attacks such as SQL (structured query language) injection and cross-site scripting (XSS). WAFs monitor and filter HTTP traffic between the web server and the Internet. They offer features such as user-defined policies, traffic logging and alerting, and rule sets that can be customized to provide the appropriate level of protection for a specific web application.

Next-generation firewalls (NGFWs) take the detection and protection game a step further and introduce machine learning (ML) and behavior analytics to allow or deny traffic. These devices conduct deep packet inspection (DPI) to determine whether the packet should be allowed or denied. NGFWs are the most popular firewall type today and provide various services and features in addition to firewall services. These services include malware scanning and filtering, network address translation (NAT) services, advanced threat intelligence, and more.

Individually, all the systems can be utilized during an investigation by reviewing the logs from each system. These logs can also be sent to a Security Incident and Event Management (SIEM) platform that enables analysts and engineers to gather data from all the sources in one location for more efficient and improved security investigations.

 ## Scanning and Penetration Testing

Scanning an organization's environment helps the organization to understand what assets it has, any associated vulnerabilities, and ways to remediate and mitigate those vulnerabilities. Vulnerability scanning can be done with open-source tools such as Network Mapper (Nmap) or commercial off-the-shelf (COTS) solutions such as Rapid7 or Tenable. The purpose of these scans is to examine risks that may affect the organization continuously. It also helps the organization prioritize remediation efforts and track progress.

A vulnerability scan differs from a ***penetration test*** (often shortened to *pentest*) in that vulnerability scans are passive in nature. The scan is looking for open vulnerabilities that could lead to exploitation. With pentesting, the goal is to test an organization's technology and the safeguards currently in place by attempting to exploit vulnerabilities found during a vulnerability scan. Once a pentest is complete, the results are shared with the stakeholders for remediation or mitigation. Pentests also enable teams to test their incident response plans and make changes as needed before a threat actor enters the scene.

Exam Preparation Tasks

As mentioned in the Introduction, you have a couple of choices for exam preparation: the exercises here, Chapter 13, "Final Preparation," and the exam simulation questions in the Pearson Test Prep Software Online.

Review All Key Topics

Review the most important topics in this chapter, noted with the Key Topics icon in the outer margin of the page. Table 3-3 lists a reference of these key topics and the page numbers on which each is found.

Table 3-3 Key Topics for Chapter 3

Key Topic Element	Description	Page Number
Section	Malware	39
Section	Distributed Denial-of-Service Attack	43
Section	Detection Tools	45
Paragraph	Firewalls and their uses	46
Section	Scanning and Penetration Testing	48

Define Key Terms

Define the following key terms from this chapter and check your answers in the glossary:

tactics, techniques, and procedures (TTPs), malware; virus; worm; Trojan; ransomware; advanced persistent threat (APT); distributed denial-of-service (DDoS); synchronization (SYN) flood; User Datagram Protocol (UDP) flood; Hypertext Transfer Protocol (HTTP) flood; man-in-the-middle (MITM) attack; side-channel attack; intrusion detection system (IDS); network intrusion detection system (NIDS); host-based intrusion detection system (HIDS); intrusion prevention system (IPS); firewall; packet filtering firewall; proxy, application-aware firewall; web-application filtering firewall (WAF); next-generation firewall (NGFW); scanning; penetration test

Q&A

The answers to these questions appear in Appendix A. For more practice with exam format questions, use the Pearson Test Prep Software Online.

1. Why is threat intelligence sharing important in cybersecurity?

2. What are the key factors contributing to the effectiveness of ransomware as a cyber threat?

3. What is a distributed denial-of-service (DDoS) attack?

4. What device combines the power of detection and prevention and adds behavior analytics and machine learning to the mix for improved security?

5. How does a pentest differ from a vulnerability scan?

References

NIST SP 1800-15, *Securing Small-Business and Home Internet of Things (IoT) Devices*: https://nvlpubs.nist.gov/nistpubs/SpecialPublications/NIST.SP.1800-15.pdf

Newman, Andrew. "How Has Antivirus Software Evolved, and Where Might the Industry Be Heading?" *Forbes*, March 9, 2022: https://www.forbes.com/sites/forbestechcouncil/2022/03/09/how-has-antivirus-software-evolved-and-where-might-the-industry-be-heading/?sh=6016e8db5e0f

Holzberg, Melissa. "Hackers Got $5 Million: Colonial Pipeline Reportedly Paid a Ransom in Cryptocurrency, Contrary to Claims." *Forbes*, May 13, 2021: https://www.forbes.com/sites/melissaholzberg/2021/05/13/hackers-got-5-million-colonial-pipeline-reportedly-paid-a-ransom-in-cryptocurrency-contrary-to-claims/?sh=2b72afbb799e

Wright, Gavin, and Alexander S. Gillis. "What Is a Side-Channel Attack?" *Security*, April 6, 2021: https://www.techtarget.com/searchsecurity/definition/side-channel-attack?Offer=abt_pubpro_AI-Insider

"Top 10 Most Dangerous Malware of All Time." Dynamic Solutions Group, December 21, 2022: https://www.dsolutionsgroup.com/top-10-most-dangerous-malware-of-all-time/

This chapter covers the following topics:

- **Physical access controls:** Understanding what physical access controls are and their importance

- **Physical security controls:** Ways to implement physical security controls

- **Monitoring physical security:** Ways to monitor controls in place

- **Authorized versus unauthorized access:** Differences between the two

CHAPTER 4

Physical Access Controls

Physical access controls are typically the first line of defense when protecting and securing an organization. These controls help reduce the chance of damage to the organization or theft of its property. Access controls come in many forms, such as badging systems, gates and barriers, and policies and procedures to follow to determine whether authorized and unauthorized individuals should be allowed into a space. In this chapter, we will go deeper into these areas and why they are important.

This chapter covers the following Certified in Cybersecurity exam objectives:

- 3.1 Understand physical access controls

  - 3.1a Physical security controls (e.g., badge systems, gate entry, environmental design)

  - 3.1b Monitoring (e.g., security guards, closed-circuit television (CCTV), alarm systems, logs)

  - 3.1c Authorized versus unauthorized personnel

"Do I Know This Already?" Quiz

The "Do I Know This Already?" quiz allows you to decide whether you need to read this entire chapter or skip to the "Exam Preparation Tasks" section. If you doubt your selection of answers to these questions or your own assessment of your knowledge of these topics, you may want to read the entire chapter. Table 4-1 lists the major headings in this chapter and their corresponding "Do I Know This Already?" Quiz questions. You can find the answers in Appendix A, "Answers to the 'Do I Know This Already?' Quizzes and Q&A Sections." Good luck!

Table 4-1   "Do I Know This Already?" Section-to-Question Mapping

Foundation Topics Section	Questions
Physical Security Controls	1–5
Monitoring for Physical Security	6–9
Authorized versus Unauthorized Personnel	10

CAUTION   The goal of self-assessment is to gauge your mastery of the topics in this chapter. If you do not know the answer to a question or are only partially sure of the answer, you should mark that question as wrong for purposes of the self-assessment. Giving yourself credit for an answer you correctly guess skews your self-assessment results and might provide you with a false sense of security.

1. Which of the following is *not* an example of physical access controls?

    a. Locks

    b. Gates

    c. Cybersecurity software

    d. Fences

2. Which type of badging system uses RFID technology for access control?

    a. Proximity cards

    b. Smart cards

    c. Biometric IDs

    d. Turnstiles

3. What is the purpose of using gates for physical protection?

    a. To visually identify authorized personnel

    b. To track where access cards are used

    c. To limit physical access to facilities

    d. To integrate with badging systems

4. What is a drawback of using turnstiles for access control?

    a. They are easily customizable for different organizations.

    b. They can be integrated with badging systems.

    c. They can cause delays and bottlenecks in traffic.

    d. They provide the same level of security as solid gates.

5. Which access control method is based on unique characteristics like fingerprints or facial recognition?

    a. Badging systems

    b. Access codes or PINs

    c. Biometric authentication

    d. Gate

6. Which of the following is *not* a type of CCTV camera?

    a. Fixed cameras

    b. Dome cameras

    c. Pan-tilt-zoom (PTZ) cameras

    d. Mobile cameras

7. What is the role of security guards in physical security?

    a. They monitor CCTV systems.

    b. They set up access control systems.

    c. They patrol and monitor the premises.

    d. They manage logs and documentation.

8. What can trigger alarm systems in physical security?

    a. Unauthorized access to areas

    b. Motion when no one should be present

    c. Lapses in CCTV coverage

    d. All of these answers are correct.

9. How is the retention of access logs and other documentation determined?

    a. By the organization's data retention policy

    b. By the manager of the security team

    c. By stakeholder consensus

    d. By the discretion of individual employees

10. How do security guards determine whether someone is authorized or unauthorized personnel?

    a. They check the person's identification.

    b. They analyze the person's body language.

    c. They rely on the person's job title.

    d. They make a judgment based on the person's appearance.

Foundation Topics

Let's dive into the world of physical access controls. These measures and procedures are put in place to safeguard physical assets and regulate entry into buildings, rooms, and other areas of importance. It's important to note that these controls are designed to restrict access until specific authorization has been granted.

Physical controls are integral to an organization's overall security, especially when protecting sensitive data. In areas where confidential information is stored, it's critical to have secure physical access controls in place. These controls help prevent unauthorized access, which can potentially compromise sensitive data, lead to data theft, or threaten an organization's security.

Examples of physical access controls include locks, gates, and fences. These barriers are meant to keep unwanted individuals out and allow only authorized personnel access to restricted spaces. This ensures that valuable resources and equipment are protected from harm, tampering, or theft.

Physical Security Controls

There are several factors that organizations should consider when implementing physical security controls. The nature of the business helps determine what type of security is needed. If the organization stores or processes top-secret information, armed security guards or security fences may be the best choice to enhance security. Conversely, an unarmed security guard and cameras may suffice for a retail store. Where a facility is located will also determine what type of access control is appropriate and how much control is needed. Regulations can also play a part in the decision-making process for physical security controls. An organization's risk assessments and security planning should include all these considerations, plus others that may relate directly to the organization's industry.

Risk assessments can also help organizations better understand how to balance security convenience when planning which controls to implement. It's pointless to implement a control that people circumvent because it causes inconvenience. Security measures shouldn't hinder employee productivity or operations while mitigating risks and ensuring unauthorized individuals cannot gain access.

Badge Systems

Badge systems allow organizations to control access to facilities, secure areas, computer systems, and places only authorized employees should be able to access. Simply stated, these systems are designed to control who can access what, physically. Badges also log the activity of the employee as they enter different areas of the organization.

Badges are commonly used to identify authorized personnel visually. Badges often contain the individual's name, a photograph, and some sort of unique identifier such as employee ID number (see Figure 4-1). Badges can be easily displayed and verified by security personnel and access control systems. In conjunction with other physical security controls, additional security is added to a facility with the use of badges and access control cards.

Olivia Nguyen
Database Administrator
ID# YYZ90210
Building 3A

Figure 4-1   Sample Badge

Here are three types of badge systems to consider:

■ *Proximity cards*: Use radio frequency identification (RFID) technology to communicate with card readers and allow access based on proximity to the reader. Proximity cards are part of the contactless card technology in that you don't have to insert the card into a device reader. These cards are commonly used in office buildings, hotels, healthcare facilities, and other industries.

- *Smart cards:* Have an embedded microchip containing data for identification and authentication. This data typically includes a password, personal identification number (PIN), private key, and other access information that is needed. Smart cards perform various calculations to confirm someone's identity and what they have access to. This technology is commonly used by entities with highly sensitive or classified data with strict access control guidelines. Many government agencies and organizations use smart cards to control physical access to facilities and resources on the computer network.

- *Biometric IDs:* Combine the power of biometric identification with smart card technology. Biometric ID cards can store fingerprint data, retina data, and other types of information that relate to someone's identity. By adding the smart card functionality to the mix, there is added security, such as embedded chips. Many universities and research institutions are evaluating the risks and benefits of moving to these types of cards for enhanced security in the campus community. We will briefly discuss biometric identification later in this chapter.

These are the most common badging types you will encounter when working in most environments. They provide a means to verify who is authorized to access specific spaces and data and who is not.

Badges allow organizations to limit physical access to facilities and data based on job function, security clearance, and specific physical locations in the building.

NOTE A *security clearance* is a status granted to individuals that allows them access to classified information after an in-depth security investigation has been conducted. Security clearances range from confidential (least restrictive access) to top secret (most restrictive access). Clearances are typically granted to individuals who work or have applied to work within the U.S. federal government. As an example, the U.S. government issues security clearances to its employees after they have been thoroughly screened. Individuals do need to be U.S. citizens to obtain a security clearance in the United States. Other countries might have different requirements for clearance.

Access to restricted areas, secure zones, and other access points are based on the principle of "least privilege," which means employees are given access only to those areas required to do their job. Badging systems help monitor and control this access and can be adjusted as needed as roles and responsibilities change. Each organization should have a set of policies and procedures for issuing badges to employees and revoking access when it is no longer needed. Employees will need to be trained on how to use the badge and how to store the badge securely when not in use. Each organization should also have a policy in place that instructs employees what to do if their badge is lost or stolen and what steps the employee and the employer should take to ensure no unauthorized access is granted.

Badge systems provide an effective way for organizations to protect their physical space, quickly verify if someone is authorized or not, and take action if unauthorized access is attempted.

Gates for Physical Protection

Gates are a great way to protect access to a facility physically. They help deter and delay intruders. Using some sort of gate or barrier system can also provide a single point of entry (SPOE), adding more security protections. Gates also serve as a physical deterrent to threat actors, as they are typically controlled and monitored by badging systems, security guards, or CCTV. (Security guards and CCTV are discussed later in this chapter.) Different types of gates are available for physical security, such as gates used by pedestrians while walking or electronic sliding gates sometimes seen at private locations. Each organization can customize the gates to fit their needs and security requirements. Gates and barriers can also integrate with badging systems to allow or deny an employee access based on their authorization levels and their need to know.

 ## Types of Gate Entry Systems

When considering gates and barriers, organizations should first look at whether local ordinances, zoning requirements, and building codes require specific types of gates and barriers for their location. Whichever system is chosen, the materials used should be able to resist intrusions and be of a certain height, typically at least six feet, when thinking about gates and fences. The placement of these barriers is also important. They should be placed at appropriate distances to prevent a vehicle from gaining enough momentum to breach the entry point. Let's look at a few types of gate systems and what they require.

Turnstiles

Turnstiles, such as shown in Figure 4-2, are commonly used in train and subway stations, stadiums, amusement parks, and similar venues with a high rate of pedestrian traffic. If you have ever taken the train or gone to a concert, you might have utilized a turnstile to gain access to the facility. These electronic barriers are typically used to control pedestrian traffic because they allow entry of only one person at a time into a facility. Often, access to the facility requires valid credentials (or tickets) to pass through the turnstile. Turnstiles are also used to prevent tailgating. Tailgating is when an unauthorized person attempts to gain access to a facility or space by closely following an authorized employee.

Figure 4-2   Turnstiles (Image Credit: Serjio74/Shutterstock)

Barrier Gates

Barrier gates are typically used to regulate the flow and access of vehicle traffic entering and exiting a physical location. They use a horizontal "arm" that raises and lowers to give access, as illustrated in Figure 4-3. The arm is a physical barrier that serves as a deterrent to threat actors. Like turnstiles, these systems can be integrated with badge systems and security guards and are easy to use once installed. Implementing barrier gates is a great access control measure, but they do not provide the same level of security as a solid gate. A vehicle can be driven through the arm to gain access to the premises.

Bollards

Bollards, as illustrated in Figure 4-4, are beams or poles that control the flow and safety of pedestrian and vehicle traffic around a facility. These systems provide physical security at night or after hours while still allowing access during the day. The beams can be either movable or stationary or be raised and lowered manually or automatically using hydraulics, based on the needs of the organization. Bollards are used a lot around government buildings or places that contain highly sensitive data. The primary drawback of bollards is that they can be difficult to implement around existing buildings due to lack of space to install them. They can also slow down emergency personnel.

Figure 4-3   Barrier Gates (Image Credit: Fedor Selivanov/Shutterstock)

Figure 4-4   Bollards (Image Credit: Ratchat/Shutterstock)

Access Control

Access to the operational controls of a gate or barrier system should be restricted to authorized personnel who need access to the gate or barrier. Often, these systems integrate with a badge system and may require an access code or PIN to verify the user is authorized to access the space or data they are trying to access. Authorized personnel can easily control, manage, and change the code within an access control system, allowing them to adjust operational controls as needed.

Biometric authentication, such as through the use of fingerprints and facial recognition, provides other ways that authorized access may be granted. Today, we have the ability to log in to smart phones, tablets, and computers with these types of authentication methods. Based on the device settings and what permissions are granted, users can gain access to facilities and data based on their unique physical characteristics. This form of authentication is great because it is hard to fake a fingerprint or someone's face when trying to gain unauthorized access, contrary to what we see in movies and TV series!

As mentioned previously, gate and barrier systems can also integrate with badging systems to synchronize access across the systems. This integration allows an employee to use their badge to gain physical access to an environment. When the badge is used, the employee's permissions are checked in real time against the database to see what level of access, if any, they should have. This also reduces the risk of unauthorized access and provides an additional layer of security.

Environmental Design

Environmental design can also play an important role in physically securing a facility. When considering the design of physical access controls, consider the Crime Prevention Through Environmental Design (CPTED) concept. CPTED is a multidisciplinary approach to crime prevention that uses environmental design strategies to deter criminal activity. An organization should consider the following four principles:

- *Natural surveillance* is using people, such as security guards, or technology, such as lighting, to observe an area. The presence of these measures keeps intruders out because they do not want to be observed.

- *Natural access control* such as bollards, landscaping, gates, and other physical features can be used to control the flow of traffic and pedestrians.

- *Territorial reinforcement* creates clear boundaries between public and private spaces, reinforcing "ownership" of the property by the authorized users.

- *Maintenance* is an ongoing task to ensure the surrounding property and the access controls in place are still effective. If an area looks outdated, threat actors might be more likely to attempt to gain access to the premises.

Following this method will allow organizations to make informed decisions about current locations and future locations when it comes to physical security.

Environmental controls also aid in the previously mentioned SPOE strategies, helping to reduce the number of physical entry points an organization's campus or building has. Having a single entry point from an environmental standpoint helps an organization strictly control the process of identifying who is and is not authorized to access the premises. This approach helps regulate entry and deters unauthorized access. In an emergency situation, bollards can be raised to stop someone from leaving without permission fairly quickly. Similarly, the SPOE strategy can prevent unauthorized personnel from leaving without first being questioned.

 # Monitoring for Physical Security

Once access controls are put in place, organizations must monitor these systems and take action if unauthorized guests gain access to the facility. Monitoring can be conducted in various ways, such as using security guards, CCTV, or reviewing the access logs.

Security Guards

In a previous life, I (Mari Galloway) was an armed *security guard* at the headquarters of the U.S. Department of State in Washington, DC. My job was to patrol and grant access to the State Department based on whether those entering the facility were visitors or authorized personnel.

There were multiple checks to gain access to the property and then again to access the actual building. We checked every person's identification, whether it was a smart card, driver's license, or other form of identification, and then granted access if appropriate. At the State Department, many types of barriers and gates were used, such as bollards and control arms, which both detected and prevented unauthorized access.

The role of the security guard is to patrol and monitor the premises for any signs of unauthorized access, suspicious activity, or security breaches. Guards are essentially the first line of defense when it comes to physical security and serve as a physical deterrent. They use CCTV to monitor and ensure the safety and security of the building. The use of CCTV also allows for faster threat detection. Security guards check the identification of all those entering the premises and can allow visitors into the space based on what they need and where they need to go. In addition to their surveillance duties, security guards are also trained in emergency response for fires and medical emergencies. They have a clear understanding of evacuation routes, assembly points, and emergency communications systems within the facility.

Training for security guards should be ongoing to ensure they are versed in the newest threats and monitoring techniques. Training such as live simulations should also be conducted for incident response purposes. Guards should also be trained and encouraged to build positive relationships with employees and visitors to help with information gathering should incidents or events occur. We want people to approach guards with critical issues they are observing so those concerns can be addressed promptly.

Closed-Circuit Television

A *closed-circuit television (CCTV)* system is a network of cameras strategically placed to monitor and record activities in and outside a facility. Several countries and cities also use this technology to monitor suspicious or illegal activity. CCTV setups can include any or all of the following camera types:

- **Fixed cameras:** Cameras that are stationary and capture a specific field of view.

- **Pan-tilt-zoom (PTZ) cameras:** Cameras that can be controlled from a control room and can be moved to get a better view of a situation.

- **Dome cameras:** Cameras that are typically used indoors and are more aesthetically pleasing.

- **Bullet cameras:** Weather-resistant cameras that are cylindrical (like bullets) and mounted on poles to provide a wide view of an area or building.

Combining all these types of cameras in a CCTV system allows an organization to have a full internal and external view of what is going on around its facility.

A networked video management system (VMS) is a combination of hardware and software components used to manage and control video surveillance cameras across different locations. VMS provides functionality such as live video viewing, camera configuration, video playback, and access control integration. Users can set up notifications for alerts, video analytics, motion detection, and more advanced options.

Where these cameras are placed is critical to the success of managing access controls. Understanding what is considered critical in an organization helps determine where cameras are placed. Ideally, cameras should be located where entry and exit points exist in a facility. These can include parking lots, high-traffic areas, places where valuable assets are stored such as vaults, and any area prone to a potential security breach such as a server room. Cameras should be placed in locations that provide the best view of the area being surveilled. They should also be out of reach to prevent tampering with or destroying the camera. Blind spots, lighting, and camera resolution all play a role in finding the best location for camera placement.

No one wants their brand-new cameras placed where the sun can obstruct the camera view, thereby causing a gap in security.

Once CCTV systems are installed, they must be monitored. Standard operating procedures (SOPs) should be in place for employees to understand what they should do if they view suspicious activity. Typically, the CCTV network is monitored by security guards who are trained in how to utilize this type of technology. Because these cameras are recording continuously, how long data is stored—data retention—is based on the legal requirements of the jurisdiction the organization falls in and organizational policies. Access to this data should also be restricted to those with a need to know and law enforcement should an incident occur.

Alarm Systems

An *alarm system* provides an additional layer of physical security by sounding an alert if someone tries to circumvent another physical security measure to gain access to areas they are not authorized to access. A comprehensive alarm system includes various sensors placed on doors, windows, and other access points within the organization to detect unauthorized access and alert personnel. It may also include motion detectors that send alerts when motion is detected during a time when there should not be movement.

When an alarm is triggered, organizations will activate their incident response plan to investigate and triage the alarm. Depending on the severity of the alarm, the incident response team will notify the stakeholders to jump into action. The incident response plan identifies when stakeholders should be contacted and by whom. Clearly defined incident response procedures are important to mitigate any issues in a quick and timely fashion. Security guards typically monitor these alarms and can react quickly when incidents occur. There are also offsite, remote monitoring systems that track all alerts for various organizations. Smaller organizations may use a monitoring center if they don't have personnel in-house, which allows for two-way communication between the organization and the monitoring team to verify and confirm that an event is occurring.

Logs and Documentation

Logs are generated when access is granted or denied to entry points of a facility. These logs can then be reviewed if an alarm is triggered, for further investigation. These logs, along with other network and system logs, are usually reviewed by the security operations team in a SIEM, if applicable. In smaller organizations the physical security team may review those logs when an alarm is triggered.

Access logs and entry and exit attempts create an accountability trail as they record the who, what, when, and where of the access. These logs also record failed access attempts, which can help with potential security breaches and determine the root cause of issues in emergency situations. This same type of information is available in visitor logs. Logs can also assist in creating new policies and procedures for investigations.

The length of time that logs should be retained is based on a number of factors. An organization should have a data retention policy that dictates how long data should be retained and when it should be deleted. The policy should comply with legal and regulatory requirements such as the EU General Data Protection Regulation (GDRP) and, if applicable, the U.S. Health Insurance Portability and Accountability Act (HIPAA). Logs should be kept in a secure location to prevent unauthorized access to that data. Access logs should be reviewed on a regular basis to help identify anomalous behaviors that could be potential security breaches or insider threats. Automated tools are available to help with this review and monitoring process.

Authorized Versus Unauthorized Personnel

As previously discussed in this chapter, authorized personnel typically are issued badges that give them access to the premises, buildings, rooms, and systems based on their job function or what they need to accomplish. For individuals who are unauthorized or visitors, a few additional checks may be required. Unauthorized personnel can include contractors and vendors where their authorization depends on the permission granted by the organization. Unauthorized personnel will still need to show identification and provide a valid reason for needing access. This information is tracked via logs by the security guards to ensure that these visitors take care of their business in a timely manner. Visitors may also need to be escorted while they are in the facility, which typically is done by security guards or the visitor's point of contact at the organization.

Exam Preparation Tasks

As mentioned in the Introduction, you have a couple of choices for exam preparation: the exercises here, Chapter 13, "Final Preparation," and the exam simulation questions in the Pearson Test Prep Software Online.

Review All Key Topics

Review the most important topics in this chapter, noted with the Key Topics icon in the outer margin of the page. Table 4-2 lists a reference of these key topics and the page numbers on which each is found.

Table 4-2 Key Topics for Chapter 4

Key Topic Element	Description	Page
Section	Badge Systems	56
Section	Types of Gate Entry Systems	59
Section	Monitoring for Physical Security	63
Section	Authorized Versus Unauthorized Personnel	66

Define Key Terms

Define the following key terms from this chapter and check your answers in the glossary:

badge system, proximity cards, smart cards, biometric IDs, turnstiles, bollards, security guards, closed-circuit television (CCTV), alarm system

Q&A

The answers to these questions appear in Appendix A. For more practice with exam format questions, use the Pearson Test Prep Software Online.

1. What are three types of badge systems used to grant access to a facility or room?

2. What type of camera should be used if an organization wants to move the camera to get a better view of a location?

3. What type of physical controls help create a single point of entry to a facility?

4. What software is used to control and monitor CCTV setups?

5. What are two ways to protect and monitor an organization for a physical security breach and what purpose do they serve?

References

Dail, Vincent. "Biometric Identification Cards, the Future of Personal Identification." *Biometric-Security-Devices*, 2021: https://www.biometric-security-devices.com/biometric-identification-cards.html

U.S. Customs and Border Protection. "Background Investigations." *U.S. Customs and Border Protection*, 2024: https://www.cbp.gov/careers/car/bi

The International Crime Prevention Through Environmental Design. "Primer in CPTED – What is CPTED?": https://www.cpted.net/Primer-in-CPTED

Rouse, Margaret. "What is a bullet camera?" *Techopedia*, September 23, 2016: https://www.techopedia.com/definition/4694/bullet-camera

Isarsoft. "What is Video Management Software (VMS)?" January 17, 2024: https://www.isarsoft.com/knowledge-hub/vms

National Crime Prevention Council. "Crime Prevention Through Environmental Design Guidebook." October 2003: https://rems.ed.gov/docs/Mobile_docs/CPTED-Guidebook.pdf

This chapter covers the following topics:

- **Logical access controls:** Definitions of logical access controls

- **Principle of least privilege:** Concept to separate access based on need to know

- **Segregation of duties:** Concept of separation of duties

- **Discretionary access control (DAC):** Policy defined by user

- **Mandatory access control (MAC):** Policy defined by system

- **Role-based access control (RBAC):** Policy defined by the user's function/role in the company

CHAPTER 5

Logical Access Controls

In this chapter, we'll examine logical access controls. Access controls are a fundamental aspect of cybersecurity. Logical access controls enable key security principles, including the principle of least privilege, segregation of duties, DAC, MAC, and RBAC. We'll also briefly look at automation and identity and access management (IAM).

This chapter covers the following Certified in Cybersecurity exam objectives:

- 3.2 Understand logical access controls

  - 3.2a Principle of least privilege

  - 3.2b Segregation of duties

  - 3.2c Discretionary access control (DAC)

  - 3.2d Mandatory access control (MAC)

  - 3.2e Role-based access control (RBAC)

"Do I Know This Already?" Quiz

The "Do I Know This Already?" quiz allows you to decide whether you need to read this entire chapter or skip to the "Exam Preparation Tasks" section. If you doubt your selection of answers to these questions or your own assessment of your knowledge of these topics, you may want to read the entire chapter. Table 5-1 lists the major headings in this chapter and their corresponding "Do I Know This Already?" Quiz questions. You can find the answers in Appendix A, "Answers to the 'Do I Know This Already?' Quizzes and Q&A Sections." Good luck!

Table 5-1 "Do I Know This Already?" Section-to-Question Mapping

Foundation Topics Section	Questions
Need to Know and Least Privilege	1–2
Segregation of Duties	3
Security Models	4–7
IAM and Automation	8

CAUTION The goal of self-assessment is to gauge your mastery of the topics in this chapter. If you do not know the answer to a question or are only partially sure of the answer, you should mark that question as wrong for purposes of the self-assessment. Giving yourself credit for an answer you correctly guess skews your self-assessment results and might provide you with a false sense of security.

1. Which of the following best describes logical access controls?

    a. Access controls that regulate physical access to computer systems

    b. Access controls that restrict access to software, applications, and databases based on user privileges

    c. Access controls that separate critical tasks and responsibilities among multiple individuals

    d. Access controls that monitor and audit user access to information systems

2. What is the principle of least privilege?

    a. Users are only provided with the information they need to complete their job.

    b. Users are granted the least amount of permission necessary to complete their job function.

    c. Users have access to all the privilege and control in the organization.

    d. Users have limited access to information or systems.

3. What is the purpose of segregation of duties?

    a. To ensure efficient completion of tasks

    b. To reduce the risk of unauthorized or fraudulent activities

    c. To grant complete control over a process to one person

    d. To increase efficiency in task completion

4. What is the main difference between mandatory access control and discretionary access control?

    a. MAC allows subjects to override access control policies, while DAC does not.

    b. MAC is focused on data integrity, while DAC is focused on confidentiality.

c. MAC implements zero trust in its control mechanism, while DAC separates subjects into trusted and untrusted groups.

d. MAC is used in government agencies and defense organizations, while DAC is used in corporate environments.

5. Which access control model focuses on confidentiality by controlling access based on security levels and preventing information leakage?

   a. Role-based access control

   b. Mandatory access control

   c. Discretionary access control

   d. Biba Model

6. Which security model focuses on controlling access based on the user's assigned role?

   a. Mandatory access control

   b. Bell-LaPadula Model

   c. Clark-Wilson Model

   d. Role-based access control

7. What is the purpose of an access matrix in access control?

   a. To map permissions to each user or role in the organization

   b. To enforce separation of duties in a constrained access control model

   c. To visualize the hierarchy of permissions in a hierarchical access control model

   d. To centralize user management and access control in an IAM system

8. Which technology can IAM utilize to enhance security by requiring users to provide multiple forms of authentication when accessing objects?

   a. Single sign-on

   b. Automation scripts

   c. Security orchestration, automation, and remediation tools

   d. Multi-factor authentication

Foundation Topics

In Chapter 4, "Physical Access Controls," we discussed the importance of physical access controls as the first layer of defense from external actors. In this chapter we turn to logical controls (software and policies) used within the organization to regulate access to software, applications, databases, and other digital resources based on user privileges and credentials. Logical access controls are of utmost importance in ensuring the security and integrity of computer systems and information. Having logical controls in place helps with maintaining the confidentiality, integrity, and availability (CIA) of data.

Let's first take a look at a few concepts that help with implementing logical access controls.

Need to Know and Least Privilege

There are a variety of concepts that are important to note when considering logical access controls for an organization. These concepts help an organization place restrictions on which systems and information users are authorized to access. The concept of *need to know* is that users gain access only to information they need to know or have access to in order to complete their job functions and shouldn't have access to any other information. An organization determines which information each employee should have access to and then implements role-based access controls (RBAC) to grant the least amount of permissions necessary to access that information. This is the *principle of least privilege (POLP)*. In a nutshell, "need to know" is about what information an employee should know, while POLP is about implementing the correct access controls to take action on that information.

For example, suppose that you are assigned the IT role of a company and your privileges are restricted to that role. In that case, you won't have access to financial- or HR-related files, such as onboarding data or employee compensation data, because you don't need to know that information.

Access controls come with different levels of privilege. Privilege levels determine which files and computer resources a user can access and which actions they can take after accessing those files and resources. The higher the level, the more access and control the user has.

The following are three common privilege levels:

- **Administrator:** Typically, all the privileges—think root—and thus is a target for threat actors

- **User:** Typically, has limited access to only the files and resources needed to complete their day-to-day job

- **Guest:** Very limited access to information or systems

Each organization will have different privilege levels based on their organizational needs.

Implementing POLP and need to know is a great way to minimize an organization's attack surface, as individuals are limited in what they can access and what they can do once they have access. This also reduces the risk of data breaches because access is being monitored. POLP also helps to reduce human error. If a threat actor gains access to an account, the permissions for that account will prevent that user from accessing other data or systems they don't have authorization for.

POLP adds an additional layer of security to continue to protect the data and systems, but it can be complex to implement because an organization must have a clear understanding of job roles and descriptions and what access each role needs. This causes teams to spend additional time monitoring access control levels and updating as employees move between teams or exit the company. Implementing too much control usually is met with resistance from employees if the controls start to hinder or impede their work. Automation (discussed later in this chapter) is a great way to assist with keeping controls in line.

Segregation of Duties

Another key concept when implementing logical access controls is ***segregation of duties (SOD)***, also known as *separation of duties*, which refers to dividing critical tasks and responsibilities among multiple individuals to ensure that one person doesn't have complete control over a process. SOD helps to reduce error and fraud. If you have ever watched a bank heist movie, you've likely seen an example of SOD in action. Such movies typically show that opening the vault requires two bank employees with different keys simultaneously turning their keys to open the vault. SOD is implemented so that one person doesn't have complete access to sensitive information or systems, which ensures that checks and balances are happening.

SOD comes from the accounting world and involves separating four key functions when dealing with a transaction or task: authorization, custody, record-keeping, and reconciliation. Ideally, a different employee would be responsible for each of the four functions. This adds an extra layer of control and oversight to critical processes and reduces the risk of unauthorized or fraudulent activities.

Along with the various good reasons to separate duties and responsibilities, SOD does have some disadvantages. The framework that SOD uses, by its nature, is a disadvantage. Requiring multiple people to complete a task that one person could perform takes more time and is more cumbersome. It also reduces efficiency, requires coordination of schedules, and can increase costs if additional people need to be hired to implement SOD.

Security Models

Security models are used to specify and enforce security policies in an organization. These models provide varying levels of security to ensure access is granted to authorized users only. The following are a few key terms to keep in mind as we go through the three different models covered on the Certified in Cybersecurity exam:

- **Subject:** User or resources run by users capable of accessing objects
- **Object:** The resource or data the subject wants to access in a system

Think of a security model as a blueprint to protecting data and information for an organization. A security model provides the plan of action organizations should be taking when securing their information.

Discretionary Access Control

Discretionary access control (DAC) is a security model that grants or restricts access to objects based on the discretion of the data owner. DAC is discretionary because the object owner can transfer access to other subjects without approval of an administrator. The owner decides who can access specific resources and sets the access permissions accordingly. With DAC, unauthorized subjects can't see object characteristics, and several failed access attempts deny access or enforce additional authentication measures.

DAC is implemented through the use of an access control list (ACL) for each object. The ACL defines what access users should have and what they can do with that access (read or update). Perhaps the most commonly recognized form of DAC is implemented in the Unix file system. With this system, the owner of an object can grant read (-r), write (-w), and execute (-x) permissions for users, groups, and others. Figure 5-1 shows what DAC controls look like.

DAC provides organizations with a flexible means of adding security to objects. It also allows owners to delegate access control decisions without consulting an administrator, enabling them to ensure access rights can be tailored to meet the specific needs and security policies of the organization.

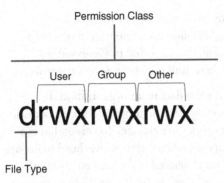

Figure 5-1 Discretionary Access Control Permissions

There are some disadvantages to implementing DAC. DAC uses access control lists (ACLs) to enforce an action. ACLs list who has access to an object and what they can do with it. Maintaining ACLs can be a challenge if the number of users and resources increases. There also isn't a centralized control center to manage the ACLs, making changes to ACLs more difficult and time consuming. A conflict of interest can arise for users that are in multiple nested working groups in the system, causing no or limited access to objects.

After implementing DAC, organizations also need to regularly review access to objects and clean up where needed. Object owners should implement the principle of least privilege and only assign the minimum permissions needed to complete the task. Organizations must also monitor these controls and access logs for unusual access patterns.

Mandatory Access Control

Mandatory access control (MAC) is a security model that enforces access control based on classification levels and security labels. A classification level indicates the relative importance of classified information for national security and determines the specific security requirements for that information. The U.S. government uses Public/Non-classified, Confidential, Secret, and Top Secret to identify the security level. These levels may differ in other countries. MAC is typically used in environments that have high security requirements, such as government agencies or defense organizations.

MAC access decisions are made by a central authority or security policy; subjects do not have the ability to override the policy. The system owner or administrator has the authority to change access permissions. This is different from DAC, which allows a subject to give access to objects and provides more strict security controls. MAC implements a zero-trust policy in its control mechanism, requiring all users to be authenticated and verified before accessing objects. Subjects are no longer separated into trusted and untrusted groups. Although implementation of a zero-trust policy is beyond the scope of this book and the Certified in Cybersecurity exam, it is good information to understand when thinking about access controls.

MAC is one of the most secure ways to protect the data in an organization. It provides a high level of security and protection against unauthorized access because it is implemented from a security policy that users can't change. To this end, it is a complex system to implement and requires higher administrative overhead to ensure that the data stays up to date and that stale data is deleted and removed. MAC also doesn't scale well, and it can interfere with users' work because they have to request access to each new piece of data they might need to complete their job.

The following are a few notable MAC models that focus on various parts of the CIA triad. Figure 5-2 shows how mandatory access controls are implemented.

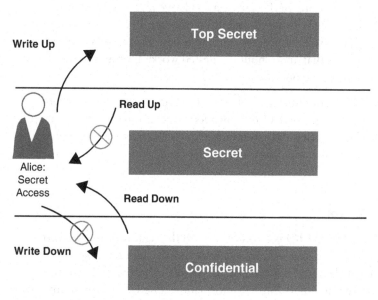

Figure 5-2   Mandatory Access Control Permissions

- **Bell-LaPadula Model:** Emphasizes confidentiality. It uses the concept of security levels (such as Top Secret, Secret, and Confidential) to control access and prevent information from being leaked to unauthorized users.

- **Biba Model:** Emphasizes integrity. It prevents subjects with lower integrity levels from modifying or corrupting objects with higher integrity levels.

- **Clark-Wilson Model:** Emphasizes data integrity and consistency. It achieves this by enforcing specific procedures and rules for subject access and modification of objects, promoting controlled and authorized changes.

Role-Based Access Control

The third security model to be familiar with for the Certified in Cybersecurity exam is *role-based access control (RBAC)*. Figure 5-3 shows how RBAC may be implemented. This model grants or restricts access to objects based on the user's assigned role. The permissions are defined by the job functions and responsibilities rather than individual user accounts, simplifying access management and reducing overhead. RBAC provides access to what an employee needs while restricting access to what they don't need based on their role in the organization. This also helps prevent unauthorized access to sensitive data.

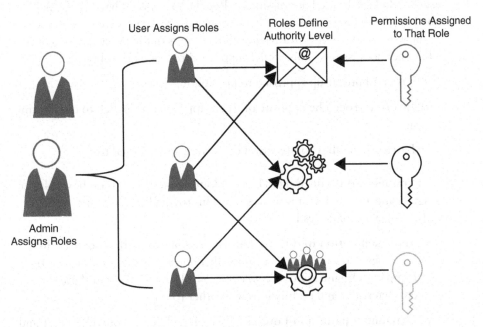

Figure 5-3   Role-Based Access Control Permissions

For instance, someone in IT wouldn't need access to financial information unless their role was specific to finance and they needed access. With RBAC, organizations can restrict access to the financial information to specific roles or groups of roles in the finance department and restrict or deny access to those in the IT department.

There are three types of access control models within RBAC:

- **Core:** The foundation of RBAC models, the core model describes the key elements of an RBAC system. When implementing RBAC, keep in mind these key elements:

    - **Role assignment:** A subject can only exercise privileges when assigned a role.

- **Role authorization:** The system authorizes a subject's active role. The system confirms the subject is authorized to access the object based on their role.

- **Permission authorization:** A subject can only apply permissions granted to the subject's active role. This means that users should only access resources that their assigned role permits.

- **Hierarchical:** Builds on the core model by stacking permissions. This allows for sharing and inheritance of permissions between roles. For example, a Guest user would have limited permissions, a Regular user would have all the permissions of the Guest user and whatever new permissions were assigned, and so on, with the Administrator having all the access of the previous users plus additional permissions. This model supports three hierarchical types:

  - **Tree:** A bottom-up approach to distributing access

  - **Inverted tree:** The opposite of tree, a top-down approach to distributing access

  - **Lattice/hybrid:** A combination of the tree and inverted tree

- **Constrained:** Constrained models add additional restrictions on how roles are assigned and accessed within the system. This particular type of model helps with segregation of duties in two ways:

  - **Static separation of duties:** This is based on where the user is in the hierarchy. No single user has mutually exclusive roles, as defined by the company. Organizations are able to control which roles can share characteristics and permissions with other roles.

  - **Dynamic separation of duties:** This is based on the role of the user and implements the least privilege principle. Users can be in multiple roles but cannot act in both roles at the same. For example, the person making the purchase can't also approve the purchase even if in the approver role. This helps prevent unauthorized role usage.

A great way to visualize access and permissions in RBAC is with a matrix. An access matrix is a table that defines the permissions and access rights of each user or role in the organization. The matrix lists users, resources (files, folders, systems, and so on), and the corresponding actions that can be performed on those resources. Next, permission assignments are mapped to each user or role to specify what actions they can perform.

Making sure this access matrix is updated regularly and then implemented into whichever system is chosen helps to keep access organized and maintained. This also ensures permissions still align to roles. As with any model, RBAC can be complex to set up and maintain and increases the administrative overhead due to monitoring and updating, but RBAC still serves as a model of choice in organizations.

IAM and Automation

Identity and access management (IAM) is a framework that manages and controls user identities, their access rights, and authentication across systems and applications. These systems centralize user management and access control, allowing changes and updates to access rights to occur more quickly. IAM may also use technologies such as single sign-on (SSO) and multi-factor authentication (MFA) for added security when users are trying to access objects. Having a well-defined IAM vision and a detailed understanding of roles and permissions are the few first steps in managing and maintaining whatever security model is chosen. With the use of automation scripts or security orchestration, automation, and remediation (SOAR) tools, organizations can grant or revoke permissions, update passwords, and identity information on a more automatic basis. In-depth discussion of these topics is beyond the scope of this book and the Certified in Cybersecurity exam, but they are important concepts to consider when thinking about access control.

Exam Preparation Tasks

As mentioned in the Introduction, you have a couple of choices for exam preparation: the exercises here, Chapter 13, "Final Preparation," and the exam simulation questions in the Pearson Test Prep Software Online.

Review All Key Topics

Review the most important topics in this chapter, noted with the Key Topics icon in the outer margin of the page. Table 5-2 lists a reference of these key topics and the page numbers on which each is found.

Table 5-2 Key Topics for Chapter 5

Key Topic Element	Description	Page
Paragraph	Need to Know and Least Privilege	74
Paragraph	Segregation of Duties	75
Paragraph	Discretionary Access Control	76
Paragraph	Mandatory Access Control	77
Paragraph	Role-Based Access Control	79

Define Key Terms

Define the following key terms from this chapter and check your answers in the glossary:

need to know, principle of least privilege (POLP), segregation of duties (SOD), discretionary access control (DAC), mandatory access control (MAC), Bell-LaPadula Model, Biba Model, Clark-Wilson Model, role-based access control (RBAC)

Q&A

The answers to these questions appear in Appendix A. For more practice with exam format questions, use the Pearson Test Prep Software Online.

1. What are the three permissions used with discretionary access control?

2. What are the core elements of role-based access control (RBAC)?

3. Which mandatory access control model focuses on confidentiality of information using security levels?

4. What can automation help an organization accomplish?

References

NIST SP 800-192. "Discretionary Access Control (DAC)": https://csrc.nist.gov/glossary/term/discretionary_access_control

NIST. "Role-Based Access Control": https://csrc.nist.gov/CSRC/media/Presentations/Role-based-Access-Control-an-Overview/images-media/alvarez.pdf

Quist, Arvin S. "Security Classification of information" April 1993: https://sgp.fas.org/library/quist2/chap_7.html

McCarthy, Maile and Brown, Schuyler. "Definitive Guide to Role-Based Access Control" *StrongDM*, December 22, 2023: https://www.strongdm.com/rbac

This chapter covers the following topics:

- **Network security:** Understanding network security.

- **OSI model:** Understanding how device communication works across the network and the ports and protocols used.

- **TCP/IP model:** Describing the differences between the models and their uses.

CHAPTER 6

Computer Networking Fundamentals

In this chapter we begin by discussing what computer networking is and the various types of networks. Next, we'll discuss the Open Systems Interconnection (OSI) model, including the ports and protocols that help packets traverse the network. Finally, we'll take a quick look at the layers of the TCP/IP model and how they relate to the OSI model.

This chapter covers the following Certified in Cybersecurity exam objectives:

■ 4.1 Understand computer networking

  ■ 4.1a Networks (e.g., Open Systems Interconnection (OSI) model, Transmission Control Protocol/Internet Protocol (TCP/IP) model, Internet Protocol version 4 (IPv4), Internet Protocol version 6 (IPv6), Wi-Fi)

  ■ 4.1b Ports

  ■ 4.1c Applications

"Do I Know This Already" Quiz

The "Do I Know This Already?" quiz allows you to decide whether you need to read this entire chapter or skip to the "Exam Preparation Tasks" section. If you doubt your selection of answers to these questions or your own assessment of your knowledge of these topics, you may want to read the entire chapter. Table 6-1 lists the major headings in this chapter and their corresponding "Do I Know This Already?" Quiz questions. You can find the answers in Appendix A, "Answers to the 'Do I Know This Already?' Quizzes and Q&A Sections." Good luck!

Table 6-1 "Do I Know This Already?" Section-to-Question Mapping

Foundation Topics Section	Questions
Understanding Computer Networking	1–5
Ports and Protocols	6, 7
OSI Model	8–12
TCP/IP Model	13

CAUTION   The goal of self-assessment is to gauge your mastery of the topics in this chapter. If you do not know the answer to a question or are only partially sure of the answer, you should mark that question as wrong for purposes of the self-assessment. Giving yourself credit for an answer you correctly guess skews your self-assessment results and might provide you with a false sense of security.

1. Which type of network is typically limited in range from a few centimeters to a few meters and connects devices within an individual's workspace?

   a. Local-area network

   b. Wide-area network

   c. Personal-area network

   d. Metropolitan-area network

2. Which networking device transmits data packets between connected devices on the LAN?

   a. Modem

   b. Network interface card

   c. Wireless access point

   d. Switch

3. Which type of network provides local wireless connectivity and is commonly found in settings like cafes, airports, and public spaces?

   a. Wide-area network

   b. Wireless local-area network

   c. Metropolitan-area network

   d. Personal-area network

4. What is the purpose of a metropolitan-area network?

   a. Connect multiple LANs across a city or large area

   b. Provide local wireless connectivity

   c. Connect devices within an individual's workspace

   d. Connect multiple WANs via radio waves or telephone lines

5. Which ports range from 0 to 1023 and are used for common services in network communications?

   a. Dynamic ports

   b. Registered ports

    c. Well-known ports

    d. Virtual ports

6. What is the main advantage of using fiber-optic cables in a wide-area network?

    a. Ability to connect devices within an individual's workspace

    b. Wireless connectivity for local network access

    c. High-speed data transmission over long distances

    d. Cost-effectiveness for small to medium-sized networks

7. Which transport layer protocol ensures reliable, ordered, and error-checked data transfer?

    a. TCP

    b. UDP

    c. SMTP

    d. HTTP

8. Which transport layer protocol is commonly used in multimedia applications that require real-time transmission and is prone to occasional packet loss?

    a. TCP

    b. UDP

    c. FTP

    d. SNMP

9. Which layer in the OSI model is responsible for data delivery between networks?

    a. Physical layer

    b. Transport layer

    c. Network layer

    d. Application layer

10. Which technique is used to conserve IPv4 address space by assigning a single public IP address to a device within a network?

    a. NAT

    b. DHCP

    c. IPsec

    d. SNMP

11. Which sublayer of the data link layer is responsible for flow control and handles communication between the MAC and network layers?

     a. Logical Link Control (LLC)

     b. Media Access Control (MAC)

     c. Physical layer (PHY)

     d. Transport layer (TCP/UDP)

12. Which wireless encryption standard is considered obsolete?

     a. WPA

     b. WPA2

     c. WPA3

     d. WEP

13. Which layer in the TCP/IP model combines the physical and data link layers of the OSI model?

     a. Application layer

     b. Transport layer

     c. Internet layer

     d. Network access layer

Foundation Topics

Understanding Computer Networking

A computer network is a system that interconnects two or more physical or logical machines, using networking devices such as computers and servers to enable them to share information and resources. These devices are connected through wired and wireless connections, enabling effective communication and data transmission.

The Advanced Research Projects Agency Network (ARPANET) became the first connected network in 1969. This network used the Transmission Control Protocol (TCP)/Internet Protocol (IP) suite of tools to facilitate communication between networked devices. The TCP/IP model is based on standard protocols and is the backbone of the Internet we use today. We discuss this model later in this chapter.

Computer networks play a crucial role in providing the infrastructure for organizations to carry out their day-to-day tasks. Through the network, users can use their devices to transmit and receive information, access file shares and applications, and communicate through email and video conferencing applications.

The size and geographic location of computer networks vary based on specific needs. Let's explore five types of computer networks:

- *Personal-area network (PAN):* A PAN is a network of devices connected within an individual's workspace. A PAN typically includes smartphones, computers, tablets, and other mobile devices. The range of a PAN is usually limited in range from a few centimeters to a few meters, and devices are often connected wirelessly or via Bluetooth, such as headphones or other peripheral devices.

Figure 6-1 illustrates a typical PAN topology.

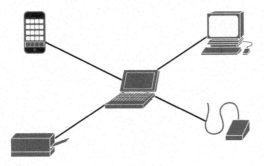

Figure 6-1 Personal-Area Network

■ **Local-area network (LAN):** A LAN is a network in a single physical location, such as an office building, school, or home. LANs are the most common type of network and can vary in size from small, connecting two computers, to large, connecting hundreds or thousands of computers. They enable users to connect to internal networks for purposes of printing, file sharing, accessing shared applications and databases, and accessing other resources necessary for business operations. Devices in a LAN are connected either through Ethernet cables or wirelessly. Additionally, LANs offer high-speed Internet access due to their relatively smaller size compared to other networks discussed later. Typical devices used in a LAN include the following devices:

  ■ **Switches:** Transmit data packets between connected devices in the network. These devices operate at Layer 2, the data link layer, of the OSI model (discussed in an upcoming section).

  ■ **Network interface cards (NICs):** Installed on individual computer systems to enable connection to a network. These cards aid in communication between devices.

  ■ **Wireless access points (WAPs):** Allow wireless-enabled devices to connect to the network.

  ■ **Servers:** Host shared applications that organizations need access to, such as email services, collaboration tools, virus protection, and storage.

  ■ **Modems:** Connect to the Internet service provider (ISP) network to give systems Internet access.

  ■ **Cables:** Required for wired connectivity. Cable types include untwisted shielded pair (UTP) cables, used for Ethernet access, and fiber-optic cables, discussed in the context of WANs later in this list.

Figure 6-2 illustrates a typical LAN topology.

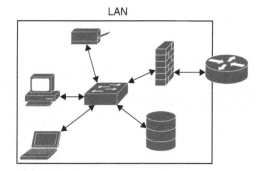

LAN

Figure 6-2   Local-Area Network

- *Wireless local-area network (WLAN):* A WLAN is similar to a LAN but provides local wireless connectivity. Devices can connect to a WLAN network using Wi-Fi-enabled devices. WLANs are commonly found in settings like cafes, airports, public spaces, and office settings where users can access the Internet wirelessly.

- *Metropolitan-area network (MAN):* A MAN connects multiple LANs across a city, providence, or large geographical area to provide access to shared resources and data. A MAN is larger than a LAN but smaller than a WAN. Examples of MANs include cable networks and telephone systems. Modems and cables (such as fiber optic) are typically used to connect LANs in a MAN.

Figure 6-3 illustrates a typical MAN topology.

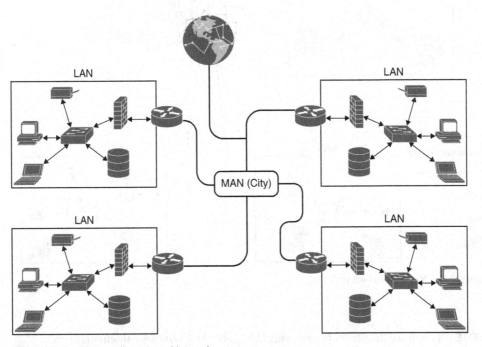

Figure 6-3   Metropolitan-Area Network

- *Wide-area network (WAN):* A WAN contains multiple LANs and MANs connected via radio waves or telephone lines. A WAN provides connectivity to a large number of systems and shared resources to business offices located further away from each other, connecting a large number of computers over a wide area. The Internet is a WAN that communicates over fiber-optic cable, which can transmit large amounts of data at high speeds. Fiber-optic cables are the width of a human hair and transmit data using light waves instead of electricity. Cables are made from silica glass that allows the light to bounce through the cable without issue.

Figure 6-4 illustrates a typical WAN topology.

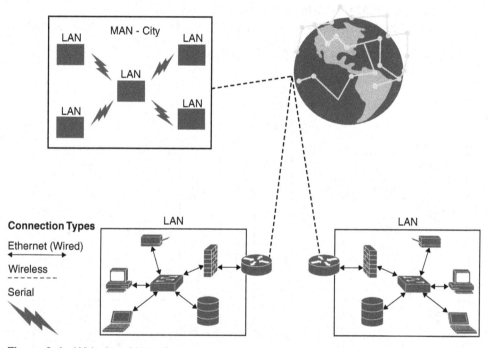

Figure 6-4   Wide-Area Network

NOTE   For more details on fiber-optic cables, visit https://www.cablematters.com/Blog/Networking/fiber-optic-cable-types-a-complete-guide.

Table 6-2 provides an overview of common network types; however, note that this is not an exhaustive list.

NOTE   To learn more about additional types of networks, visit https://www.geeksforgeeks.org/types-of-computer-networks/.

Table 6-2 Network Type Comparison

Network Type	Name	Coverage Area	Ownership	Technology
PAN	Personal-area network	Covers a small area or room	Personal (individual or household)	Bluetooth, Zigbee
LAN	Local-area network	Covers a limited geographical area, such as an office building or a campus	Private (organization or institution)	Ethernet, Wi-Fi
MAN	Metropolitan-area network	Spans across a city or metropolitan area	Public (government or municipality), private (organization or institution)	Ethernet, fiber-optic
WAN	Wide-area network	Spans across a wide region, such as a country or globally	Public (telecommunications company or ISP)	MPLS, Internet

Next, we discuss how data is transmitted between devices using the OSI model.

Ports and Protocols

In order for devices and systems to communicate, they rely on a variety of ports and protocols. *Ports* are the starting and ending points for network communications between computer devices. Ports identify where the data should go. There are 65,535 ports available, categorized as follows:

- **Well-known ports:** These ports range from 0 to 1023 and are used for common services. For example, port 80 is commonly used for Hypertext Transfer Protocol (HTTP), port 443 is commonly used for Hypertext Transfer Protocol Secure (HTTPS), and port 22 is for Secure Shell (SSH), to note a few examples. Well-known ports and their associated services are considered permanent and cannot be changed.

- **Registered ports:** Falling within the range of 1024 to 49151, registered ports are assigned to specific services that organizations wish to register for proprietary applications. An example of a registered port is 3389, used by Microsoft's Remote Desktop Access (RDP).

- **Dynamic ports:** Ranging from 49151 to 65535, dynamic ports are available for any application to use for communication. This flexibility allows users to initiate communication through a web browser over port 80 or 443 while the response is received on an available higher port. Dynamic ports are considered ephemeral, meaning they are temporary in nature. Once the connection is terminated, the port becomes available for use.

A *protocol* provides a framework for reliable and efficient communication between devices on a network. It defines the syntax, formatting, and semantics of the message being sent. The protocol also outlines the actions that should be taken during communication, such as error handling and data validation. We will discuss protocols further in the next section.

OSI Model

The International Organization for Standardization (ISO) created the *Open Source Interconnection (OSI) model* in the 1970s as a vendor-neutral, conceptual model used to visualize and describe the logical communication between devices. This model uses a universal set of protocols for interoperability between systems. The OSI model contains seven layers that serve different functions and purposes as a packet traverses the network. The model is typically broken up into the three upper layers (application, presentation, session) and the four lower layers (transport, network, data link, physical).

As shown in Figure 6-5, as the data moves along the stack, header information is added (*encapsulation*) or removed (*decapsulation*) at each layer to help securely and efficiently guide packets to their destination. The important features depicted in the middle column of Figure 6-5 are introduced in the following discussion of the OSI layers.

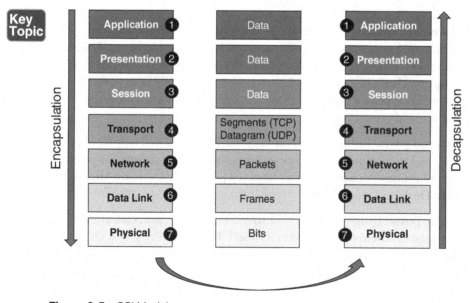

Figure 6-5   OSI Model

A *packet* is a unit of data, a small piece of a larger message sent across the network. When data is transmitted across the network, messages are broken down into smaller, more manageable pieces for more efficient delivery. Packets generally contain the following parts:

- *Header*: Contains information about the packet, the source and destination information, sequence numbers, and other control information to help deliver the packet to the correct destination.

- *Payload*: This is the data that is being transmitted, such as an email or data from or to a website.

- *Trailer*: This is optional but contains error detection and parity checks.

While the maximum packet size is 64KB, packets sent across the network are significantly smaller for more efficient transmission. Packet size can be set to an amount an organization wishes, but the size shouldn't exceed the hardware Maximum Transmission Unit (MTU). For Ethernet networks, that limit is 1500 bytes. The process for breaking these packets up is known as *data fragmentation*.

NOTE Use a mnemonic device to help remember the layers of the OSI model, such as All People Seem To Need Data Processing.

Figure 6-5 shows an example of a letter being written and sent through the postal service to represent how data traverses the network. The sender writes a letter (Application) to her friend that is placed in an envelope (Presentation) and addressed (Session). This letter is then placed in the mailbox for pickup and delivery by a postal worker (Transport). The postal worker takes the letter to the post office (Network), where it is sorted (Data Link) for delivery to the friend's mailbox (Physical).

Application Layer (Layer 7)

The *application layer* is the topmost layer of the OSI model, closest to the end user. This layer ensures that end users can exchange data with other applications on different devices and networks. *Data* is presented to the end user via web browsers, email clients, and other applications. Layer 7 devices that provide security to an organization include firewalls, IDS/IPS, and endpoint security tools.

The application layer is not an actual application but a set of protocols and services that facilitate communication between applications. This layer communicates down to the presentation layer to ensure the data is in the correct format for delivery. Table 6-3 outlines the common protocols and ports used at the application layer.

Table 6-3 Application Layer Protocols

Protocol	Name	Purpose	Port(s)
DNS	Domain Name System	Translates domain names into IP addresses; phone book of the Internet	53
FTP	File Transfer Protocol	Transfer files from one system to another	20, 21*
HTTP(S)	Hypertext Transfer Protocol (Secure)	Use for communication between web browsers and web servers	80, 443
SMTP	Simple Mail Transfer Protocol	Used for email communications	25
SNMP	Secure Network Management Protocol	Gathers data about devices on the network	161, 162
Telnet	Telecommunications Network	Used to manage files over the Internet; SSH (22) is the more secure way to access files remotely	23

*Port 21 used by default for FTP. Port 21: Control port, Port 20: Data channel.

Presentation Layer (Layer 6)

The *presentation layer* translates data to be presented in the correct format for the recipient. This allows communication with both the application layer and the lower layers. If something is being sent via email, the presentation layer formats it for email delivery. If pictures are being sent, the presentation layer formats them as .jpeg or other image and video formats. This layer is also responsible for data encryption and compression. Data compression reduces the size of a data packet for faster transmission.

Secure Socket Layer (SSL) and Transport Layer Security (TLS) are protocols typically used over port 443, HTTPS. They enhance the security of transmitted data. Chapter 8, "Data and the System," discusses data encryption in more detail.

Session Layer (Layer 5)

The *session layer* establishes, manages, and terminates sessions with applications on different systems. This layer connects the upper and lower layers, preparing the data and connection for secure transmission. While there are no specific ports or protocols for this layer, the session layer relies on transport layer protocols such as Remote Procedure Call (RPC) and NetBIOS to establish connections in networked environments.

Transport Layer (Layer 4)

The *transport layer* is responsible for data delivery between networks. Once the data is packaged, the transport layer determines which delivery method is best for it: Transmission Control Protocol (TCP) or User Datagram Protocol (UDP). These packages are considered packets. Error checking also occurs here to ensure that data is correctly transmitted or fixed for retransmission. TCP packets are segments of data sent from the transport layer, while UDP packets are datagrams, which is a network unit that doesn't need a response.

TCP ensures reliable, ordered, and error-checked data transfer using a three-way handshake, as illustrated in Figure 6-6. The handshake establishes a secure connection between a client and a server by exchanging acknowledgment (ACK) and synchronization (SYN-ACK) packets between the sending and receiving systems. Once the final acknowledgment (ACK) is received, the connection is established and data is transmitted. To ensure successful delivery, each segment has header and sequencing information for the receiving systems to reassemble the message. TCP is connection-oriented as it requires a successful connection before data is transmitted.

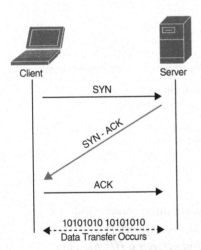

Figure 6-6 TCP Three-Way Handshake

UDP is a connectionless protocol that offers faster delivery but sacrifices reliability because it doesn't require delivery confirmation. Unlike TCP, UDP does not establish a connection before communication begins. UDP is commonly used in multimedia applications, such as streaming video or live audio, that require real-time transmission and function properly despite occasional packet loss. Due to UDP's lack of error-checking and retransmission mechanisms, however, there is no guarantee that all segments will reach the destination or arrive in the correct order.

Network Layer (Layer 3)

The *network layer* takes segments sent from the transport layer and determines the best path to route the data based on their Internet Protocol (IP) address. These segments are encapsulated with header information to continue their journey through the network. IP addresses are logical addresses that help *packets* reach their final destination. These addresses are like the physical address used on a letter. We discuss the IP protocol next.

Routers are used at this level to connect two or more networks together for communication. Each router contains a routing table that identifies all the "hops" in a network a packet could travel to reach its destination. The Internet is a network of routers worldwide that move packets along the best path. In our postal example, each post office would be a router moving the letter to its correct destination. This layer also handles network congestion and packet fragmentation and reassembly as needed. Table 6-4 lists and describes the additional protocols that operate at the network layer.

Table 6-4   Network Layer Protocols

Protocol	Name	Purpose
ICMP	Internet Control Message Protocol (Ping and Traceroute)	Checks if devices on a network are reachable and sends a response to the original host
IPsec	Internet Protocol Security	Suite used to encrypt network communications; built into IPv6
IGMP	Internet Group Management Protocol	Used to manage group membership for hosts, routers, and other devices

Internet Protocol

The *Internet Protocol version 4 (IPv4)* is the most common connectionless protocol that provides "best effort delivery" and is used at the network layer. IP logical addresses are either IP version 4 or *Internet Protocol version 6 (IPv6)*. They determine which network and device a packet should be routed to.

IPv4 was introduced in 1982 as an upgrade to previous IP versions. There are approximately 4 billion IPv4 addresses in use or available today. IPv4 addresses are 32-bit dotted-decimal notation addresses that identify the *network* and *host* to which a packet is transferred. These addresses are broken into four octets separated by a decimal, as illustrated in Figure 6-7.

192 . 168 . 110 . 125

8 Bits = 1 Byte   8 Bits = 1 Byte   8 Bits = 1 Byte   8 Bits = 1 Byte

32 Bits = 4 Bytes

Figure 6-7   Sample IPv4 Address

As outlined in Table 6-5, the original IP addressing system (prior to IPv4) consisted of five classes that offered a fixed number of addresses per subnet, known as *classful* IP addressing.

Table 6-5   Classful IP Addressing

Class	First Octet of IP Address	Subnet Mask	Purpose
Class A	1–126	255.0.0.0	Large networks
Class B	128–191	255.255.0.0	Medium networks
Class C	192–223	255.255.255.0	LANs
Class D	224–239	—	Multicast traffic
Class E	240–254	—	Research

Each octet goes from 0 to 255, allowing for 256 addresses each. IP addresses that end with 0 or 255 are reserved for other purposes. If an IP address ends in 0, it is the network identifier. If an IP address ends in 255, it is the broadcast IP address and all systems on that network will respond to messages from that address.

However, this system had limitations, such as inflexibility in addressing, inefficient use of address space, and the inability to accommodate network growth. In response, *classless inter-domain routing (CIDR)* was introduced in 1993. CIDR allows for a more flexible allocation of IP addresses with various subnet sizes without the constraints of class boundaries. This has led to more efficient use of address space and has facilitated the rapid expansion of the Internet and networking technologies.

The example in Figure 6-8 shows the IP header information used to route packets to their destinations. There are 14 fields, of which 13 are required.

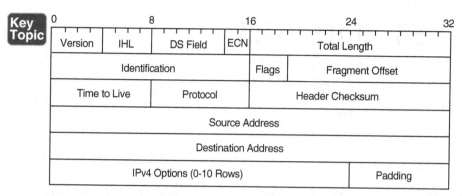

Figure 6-8 IPv4 Header

Network address translation (NAT) is a technique to conserve IPv4 address space. It enables an organization to connect its internal network to the Internet using private IP addresses by assigning a single public IP address to a device within its network. This device, known as a *NAT gateway*, acts as an intermediary, translating the private IP addresses of internal devices into the public IP address for external communication. NAT helps mitigate the scarcity of IPv4 addresses by allowing multiple devices to share a single public IP address, promoting efficient utilization of available addresses while providing a secure connection between the internal network and the Internet.

NOTE Private IP addresses are reserved address ranges for use on interworks. These IPs are not routable to the Internet:

- 10.0.0.0–10.255.255.255
- 172.16.0.0–172.31.255.255
- 192.168.0.0–192.168.255.255

IPv6 was created to account for the rising number of devices on the Internet as well as to address security concerns with IPv4. IPv6 addresses are 128-bit, broken into eight groups separated by colons, known as *hexadecimal notation*. This means the address space available for use is enormous. IPv6 addresses are assigned to interfaces instead of nodes, allowing multiple interfaces on a device to have an IP address.

There are a few advantages to using IPv6 over IPv4. IPv6's vast number of addresses allows for fewer network collisions. IPv6 addresses do not require NAT. Their header format allows for simpler, more efficient routing. IPv6 addresses can also be automatically configured, which doesn't require a server on the network to assign the address to an endpoint.

IPv6 addresses include three parts:

- **Prefix (48 bits):** Defines the public topology assigned by the ISP
- **Subnet ID (16 bits):** Defines the private network set up in the organization
- **Interface ID (64 bits):** Token that is configured from the media access control (MAC) address or manually

When there are continuous zeros in the address, these zeros are compressed using colons and single zeros. Figure 6-9 shows the full version and compressed versions.

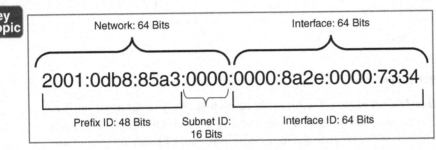

Simplified Versions

2001:0db8:85a3::8a2e:0000:7334

2001:0db8:85a3::8a2e:0:7334

Figure 6-9 Sample IPv6 Address

NOTE IPv6 has prefixes similar to private IPs for special use. These include

- 2002::/16—Indicates that a 6to4 routing prefix follows
- fe80::/10—Indicates that a link-local address follows
- ff00::/8—Indicates that a multicast address follows

The header information also looks a little different than that of an IPv4 header. The sample in Figure 6-10 shows the IPv6 header format.

IPv6 also incorporates enhancements such as improved security, built-in quality of service (QoS) support, and simplified network configuration.

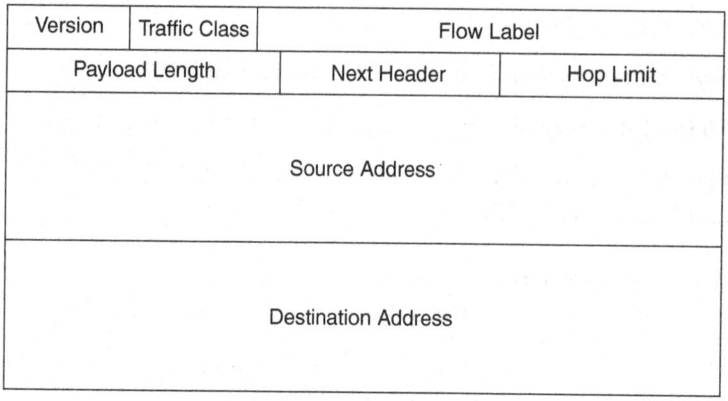

Version	Traffic Class	Flow Label	
Payload Length		Next Header	Hop Limit
Source Address			
Destination Address			

Figure 6-10   IPv6 Header

Data Link Layer (Layer 2)

The *data link layer* is responsible for node-to-node delivery of information, error free. Packets are encapsulated into frames and sent bit by bit to the physical layer for decapsulation on the receiving system. With framing, a header and trailer are added to the packet that provide information about the data in the packet, the MAC address of systems involved, and the frame start and end information. This allows the frames to be reassembled on the receiving end so the user gets the message.

Devices such as switches and bridges are typically seen operating at this layer.

There are two sublayers of the data link layer:

- *Logical Link Control (LLC)*
- *Media Access Control (MAC)*

The LLC sublayer is responsible for sending each frame to the next destination along its journey, known as *flow control*. This layer handles the communication between the network layer and the MAC sublayer.

The MAC layer is the lower level of the data link layer and connects the LLC to the physical layer. This is where the hardware address lives. The MAC address is hard-coded and burned on all NICs by the manufacturer and is unique to every device. Data encapsulation and error control are handled by the MAC sublayer as well.

As illustrated in Figure 6-11, a MAC address is a 12-digit, 48-bit hexadecimal number that is broken into two parts: the organizationally unique ID (OUI) or manufacturer ID and the NIC ID, which is device-specific. The OUI is specific to the vendor that developed the system. Here are the OUIs of some popular vendors:

- Google: 60:70:6C

- Apple: 60:FD:A6

- Microsoft: 70:F8:AE

Figure 6-11 Sample MAC Address

MAC addresses may also use colons and periods to separate each octet. Unicast MAC addresses are used for one-to-one communication between specific devices. Multicast MAC addresses facilitate one-to-many communication within a group of devices. Broadcast MAC addresses enable one-to-all communication across the entire local network. The broadcast destination address is noted as FF-FF-FF-FF-FF-FF, which equals all 1's in binary form. To learn more about binary, visit https://careerkarma.com/blog/learn-to-code-in-binary/.

Protocols

A variety of protocols are used at the data link layer. Common protocols include the following:

- **Address Resolution Protocol (ARP):** ARP maps an IP address (Layer 3) to a MAC address (Layer 2). This mapping is then added to the ARP tables of devices on the network for future frame routing.

- **Point-to-Point Protocol (PPP):** PPP is a popular protocol to establish a direct connection between two nodes over different physical media, such as serial cables, Ethernet, or wireless connections. It operates at the data link layer and offers features like authentication, error detection, and encryption. PPP is commonly used in dial-up connections, DSL, and virtual private networks (VPNs).

- **Synchronous Data Link Protocol (SDLC):** SDLC is a communication protocol developed by IBM, used for reliable and error-free transmission of data in point-to-point and multipoint networks. It implements error-checking and flow-control mechanisms to ensure data integrity and efficient data transfer.

Wireless

Wireless networks provide the capability to connect devices without the use of physical cables or wires. They rely on radio waves to transmit and receive data across the network. The technology commonly used for wireless networks is known as *Wi-Fi*.

Wi-Fi operates based on the IEEE 802.11 standards, which define the protocols and specifications for wireless communication. These standards enable devices to communicate with each other within a LAN or connect to the Internet.

The main components of a Wi-Fi network include

- *Access point (AP)*: The access point serves as a central hub that connects wireless devices to the network. It broadcasts the wireless signal and allows devices to communicate with each other and access resources. To connect, users must know the AP's service set identifier (SSID).

- *Wireless network interface card (WNIC)*: As stated previously, NICs are installed on individual computer systems to enable connection to a network. These cards aid in communication between devices. A wireless NIC allows for communication with wireless-enabled devices.

- *Router*: The router connects the wireless network to the Internet. It routes data packets between the local network and the Internet, enabling devices to access online resources.

Wi-Fi networks use radio frequencies to transmit data. The 2.4-GHz and 5-GHz bands are the primary frequency ranges used by Wi-Fi networks. Wi-Fi standards like 802.11b/g/n operate in the 2.4-GHz band, while newer standards like 802.11ac/ax operate in the 5-GHz band, offering faster speeds and better performance. Table 6-6 outlines the 802.11 wireless standards; however, this is not an exhaustive list of wireless standards. To learn more, visit https://www.ieee802.org/.

Table 6-6 Wireless Standards

Standard	Year Introduced	Frequency Band	Maximum Data Rate	Encryption
802.11b	1999	2.4 GHz	11 Mbps	WEP, WPA, WPA2
802.11g	2003	2.4 GHz	54 Mbps	WEP, WPA, WPA2
802.11n	2009	2.4/5 GHz	300–900 Mbps	WEP, WPA, WPA2

Standard	Year Introduced	Frequency Band	Maximum Data Rate	Encryption
802.11ac	2013	5 GHz	433–6933 Mbps	WEP, WPA2, WPA3
802.11ax	2019	2.4/5 GHz	600–12000 Mbps	WEP, WPA2, WPA3

Wired Equivalent Privacy (WEP) was the first wireless encryption standard and, as the name indicates, was intended to provide security equivalent to wired networks. While it served its purpose for a while, WEP's critical security vulnerabilities were soon discovered. Weak security with short key lengths, static key authentication, and various other flaws made WEP an unreliable choice for securing wireless networks. In response, Wi-Fi Protected Access (WPA) was introduced, significantly enhancing wireless security with dynamic key authentication. WPA2 and WPA3 provide even stronger security measures to protect network traffic against brute-force attacks, network exploiting techniques, and more. WEP is deemed obsolete and should be replaced by WPA2 or higher encryption methods.

Table 6-7 shows the difference between various wireless encryption standards and protocols.

Key Topic

Table 6-7 Wireless Encryption Comparison

Encryption	Year	Security Level	Key Size	Authentication	Additional Notes
Wired Equivalent Privacy (WEP)	1997	Weak	40/104 bits	Shared static key	Replaced by WPA
Wi-Fi Protected Access (WPA)	2003	Moderate	256 bits	Pre-shared static key	Largely replaced by WPA2
WPA2	2004	Strong	256 bits	Dynamic key	Current standard for most wireless networks
WPA3	2018	Enhanced security	192/256 bits	Simultaneous authentication; individualized data encryption	Provides stronger encryption using Simultaneous Authentication of Equals (SAE) but requires hardware

Simultaneous Authentication of Equals (SAE) enables password-based authentication and a key agreement mechanism.

Physical Layer (Layer 1)

The *physical layer* is the lowest layer of the OSI model. It is responsible for transmitting and receiving raw data bits over the physical medium, such as copper wires, optical fibers, or wireless radio waves. The physical layer is concerned with the electrical, mechanical, and timing aspects of data transmission. It defines the physical characteristics of the network, including the physical connectors, signaling, voltage levels, and data transmission rates. The primary function of the physical layer is to establish and maintain the physical link between network devices, ensuring reliable and efficient data transfer.

TCP/IP Model

The *TCP/IP model* is a suite of protocols used to facilitate communication between networked devices. This is the foundation of the Internet we use today. The TCP/IP model is broken up into four distinct layers: application, transport, Internet, and network access. Figure 6-12 shows how it compares to the OSI model.

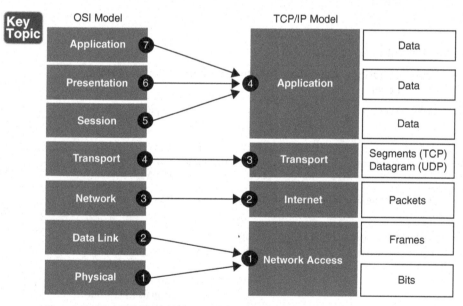

Figure 6-12   OSI Model Versus TCP/IP Model

The application layer is the top layer of the TCP/IP model and includes the functions of the application, presentation, and session layers of the OSI model. This layer interfaces with the end-user applications such as email services and web browsers. The application layer also allows users to log in to remote hosts.

The transport layer is responsible for ensuring reliable and efficient data transmission between devices. TCP and UDP are both used here for the transmission of data. TCP ensures reliable delivery of data and requires confirmation of connection and delivery. UDP provides connectionless, faster delivery of packets to the final destination. This is similar to the transport layer of the OSI model.

The Internet layer, also referred to as the network layer, is responsible for routing packets across the network. This layer uses IP to move data through the network and to determine the best path to the destination. This is the network layer in the OSI model.

The network access layer (also known as the network link layer) handles the physical transmission of the data from device to device. This layer defines the protocols that are used for communication between systems such as Ethernet and Wi-Fi. This layer combines the physical and data link layers of the OSI model.

NOTE   Do not confuse Layer 3 (network) of the OSI model with Layer 1 (network access) of the TCP/IP model. These are two distinct layers that offer very different functionality in the network.

Exam Preparation Tasks

As mentioned in the Introduction, you have a couple of choices for exam preparation: the exercises here, Chapter 13, "Final Preparation," and the exam simulation questions in the Pearson Test Prep Software Online.

Review All Key Topics

Review the most important topics in this chapter, noted with the Key Topics icon in the outer margin of the page. Table 6-8 lists a reference of these key topics and the page numbers on which each is found.

Table 6-8   Key Topics for Chapter 6

Key Topic Element	Description	Page Number
Paragraph	Understanding Computer Networking	89
Note	Points to a resource on fiber-optic cables	92
Table 6-2	Network Type Comparison	93
Section	Ports and Protocols	93

Key Topic Element	Description	Page Number
Paragraph	OSI Model	94
Figure 6-5	OSI Model	94
List	Lists packet components	95
Table 6-3	Application Layer Protocol	96
Paragraph	Describes TCP and three-way handshake	97
Table 6-4	Network Layer Protocols	98
Section	Internet Protocol	98
Table 6-5	Classful IP Addressing	99
Figure 6-8	IPv4 Header	100
Paragraph	Describes NAT and private IP address space	100
Figure 6-9	Sample IPv6 Address	101
List	Lists the main components of a Wi-Fi network	104
Table 6-7	Wireless Encryption Comparison	105
Figure 6-12	OSI Model Versus TCP/IP Model	106

Define Key Terms

Define the following key terms from this chapter and check your answers in the glossary:

> personal-area network (PAN), local-area network (LAN), wireless local-area network (WLAN), metropolitan-area network (MAN), wide-area network (WAN), ports, protocol, Open Source Interconnection (OSI) model, packet, header, payload, trailer, application layer, presentation layer, session layer, transport layer, network layer, Internet Protocol version 4 (IPv4), Internet Protocol version 6 (IPv6), classless inter-domain routing (CIDR), network address translation (NAT), data link layer, Logical Link Control (LLC), Media Access Control (MAC), Wi-Fi, access point (AP), wireless network interface card (WNIC), router, physical layer, TCP/IP model

Q&A

The answers to these questions appear in Appendix A. For more practice with exam format questions, use the Pearson Test Prep Software Online.

1. What type of devices are typically seen in a LAN?

2. What three categories do ports fall into and what are the ranges for each?

3. What are the seven layers of the OSI model?

4. At which layer of the OSI model does the ARP protocol operate?

References

Kainth, James. "The OSI and TCP/IP Model – Networking Basics." June 14, 2021: https://jameskainth.com/cyber/blog/2021/06/14/OSITCPIPModel.html

Oracle. "IPv6 Addressing overview System Administration Guide: IP Services." 2011:https://docs.oracle.com/cd/E18752_01/html/816-4554/ipv6-overview-10.html

Neso Academy. "Sub-layers of the Data Link Layer." March 11, 2020: https://www.youtube.com/watch?v=N1apF49Ih28

Arul's utilities. "MAC Address and OUI Lookup." March 26, 2024 https://aruljohn.com/mac.pl

WiFi Alliance. "Discover Wi-Fi Security." 2024: https://www.wi-fi.org/discover-wi-fi/security

Douglas. "Fiber optic Cable Types A Complete Guide." *Cable Matters Reliable Connectivity*, July 29, 2022: https://www.cablematters.com/Blog/Networking/fiber-optic-cable-types-a-complete-guide

This chapter covers the following topics and corresponding proficiencies:

- **On-premises network security infrastructure:** Describe different on-premises security measures.

- **Secure network design:** Describe the components of a secure network.

- **Cloud security infrastructure:** Describe cloud deployment and service models.

CHAPTER 7

Network Security Infrastructure

In this chapter, we will first look at various types of infrastructure that can be used to secure both the physical and logical assets in your organization. Next, we will look at how to design a network securely. Finally, we'll dive into cloud infrastructure, deployment, and service models.

This chapter covers the following Certified in Cybersecurity exam objectives:

■ 4.3 Understand network security infrastructure

   ■ 4.3a On-premises (e.g., power, data center/closets, Heating, Ventilation, and Air Conditioning (HVAC), environmental, fire suppression, redundancy, memorandum of understanding (MOU)/memorandum of agreement (MOA))

   ■ 4.3b Design (e.g., network segmentation (demilitarized zone (DMZ), virtual local area network (VLAN), virtual private network (VPN), micro-segmentation), defense in depth, Network Access Control (NAC) (segmentation for embedded systems, Internet of Things (IoT))

   ■ 4.3c Cloud (e.g., service-level agreement (SLA), managed service provider (MSP), Software as a Service (SaaS), Infrastructure as a Service (IaaS), Platform as a Service (PaaS), hybrid)

"Do I Know This Already" Quiz

The "Do I Know This Already?" quiz allows you to decide whether you need to actually read this entire chapter or skip to the "Exam Preparation Tasks" section. If you doubt your selection of answers to these questions or your own assessment of your knowledge of these topics, you may want to read the entire chapter. Table 7-1 lists the major headings in this chapter and their corresponding "Do I Know This Already?" Quiz questions. You can find the answers in Appendix A, "Answers to the 'Do I Know This Already?' Quizzes and Q&A Sections." Good luck!

Table 7-1   "Do I Know This Already?" Section-to-Question Mapping

Foundation Topics Section	Questions
On-Premises Network Security Infrastructure	1–4
Designing Secure Networks	5–8
Cloud Network Security Infrastructure	9–14

CAUTION   The goal of self-assessment is to gauge your mastery of the topics in this chapter. If you do not know the answer to a question or are only partially sure of the answer, you should mark that question as wrong for purposes of the self-assessment. Giving yourself credit for an answer you correctly guess skews your self-assessment results and might provide you with a false sense of security.

1. Which type of fire suppression system is commonly used in data centers, industrial settings, or other locations where water or foam-based systems would damage sensitive equipment or materials?

   a. Sprinkler systems

   b. Gas-based systems

   c. Foam systems

   d. Wet and dry chemical systems

2. Which of the following is not a characteristic of a memorandum of understanding (MOU)?

   a. To establish a legally binding contract between parties

   b. To outline the intended actions and responsibilities of the parties involved

   c. To resolve disputes that may arise during a partnership or collaboration

   d. To specify the timeline and deliverables for completing tasks or achieving goals

3. Which security strategy involves implementing multiple layers of security measures, such as firewalls, intrusion detection/prevention systems, and endpoint protection, to provide comprehensive data protection and impede threat actors?

   a. Network segmentation

   b. Defense-in-depth

   c. Microsegmentation

   d. Virtual Private Networks

4. Which network security technique provides enhanced protection by implementing security controls between workloads within a network

    a. Network segmentation

    b. Defense-in-depth

    c. Microsegmentation

    d. Virtual private networks

5. What is the purpose of a demilitarized zone (DMZ)?

    a. To provide a logical division within a physical network

    b. To establish secure connections between multiple networks

    c. To act as a buffer zone between an organization's internal network and the external network

    d. To ensure privacy and data protection for mobile users

6. What is the function of switches in implementing virtual local area networks?

    a. VLANs segment, manage, and control virtual networks.

    b. VLANs provide encryption for secure network connections.

    c. VLANs enforce security policies and controls for mobile devices.

    d. VLANs act as a buffer zone between an organization's internal network and the external network.

7. What is the difference between the public cloud and a private cloud?

    a. The public cloud is more secure than a private cloud.

    b. Unlike the public cloud, a private cloud is only accessible through the Internet.

    c. A private cloud is deployed for a specific organization and allows for tailored hardware and software.

    d. A public cloud allows for greater control and flexibility over assets.

8. Which cloud deployment model offers a collaborative, secure, cost-effective solution for organizations with shared needs?

    a. Public cloud

    b. Private cloud

    c. Hybrid cloud

    d. Community cloud

9. In which cloud service model is the CSP responsible for providing virtualized resources and services that can be accessed over the Internet, allowing organizations to free themselves from purchasing expensive hardware?

   a. IaaS

   b. PaaS

   c. SaaS

   d. None of these answers are correct.

10. In which cloud service model is the CSP responsible for maintaining and updating all the components necessary to run the application, while the organization is only responsible for how the application will be used and who needs access?

   a. IaaS

   b. PaaS

   c. SaaS

   d. None of these answers are correct

11. Which type of SLA allows customers to select different levels of service based on their requirements and budget?

   a. Customer SLA

   b. Internal SLA

   c. Multilevel SLA

   d. Managed service provider SLA

12. What is the purpose of a managed service provider?

   a. To provide security services to organizations

   b. To monitor customers' environment for issues and concerns

   c. To provide business continuity solutions

   d. All of these answers are correct.

Foundation Topics

On-Premises Network Security Infrastructure

In today's digital age, the physical security of on-premises network infrastructure plays a critical role in protecting sensitive data and confidential information. With cyber threats on the rise, it is crucial to prioritize physical security measures. An organization's on-premises network serves as the foundation of data protection efforts.

Inadequate security exposes organizations to various risks, including external threats, insider attacks, and physical vulnerabilities. Hackers, malware, and disgruntled employees are all potential sources of concern. Weak access controls and unsecured server rooms further compound the risks.

Maintaining strong physical security can decrease the risk of unauthorized access, data breaches, and financial losses. Strong access controls, surveillance systems, intrusion detection, and employee training programs contribute to a secure network infrastructure.

Environmental Controls

Environmental controls safeguard IT equipment and facilities from physical environmental factors such as temperature, humidity, and water damage. CCTV, security guards, and smoke and fire detectors can also monitor these systems. These controls ensure that the physical environment of an IT facility is within proper limits to prevent damage to sensitive equipment and data loss. The following list provides examples of important assets that require protection and the corresponding environmental controls that can be used to protect them:

- *Power sources*: Systems that bring power to the facility. Threat actors can take these systems offline, causing a service disruption. Implementing redundant power systems and backup generators and installing uninterruptible power supply (UPS) units help to minimize the risk of data loss or network downtime.

- *Data center*: Provides a controlled and secure environment for housing physical devices such as routers, switches, servers, and other network devices. Adding surveillance, access control, and fire suppression systems within the data center adds additional security measures.

- *Data closet*: Serves a similar purpose to a data center but on a much smaller scale. Typically, this is a room or empty space in an office building that can be secured with lockable doors, restricted access, and environmental monitoring systems.

- *Heating, Ventilation, and Air Conditioning (HVAC) systems*: Heat, cool, and circulate air throughout a facility. Maintaining proper temperature and humidity levels is crucial to prevent damage to sensitive equipment. Additionally, HVAC systems should be positioned and secured to prevent unauthorized access.

Fire Suppression Systems

Fire suppression systems are another form of environmental control. These systems help reduce and eliminate building and data center fires by using extinguishing agents such as water, foam, or other chemical compounds. Each type of system is designed to extinguish or suppress fires depending on the nature of the environment, type of fire, and potential hazards involved. Here are the most common types of fire suppression systems:

- **Sprinkler systems:** Use heat-sensitive sprinkler heads that detect high temperatures. Upon detection, the systems then expel water to smother the fire. These are the most common systems in office, commercial, and industrial buildings and cover a large space.

- **Gas-based systems:** Use chemicals in a gas form discharged into the protected enclosure to suppress the fire. Examples include CO_2, Halon, FM-200, Novec 1230, and Inergen. These agents displace oxygen and remove the heat that feeds the flames, effectively extinguishing the fire. They are often used in data centers, industrial settings, or other locations where water or foam-based systems would damage sensitive equipment or materials.

- **Foam systems:** Use a mixture of water and foaming agents to extinguish or suppress the fire. The foam forms a blanket over the fire, separating the flames from the fuel source and thus suffocating the fire. Foam suppression systems are often used in chemical and petrochemical facilities or other settings where flammable liquids are present.

- **Wet and dry chemical systems:** Use foam or chemicals sprayed from nozzles or sprinklers to extinguish the fire. Wet chemical systems are used in commercial kitchens and restaurants for oil or grease fires. On the other hand, dry chemical systems are often used in settings involving flammable liquids or gasses, such as fuel storage facilities, airports, and petroleum refineries.

In addition to these systems, tools such as fire blankets, fire extinguishers, and fire alarms can aid in fire detection and suppression. Table 7-2 provides additional details on the five classes of fire and their respective suppression method.

Table 7-2 Fire Suppression Methods

Class	Fuel	Suppression Method
Class A	Ordinary combustibles: wood, clothing, trash, etc.	Water
Class B	Flammable liquid: paint, gas, oil, etc.	Halon, fuel, dry chemical
Class C	Electrical: circuits, electrical outlets, etc.	Dry chemical, CO2
Class D	Combustible metal: magnesium, titanium, etc.	Dry chemical
Class K or F	Kitchen: cooking oil, etc.	Wet chemical, foam

Redundancy and High Availability

Redundancy and high availability are key concepts in network design that aim to ensure continuous operation and minimize downtime. *Redundancy* refers to providing multiple paths, duplicate components, or backup systems in a network, while *high availability (HA)* focuses on maintaining network accessibility and functionality with minimal interruptions. For example, redundant links allow traffic to be rerouted in case of a link failure, ensuring continuous connectivity. Similarly, redundant devices can take over the responsibilities of failed components, preventing service interruptions.

By incorporating redundancy measures, networks become more fault-tolerant. If a failure occurs, redundant paths or devices are designed to automatically take over, minimizing the impact of the failure on network availability. This fault tolerance enables quick recovery and reduces downtime, ensuring the network remains operational despite failures or maintenance activities.

On the other hand, high availability is the ultimate goal of redundancy. Redundancy contributes to high availability by providing backup options, load balancing, and fault tolerance. It helps distribute network traffic across multiple paths, prevent bottlenecks, and enable quick failure recovery.

High availability is crucial in environments where uninterrupted network connectivity is essential, such as data centers, critical infrastructure, or businesses relying heavily on network-dependent operations. HA ensures that users can access services or applications consistently without disruptions, enhancing productivity, customer satisfaction, and overall business continuity.

Memorandum of Understanding and Memorandum of Agreement

A *memorandum of understanding (MOU)* is a nonbinding written agreement that outlines two or more parties' intended actions and responsibilities. It is a foundational document that promotes effective collaboration and minimizes the likelihood of misunderstandings or disputes. A *memorandum of agreement (MOA)* is a legally binding agreement that defines the specific goals and actions that will be taken. MOAs list out specific legal terms that establish a conditional agreement.

When drafting an MOU/MOA, it is important to include the following elements:

- *Purpose of the partnership* defines the purpose or objective of the partnership. This section should outline why the parties entered the agreement and what they hope to achieve through collaboration.

- *Goals of each party* specify each party's goals. Clearly articulate the desired outcomes or milestones each party aims to accomplish in the partnership. This ensures that everyone is on the same page regarding their respective objectives.

- *Duties of each party* outline the specific duties, responsibilities, and contributions each party will fulfill throughout the partnership. This section clarifies the roles and expectations of each party, reducing the risk of confusion or disagreements later on.

- *Timeline* outlines key activities, deliverables, or milestones. This helps establish a structured framework and ensures that the parties clearly understand the expected timeline for completing tasks or achieving goals.

- *Confidentiality clause* ensures that all parties understand their obligations to maintain the confidentiality of any shared information or trade secrets.

- *Process for resolving disputes* addresses potential conflicts and how to resolve them. This can include negotiation, mediation, or arbitration to help parties find amicable solutions if issues arise.

By including these elements in an MOU/MOA, parties can establish a solid foundation for their partnership or collaboration. The MOU/MOA clarifies, sets expectations, and creates a roadmap for achieving shared goals.

Designing Secure Networks

Data protection is a major concern for organizations in today's digital landscape. Protecting devices is essential, but safeguarding the internal network is equally important to avoid security breaches and potential loss of sensitive information. Network segmentation is an effective security measure that involves dividing a network into smaller, isolated segments to increase control and protection over data. Figure 7-1 shows an example of how a network can be set up for an organization.

Segmenting a network enables organizations to establish different security controls and policies for each segment based on the criticality of the data they transmit and store. With clear boundaries, isolated segments can be monitored with greater visibility, making detecting and preventing threats from spreading easier.

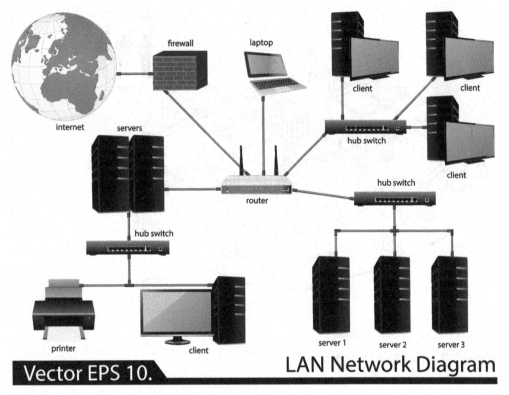

Figure 7-1 Sample Network Design (Image Credit: Ohmega1982/Shutterstock)

This security approach improves security within the organization and can enhance network performance. Network segmentation improves network efficiency by reducing network congestion and allocating additional bandwidth to segments that require it. It also simplifies compliance with regulatory requirements and makes it easier to meet data protection standards.

Defense-in-depth (DiD) is a robust security strategy that goes beyond mere network segmentation. It involves implementing multiple layers of security measures to provide comprehensive data protection by impeding threat actors and allowing security teams sufficient time to respond. This approach encompasses a diverse range of security tools, such as firewalls, intrusion detection/prevention systems, endpoint protection, and applications, to establish a multifaceted security defense. Figure 7-2 illustrates the defense-in-depth concept.

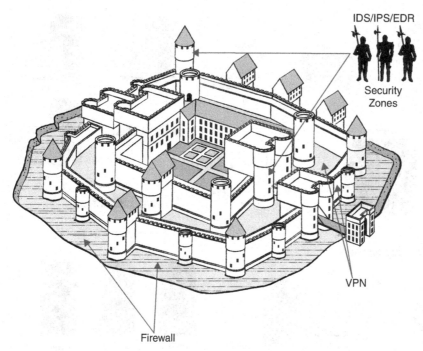

Figure 7-2 Defense-in-Depth Example

To illustrate this concept, castles serve as an excellent real-world analogy for defense-in-depth. Castles employed various layers of security to safeguard their crown jewels. Similarly, in the realm of cybersecurity, firewalls act akin to moats and gates that fortify the perimeter and control access. Guards atop the castle walls closely monitor the surroundings and permit entry through specific tunnels, mirroring the functionality of virtual private networks (VPNs), as discussed in an upcoming section.

In the event that threat actors manage to breach these initial defenses, formidable walls and locked doors within the castle function as security zones, allowing entry only to authorized personnel. Intrusion detection and prevention systems, along with endpoint detection and response tools, assume the role of vigilant guards and formidable weapons, ready to combat any attempted breach. Additionally, castle policies dictate authorized areas of access, mirroring the importance of well-defined security policies for network resources once an intruder gains entry. We discuss some of the tools used in DiD in Chapter 3, "Threats to Security."

Microsegmentation is another network security technique that provides enhanced protection by implementing security controls between workloads within a network, significantly reducing the risk of lateral movement by threat actors. With microsegmentation, each segment is isolated, and access between segments is closely monitored and controlled, making it harder for attackers to propagate or expand their reach in the event of a breach. This fine-grained security approach greatly enhances overall network security and mitigates potential risks. Figure 7-3 illustrates the difference between segmentation and microsegmentation.

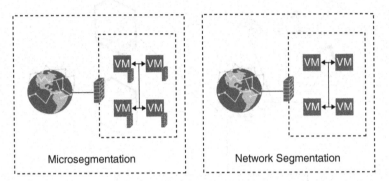

Figure 7-3 Microsegmentation Versus Network Segmentation

Demilitarized Zones

A *demilitarized zone (DMZ)* is a segregated network segment between an organization's internal network and the external, untrusted network, typically the Internet. The DMZ acts as a buffer zone that hosts servers, services, or applications that must be publicly accessible, such as web servers or email servers. By placing these resources in the DMZ, an organization can protect its internal network from direct exposure to external threats. The DMZ is fortified with firewalls and strict access controls to filter and monitor incoming and outgoing traffic and ensure that only authorized requests are allowed, thus enhancing network security.

Virtual Local Area Networks

A *virtual local area network (VLAN)* provides a logical division within a physical network, resulting in multiple isolated virtual networks. These virtual networks offer superior network management, enhanced security, and increased scalability. VLANs categorize devices based on criteria such as department, accounting, or function (e.g., help desk), rather than their physical location.

Switches are essential for VLAN implementation. They segment, manage, and control virtual networks. By assigning VLAN membership to specific ports, devices can be grouped into different VLANs based on criteria other than physical location. Switches attach a VLAN identifier to each data packet, facilitating proper routing. They also enforce VLAN policies and security controls, granting control over traffic flow between VLANs and network resource access. In summary, switches play a vital role in creating virtual broadcast domains, assigning VLAN membership, and ensuring efficient data routing within network infrastructure. Figure 7-4 illustrates VLANs in a network.

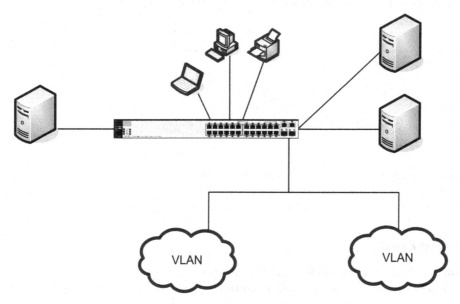

Figure 7-4   VLANs (Image Credit: Volker Schlichting/123RF)

Operating independently with unique policies and security controls, each VLAN empowers an organization to efficiently manage and troubleshoot its network, exercise fine-grained control over access to network resources, and easily scale its network infrastructure. By leveraging VLANs, an organization can achieve flexible and secure network segmentation, thereby optimizing network performance, while reducing the risk of lateral movement.

Virtual Private Networks

Virtual private networks (VPNs) provide users with a secure way to access networks, ensuring privacy and data protection. By utilizing encryption, VPNs safeguard network connections on public networks, preventing eavesdropping and interception. Additionally, VPNs obscure users' IP addresses, adding an extra layer of privacy to their online activities.

Three of the most common types of VPNs are as follows:

- *Remote access VPN*: This type of VPN allows users to connect securely to a private network or a third-party server, enabling access to files and data. Both businesses and home users benefit from remote access VPNs, as they enhance Internet security and provide access to cloud resources.

- *Site-to-site VPN*: This type of VPN is widely used in large organizations with multiple networks distributed across different locations. Site-to-site VPNs establish secure connections between these networks, facilitating secure communication and data sharing.

- *Mobile VPN*: Mobile VPNs serve as VPN services integrated into mobile device management systems or provided through dedicated applications. Mobile VPNs secure and encrypt data transmitted between mobile devices and the VPN server, ensuring privacy and data protection for mobile users.

By employing these different types of VPNs, individuals and organizations can safeguard their network connections, maintain privacy, and enhance Internet security.

 ## Network Access Control

Network Access Control (NAC) is a comprehensive security solution that combines authentication, endpoint security checking, and access controls to tightly control access to corporate or private networks. By implementing NAC, organizations gain visibility into their assets and can ensure that only authorized users and compliant devices are granted network access. Security policies, such as antivirus protection and patching, are enforced to maintain a secure network environment.

There are two types of access control in NAC: pre-admission and post-admission. *Pre-admission NAC* involves conducting compliance and authorization checks before granting access to the network. Noncompliant or unauthorized devices are denied access until they meet the necessary requirements. *Post-admission NAC* goes a step further by requiring users to reauthenticate when transitioning to different network segments where previous authorization might not have been granted. Users and devices will need to verify their identity again. This ensures that access privileges are continuously validated and monitored throughout the network, keeping security levels intact.

Some of the most common reasons for implementing NAC include the following:

- **Bring your own device (BYOD) policies:** In some organizations, employees are permitted to access their corporate network with a personal device. This can introduce a host of vulnerabilities to the network. NAC requires all devices, including BYOD, to prove authorization and compliance with security policies before access to resources is granted.

- **Guests/contractors access:** From time to time, organizations need to grant visitors and contractors access to specific corporate resources. NAC can give visitors temporary privileges separate from those of regular employees and prevent unauthorized access.

- **Internet of Things (IoT):** Due to the lack of security controls with IoT, these devices may go unnoticed on a network and are prime entry points for threat actors. A NAC solution can bring visibility to those devices and implement the necessary access controls.

By utilizing NAC, organizations can proactively protect their networks from unauthorized access, reduce the risk of security breaches, and enforce compliance with security policies across all devices and users.

Embedded Systems

Embedded systems are specialized computer systems, composed of both hardware and software, that are designed to perform specific tasks or functions at specific times. These systems are typically integrated into larger mechanical or electrical systems to carry out their designated tasks. These devices fall into one of four categories:

- **Mobile devices:** Small, portable devices such as cell phones and tablets. These devices are considered to be standalone devices, but not all standalone devices are mobile devices.

- **Network:** Networked embedded devices that communicate with the web server via a wired or wireless connection. These devices include point of sale (POS) systems and automated teller machines (ATMs).

- **Real time:** Systems that provide results immediately such as medical devices and aircraft control systems.

- **Standalone:** Devices that can produce output without a host system such as digital cameras and temperature measurement systems.

Embedded systems offer several advantages, such as customization options to meet specific requirements, low power consumption, and cost-effective development. They can also enhance performance in various industries.

However, one challenge with embedded systems is that security measures are not always built in from the start. This means that developing and implementing firmware updates to address potential security vulnerabilities may take longer. Another challenge of embedded systems is their limited resources, including processing power, memory, and energy. These limitations can make it challenging to implement complex features or accommodate future upgrades and expansion.

Overall, embedded systems provide specific functionality, but ensuring their security may require additional attention and timely updates to protect against potential threats.

Cloud Network Security Infrastructure

The cloud we see and interact with today has expanded exponentially since the first iterations of the cloud in the 1960s. During this time, John McCarthy, also the father of AI, helped create the first interactive time-sharing system. This system allowed multiple users access to the same resources on a computer simultaneously. Shortly after that, ARPANET (Advanced Research Projects Agency Network) was created by J. C. R. Licklider as the first version of the Internet. ARPANET allowed access to the nascent cloud via the Internet and from anywhere the Internet could be accessed.

The cloud didn't become popular until the late 1990s, which is when companies began to see the value in using this type of technology. In 1999, Salesforce became the pioneer of cloud computing, becoming the first company to offer applications over the Internet. Over the next two decades, the cloud became a normal part of life, from accessing banking information to media streaming to virtual assistants. Amazon Web Services (AWS), Google Cloud Platform (GCP), Microsoft Azure, and other smaller cloud service providers were created to offer various types of cloud services to customers and consumers. Cloud computing innovation continues, with the most recent trends focusing on refining the use of containers for more efficient deployment and integrating the use of AI.

Cloud computing has two main components: cloud deployment models and cloud service models. Both are discussed in turn next.

Cloud Deployment Models

Cloud deployment models refers to where the cloud infrastructure is hosted and who manages said infrastructure and cloud resources. Where data is stored and how it is accessed determines which model works best for an organization. The most popular deployment models include public, private, community, and hybrid.

Public

With the ***public cloud deployment model***, IT services and resources such as storage, servers, and networking are accessible to anyone via the Internet or a VPN. This is the most commonly used deployment model. The cloud service provider (CSP) manages and maintains the infrastructure and security of the cloud instance. Google Suite and Dropbox are two Software as a Service (SaaS) applications hosted in the public cloud. (SaaS and the other cloud service models are covered in the next section.) In a nutshell, your data is stored on a server in a data center that is located potentially anywhere in the world, and you interact with your data via the Internet from anywhere in the world. Figure 7-5 illustrates a public cloud deployment.

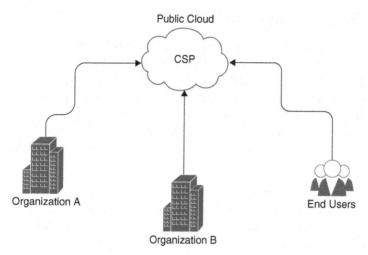

Figure 7-5 Public Cloud

Organizations that utilize public cloud offerings can reduce the need for dedicated staff to manage and maintain the infrastructure or the software they access, which leads to reduced costs. The public cloud offers flexibility and scalability when adding and removing users or services. With these benefits come some challenges using the public cloud. Organizations lose control over the underlying infrastructure because multiple users utilize the resources. The need for customization may also be a challenge for organizations with complex needs and requirements, as only basic service offerings are provided.

Private

The ***private cloud deployment model*** is similar to the public cloud deployment model, with servers, networking, storage, and all the functionality of the cloud. The difference is that each private cloud deployment is for a specific organization. This deployment can be on-premises (on-prem) at the organization's physical location or hosted on rented equipment offered by a CSP. Figure 7-6 illustrates a private cloud deployment.

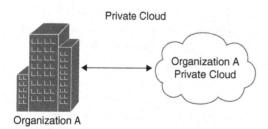

Figure 7-6 Private Cloud

One of the key advantages of a private cloud deployment is that the organization can tailor the hardware and software to meet its requirements. This ensures a better fit for the organization's unique needs and offers greater flexibility and control over its assets. The private cloud option also provides enhanced security, as the data is stored on servers that are accessible only to the organization, with the added benefit of having the in-house staff maintain the security of those systems and data. The private cloud is ideal for organizations that want to store mission-critical or sensitive data in the cloud but need to isolate it from other users of cloud resources.

The biggest disadvantage to the private cloud is cost. Costs start to grow when purchasing or renting the hardware and software to get started. These costs increase over time as updates and upgrades to infrastructure occur.

Community

The ***community cloud deployment model*** brings together organizations with similar interests to share and collaborate on cloud resources. Multiple organizations, such as government agencies, educational institutions, or healthcare providers, unite to pool their resources and share a tailored cloud infrastructure. This allows them to achieve cost savings, increase efficiency, and maximize productivity. Figure 7-7 illustrates a community cloud deployment.

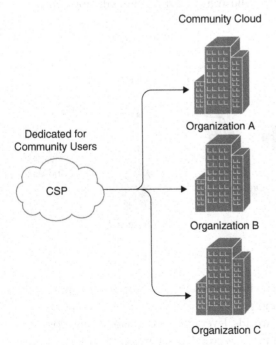

Figure 7-7   Community Cloud

Organizations can achieve economies of scale by leveraging shared resources such as servers, storage, and applications. Furthermore, the community cloud enables organizations to establish common security measures and protocols to meet industry or regulatory requirements. It provides a collaborative, secure, and cost-effective solution for organizations with shared needs, fostering a sense of community and enabling them to leverage the benefits of the cloud while working together towards their common goals.

Many sectors, including education, government, and finance, use community clouds to share information and resources.

Hybrid

The *hybrid cloud deployment model* is a mix of public and private cloud environments that provides organizations with flexibility and control over their data and applications. By using both public and private clouds, organizations can enjoy enhanced security and control while utilizing the scalability and cost-effectiveness of the public cloud for other needs. The hybrid cloud deployment model seamlessly integrates and orchestrates across both environments, enabling dynamic scaling of resources through technologies that extend infrastructure into the public cloud when required. Hybrid cloud environments can also include a community cloud such as in the healthcare field. Figure 7-8 illustrates a hybrid cloud deployment.

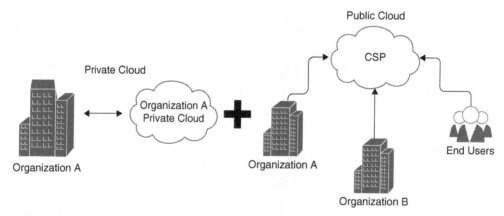

Figure 7-8 Hybrid Cloud

The hybrid cloud optimizes IT infrastructure, balancing security, control, and scalability while tailoring the cloud strategy to organizational needs. It empowers organizations to have the best of both worlds, leveraging the scalability and cost benefits of the public cloud while keeping sensitive data secure on the private cloud.

Cloud Service Models

In traditional IT environments, organizations are responsible for managing and maintaining their own systems and software, which employees and visitors use. This includes operating servers for email and web services, running virtualization software, and overseeing various applications. Managing these resources in-house can be costly and time-consuming, potentially leading to significant expenditures that impact the organization's revenue.

Cloud service models help alleviate some of this expense by sharing the responsibility of managing and maintaining systems with a cloud service provider. These models define which services an organization receives and who manages those services and resources. Cloud service models provide organizations with flexibility, scalability, and cost savings regarding cloud computing. Figure 7-9 illustrates the three main service models, discussed next, as well as a few variations (at the bottom).

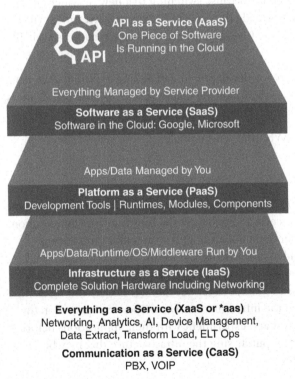

Figure 7-9   Cloud Service Models

Organizations may use a mix of cloud service models and a combination of deployment methods based on the type of information and data they are storing and processing. All of this is based on the organizational goals, what is deemed essential, and the expected outcomes for migrating to the cloud.

Infrastructure as a Service

With *Infrastructure as a Service (IaaS)*, the CSP provides virtualized resources and services that an organization can access over the Internet, thereby freeing itself from having to purchase expensive hardware for its data center needs. The CSP "leases out" resources and infrastructure such as servers, virtualization, and storage. This allows the organization the flexibility to install what it needs, scale as workloads increase with a pay-as-you-go feature, and reduce the upfront costs associated with "owned" infrastructure.

Challenges faced with IaaS include vendor dependency when leasing the infrastructure. This sometimes is described as "vendor lock," meaning an organization is locked into using one specific vendor because switching to a new provider either isn't financially feasible or doesn't provide the expected return on investment (ROI). Downtime is another challenge. If the CSP goes down, so do the resources available to organizations.

The most common uses of IaaS are for development and testing environments, data storage, and analytics. IaaS includes the following components: physical data centers, compute capabilities, software-defined networking, and storage.

Popular IaaS providers include AWS, IBM, and Google.

Platform as a Service

With *Platform as a Service (PaaS)*, the CSP provides organizations with a complete cloud solution for their business needs, accessible via the Internet from any location. The CSP manages the maintenance and updating of the infrastructure, allowing the organization to focus on building and testing its custom applications and tools. This helps the organization save time and resources on infrastructure costs. PaaS also supports getting applications to market faster because developers can focus on the app and not spend time on the infrastructure. Developers can provision the resources they need and quickly test and experiment with their applications before pushing them to market, all without purchasing the infrastructure that may be required to support the application.

PaaS has three main parts:

- Cloud resources such as virtual machines, operating systems, and storage
- Software to build and deploy applications
- A graphical user interface (GUI) to access the applications and data

API development and management is a great use case for this service model. PaaS allows developers to quickly run, manage, and secure application programming interfaces (APIs) for sharing data via integration. Another great use of PaaS is the Internet of Things (IoT). PaaS supports various programming languages (Python, Java, etc.), tools, and applications for developing and processing data from IoT devices.

Like IaaS, vendor dependency is challenging with PaaS, as platforms are typically designed as a one-size-fits-all solution. Security and compliance are also concerns, as PaaS offerings are typically in the public domain, with resources shared across multiple tenants. Depending on the data storage type, there may be better options from a security standpoint.

Popular PaaS providers include Google App Engine, Microsoft Azure App Services, and Heroku, all providing scalability and flexibility for web applications.

Software as a Service

Software as a Service (SaaS) is a model that consumers and organizations interact with daily, such as when sending and receiving emails, accessing collaboration tools like Slack or Discord, and using file-sharing applications like Google Suite or Microsoft Office 365. With SaaS, the CSP is responsible for all platform aspects, from the infrastructure to the application, while the organization is only responsible for how the application will be used and who needs access. Because this is a multitenant architecture, each organization gets a single instance of the application, which helps with data privacy.

SaaS solutions, characterized by their pay-as-you-go or subscription-based pricing, remove the necessity for an upfront total functionality purchase. This model enables organizations to access applications via the Internet or mobile devices, offering a cost-effective approach with lower initial and ongoing expenses. Benefits include rapid deployment, on-demand scalability, and other operational advantages. From a security perspective, updates to the software and underlying infrastructure are done automatically to protect the systems continuously.

The following characteristics are shared among all SaaS applications:

- Applications are built to be hosted in the cloud. Vendors can use their own infrastructure or that of a CSP to build and host their applications.

- Applications are accessible via the Internet to customers from anywhere around the world and from any Internet-connected device.

- Applications are built for multitenant use. Each customer gets its own instance of an application to access. This keeps each organization's data private and segregated from the other customers using the application.

- Applications require limited management and zero maintenance from the organization.

The CSP is responsible for maintaining and updating all the components necessary to run the application and applying the necessary security patches. The CSP is also responsible for adhering to the service-level agreement for data protection. (We discuss service-level agreements in the next section.)

Service-Level Agreement

A *service-level agreement (SLA)* is a written contract between a provider and its customers outlining the technical terms and conditions of the services provided. A cloud SLA is an agreement between a customer and a CSP that defines the quality of the cloud service. The SLA lists the requirements a CSP must adhere to when providing customer services. The following are three types of SLA:

- **Customer SLA:** The most common type of SLA, this is a contract between a service provider and its customers.

- **Internal SLA:** This type of SLA is typically between different departments in an organization.

- **Multilevel SLA:** This type of SLA is broken into tiers to allow customers to select which level of service aligns with their requirements and budget.

SLAs are important because they set the expectations of both parties when it comes to cloud computing. If an issue arises, the SLA lists actions that should be taken to resolve the issue, who is responsible for taking the action, and metrics that should be tracked while the issue is resolved. Metrics allow an organization to measure its provider's performance levels. If the CSP fails to meet its service level expectations, the SLA outlines the penalties or fines that will be incurred or legal action that should be taken.

Below are a few metrics customers should review when considering a CSP's SLA:

- *System uptime* is the amount of time a system is operational.

- *System availability* is how reliably a user can access or use the system.

- *Error rates* identify how often there are defects or issues in major deliverables. These metrics can include errors in code, missed deadlines, and other organizational concerns.

- *Security* is a vital metric when proving SLA compliance should an incident occur. This could include tracking the status of antivirus and patch updates.

- *Business results* are metrics based on an organization's existing key performance indicators (KPIs).

> **NOTE**   Uptime and availability are used interchangeably but have different metrics. Uptime is usually measured in 9s. A common standard for uptime is 99.999% or "5 nines." This means a vendor guarantees less than 5.26 minutes of downtime annually. Uptime is a part of the overall system availability.

When crafting an SLA, a few areas should be included: an overview of the agreement, who the stakeholders are and what their goals and responsibilities are, a description of all the services and metrics (including existing metrics as applicable), and a list of exclusions. The SLA should also include security standards and measures implemented, a disaster recovery plan (DRP) to restore the systems and environment, penalties for not adhering to the SLA, and any cancellation or termination clauses. An SLA should accompany every contract to protect both parties should something happen.

 ## Managed Service Provider

Managed service providers (MSPs) are outsourced services delivered to customers to support their IT needs. The employees of an MSP monitor each customer's environment for issues and concerns and report any relevant information to the customer. These employees include IT staff, analysts, engineers, and incident responders.

For security-specific services, organizations can engage a managed security service provider (MSSP) that specifically provides security services to organizations. An MSSP team works from a security operations center (SOC) and provides SOC services to customers.

Outsourcing to one of these types of services helps organizations extend their team in the event that funding is unavailable to staff IT and security teams. Having a managed service provider allows the organization to focus on business instead of technology. While the monthly costs of having a managed service can be a bit higher, it does alleviate the need to purchase expensive hardware and software, helps with business continuity, and can provide expert technical support and proactive monitoring. This ensures that the organization stays ahead of potential security threats and technology issues, allowing for smoother operations and improved overall security posture.

Numerous MSPs and MSSPs offer services around the world. Determining the best use of such a service will be based on an organization's needs and goals. The first thing is to plan how such a service would or could be used in the organization. Is it for outsourcing the entire security function or to supplement what is already in-house? Consider the cost of such a service and how it affects the organization's bottom line. Does the provider have the technical expertise and technology to perform the duties?

Compliance is also critical, as we want data and information to be stored in secure locations and have security protocols in place. Reviews are a great way to understand a service provider and make informed decisions. Finally, asking for a proof of concept (POC) allows an organization to see how operations could work with this new functionality.

Cloud Challenges

With the migration to the cloud, several challenges arise. The lack of knowledge and expertise around secure cloud environments often leads to misconfigurations, increasing the risk of data leaks. These misconfigurations are particularly evident in hybrid cloud setups, emphasizing the need to understand access control and system hardening requirements to mitigate vulnerabilities.

Password security is another significant challenge in cloud environments. Users commonly reuse passwords across multiple cloud accounts, heightening the risk of unauthorized access in the event of a security breach. Implementing password managers offers an effective solution to mitigate password reuse, thereby enhancing overall security.

Governance and compliance present additional hurdles for organizations transitioning to the cloud. As data moves between environments, adherence to federal, state, local, and international laws becomes crucial. This complexity is further compounded when data is stored across multiple locations, necessitating a comprehensive understanding of regulatory requirements and diligent adherence to ensure compliance.

In summary, addressing challenges such as misconfigurations, password security, and governance and compliance is vital for organizations navigating cloud migrations. By proactively addressing these concerns and implementing appropriate measures, organizations can mitigate risks and effectively leverage the benefits of cloud computing.

Exam Preparation Tasks

As mentioned in the Introduction, you have a couple of choices for exam preparation: the exercises here, Chapter 13, "Final Preparation," and the exam simulation questions in the Pearson Test Prep Software Online.

Review All Key Topics

Review the most important topics in this chapter, noted with the Key Topics icon in the outer margin of the page. Table 7-3 lists a reference of these key topics and the page numbers on which each is found.

Table 7-3 Key Topics for Chapter 7

Key Topic Element	Description	Page Number
Section	Environmental Controls	115
Paragraph	Covers heating, ventilation, air conditioning (HVAC)	116
Section	Fire Suppression Systems	116
Section	Redundancy and High Availability	117
Section	Memorandum of Understanding and Memorandum of Agreement	117
Paragraph	Introduces defense-in-depth, a layered approached to securing systems and data	119
Paragraph	Explains microsegmentation, a network technique that provides enhanced security to the environment	120
Section	Network Access Control	123
Section	Cloud Deployment Models	125
Section	Cloud Service Models	129
Section	Managed Service Provider	133

Define Key Terms

Define the following key terms from this chapter and check your answers in the glossary:

environmental controls; power sources; data center; data closet; heating, ventilation, air conditioning (HVAC); fire suppression systems; redundancy; high availability (HA); memorandum of understanding/agreement (MOU/MOA); defense-in-depth (DiD); microsegmentation; demilitarized zone (DMZ); virtual local area network (VLAN); virtual private networks (VPNs); remote access VPN; site-to-site VPN; mobile VPN; Network Access Control (NAC); embedded systems; cloud deployment models; public cloud deployment model; private cloud deployment model; community cloud deployment model; hybrid cloud deployment model; Infrastructure as a Service (IaaS); Platform as a Service (PaaS); Software as a Service (SaaS); service-level agreement (SLA); managed service providers (MSPs)

Q&A

The answers to these questions appear in Appendix A. For more practice with exam format questions, use the Pearson Test Prep Software Online.

1. What are four types of fire suppression systems used today?

2. What are the three types of virtual private networks (VPN) referenced in this chapter?

3. Which six elements should be included in a memorandum of understanding (MOU)?

4. What are four cloud deployment models?

5. What are three cloud service models?

References

Dooley, Kevin. "Network Redundancy and Why It Matters." *Auvik*. August 29, 2022: https://www.auvik.com/franklyit/blog/simple-network-redundancy/

"Types of Virtual Private Networks." *Geeks For Geeks*. January 24, 2023: https://www.geeksforgeeks.org/types-of-virtual-private-network-vpn-and-its-protocols/

Google Cloud. "Advantages of Cloud Computing." *Google*. 2023: https://cloud.google.com/learn/advantages-of-cloud-computing

CDW Expert. "Top 3 Cloud Computing Service Models." *CDW*. February, 13, 2023 https://www.cdw.com/content/cdw/en/articles/cloud/top-3-cloud-computing-service-models.html

IBM Expert. "What is SaaS?" *IBM*. 2023: https://www.ibm.com/topics/saas

Hertvik, Joe. "Service Availability: Calculations and Metrics, Five 9s, and Best Practices." *BMC*. July 8, 2020: https://www.bmc.com/blogs/service-availability-calculation-metrics/

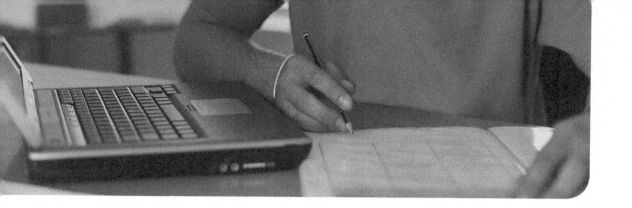

This chapter covers the following topics and corresponding proficiencies:

- **Data security:** Understand the methods used to protect data from being altered or disclosed in an unauthorized way or by an unauthorized user.

- **Encryption:** Understand the types of encryption and the ways they are used to protect data in storage and in transit.

- **Hashing:** Differentiate between encryption and hashing and describe the uses of hashing in information assurance.

- **Non-repudiation:** Differentiate between encryption and non-repudiation and understand the purpose of non-repudiation in information assurance.

- **Authentication:** Understand the need for authentication, the authentication process, the types of authentication factors, and some methods of configuration.

- **Password policy:** Describe the requirements for creating strong passwords and differentiate between technical and administrative policies.

- **Data handling:** Differentiate between the various parts of data handling and understand their importance in protecting the confidentiality and integrity of data.

CHAPTER 8

Data and the System

Now that we've covered access control and network security, let's discuss the data itself and the systems on which it is stored. Security operations is a broad topic, encompassing encryption, data handling, system hardening, configuration management, vulnerability management, patch management, and logging and monitoring, as well as several governance elements. We will discuss each of these topics in the next two chapters. As we go through each topic, we will further round out the picture of cybersecurity controls and the various interlocking processes performed every day to secure organizations. Take care to understand each one—each control interlocks in service of the defense of the organization.

The following Certified in Cybersecurity exam objectives are covered in this chapter:

- 1.1 Understand the security concepts of information assurance

  - 1d Authentication (e.g., methods of authentication, multi-factor authentication (MFA))

  - 1e Non-repudiation

- 5.1 Understand data security

  - 5.1a Encryption (e.g., symmetric, asymmetric, hashing)

  - 5.1b Data handling (e.g., destruction, retention, classification, labeling)

- 5.3 Understand best practice security policies

  - 5.3a Data handling policy

  - 5.3b Password policy

"Do I Know This Already?" Quiz

The "Do I Know This Already?" quiz allows you to decide whether you need to read this entire chapter or skip to the "Exam Preparation Tasks" section. If you doubt your selection of answers to these questions or your own assessment of your knowledge of these topics, you may want to read the entire chapter. Table 8-1 lists the major headings in this chapter and their corresponding

"Do I Know This Already?" Quiz questions. You can find the answers in Appendix A, "Answers to the 'Do I Know This Already?' Quizzes and Q&A Sections." Good luck!

Table 8-1   "Do I Know This Already?" Section-to-Question Mapping

Foundation Topics Section	Questions
Data Security	1–6
Authentication	7–10
Data Handling	11–13

CAUTION   The goal of self-assessment is to gauge your mastery of the topics in this chapter. If you do not know the answer to a question or are only partially sure of the answer, you should mark that question as wrong for purposes of the self-assessment. Giving yourself credit for an answer you correctly guess skews your self-assessment results and might provide you with a false sense of security.

1. What is data security?

    a. Protecting data from being altered or disclosed

    b. The strategic use of encryption, authentication, and data handling

    c. A synonym for information security

    d. None of these answers are correct.

2. What are the parts of a cryptographic algorithm?

    a. Fancy words, magic, numbers

    b. Key, ciphertext, key generator

    c. Coded text, random numbers, random number maker

    d. Key, ciphertext, plaintext

3. What is the difference between symmetric and asymmetric encryption?

    a. Symmetric encryption has different keys for encryption and decryption.

    b. Asymmetric encryption has the same key for encryption and decryption.

    c. The difference is the symmetry of the numbers used in the algorithms.

    d. None of these answers are correct.

    e. All of these answers are correct.

4. What are some types of cryptographic protocols, and what are they used for?

    a. AES-256; storage and transit

    b. RSA and the Diffie-Helman Key Exchange; transit

    c. TLS; transit

    d. All of these answers are correct.

    e. None of these answers are correct.

5. What are the two primary qualities of hashes?

    a. Can encrypt text in a pinch and cannot be hacked

    b. Excellent for breakfast and for snacks

    c. Irreversible but can be reverse-engineered

    d. Can encrypt text in a pinch but don't use random numbers

6. What is non-repudiation?

    a. A way to ensure that a person can't deny having taken an action, such as a digital signature

    b. A form of encryption

    c. A pillar of the CIA triad that we just forgot about

    d. A grammatical curiosity

7. What is authentication?

    a. The practice of determining the accuracy of data before use

    b. The process of checking identity before granting access

    c. A method to ensure data integrity during transmission

    d. There are various models, so all of the answers are correct.

8. How many factors of authentication are there, and how many should be used at a minimum in a secure system configuration?

    a. Two; two

    b. Five; any one will do, as these are stronger than passwords

    c. Five; two

    d. Four; three

9. Why is authentication so critical?

    a. It ensures that only authorized users gain access.

    b. It is a system's first line of defense.

    c. Without properly verifying identity, anyone could gain access to a system.

    d. All of these answers are correct.

    e. None of these answers are correct.

10. What is *not* part of implementing a strong password policy?

    a. Monitoring for compromised passwords

    b. Changing one number or character when it's time to change passwords

    c. Requiring longer passwords

    d. Making users change their passwords every 15 days

11. What are the four components of data handling?

    a. Classification, labeling, retention, destruction

    b. Classification, tagging, retention, destruction

    c. Classification, labeling, destruction, disposal

    d. Classification, retention, encryption, networking

12. What is the correct way to implement data classification?

    a. Implement classifications based on each organization's needs and data inventory.

    b. There are four categories one should always implement: Public, Confidential, Secret, and Top Secret.

    c. The analyst should copy the categories of the company they most admire.

    d. There are three categories one should always implement: Public, Confidential, and Secret.

13. What is the objective of data handling?

    a. To conserve resources for the data that actually needs protection

    b. To prevent unauthorized disclosures and leaks

    c. To ensure that passwords are secure

    d. To protect all the data

Foundation Topics

Security operations is a catch-all term for a number of security areas that form the substance of a cybersecurity program. While access control and network security control access to the system, security operations is about the design, maintenance, and protection of the system itself, as well as the data stored and processed on it. No access control setup or network security architecture is perfectly invulnerable, so it is always important to remember to secure the system and the data as a final means of defense. If you need an analogy here, think of the layout of the castle as a means to mitigate attacks. Now let's get started.

Data Security

The first item to cover in security operations is the security of the data (because it's all about the data, isn't it?). There are three areas of note here for ***data security***: encryption, authentication, and data handling. Each addresses a different aspect of data and the system on which it is stored.

Encryption

If you've ever read any detective stories or watched crime shows or mysteries, you might be familiar with the idea of using a code, as in scrambling a message such that only the intended recipient can read it. Codes and ciphers play an important role in the history of the world, from messages in wartime to protection of sensitive text in times of great strife. Today, their descendant, modern cryptography, is essential to protecting our data in storage (for example, databases and servers) and in transit (for example, when sending an email). ***Encryption*** ensures that the data itself is protected by rendering it unreadable except by those who have the key. Recalling the CIA triad, encryption gives a guarantee of confidentiality and integrity, as encrypted systems, files, and data are not easy to edit or read.

Modern cryptography is based on a complicated set of mathematical principles, such as prime number factoring, that are beyond the scope of this book and the Certified in Cybersecurity exam. Suffice it to say that modern cryptography goes far beyond merely switching around letters, as modern cryptographic algorithms produce output that is not human-readable. Through the use of random numbers as keys, encryption is not easily reversible either. So, skipping over the math, let's consider the broad aspects and categories of algorithms.

A cryptographic algorithm consists of several parts: the key, the ciphertext, and the key generator. The key is what is used to turn plaintext (unencoded text) into ciphertext (the encrypted unreadable output). A key generator, a critical part of modern algorithms, is used to create the key. Unlike codes and ciphers of old, modern cryptography works by using random number generators, a type of computer algorithm, to generate a large integer that has certain mathematical properties, such as being divisible by large prime numbers. This integer is, quite literally, the key. Using this key, a computer equipped with the necessary protocols will turn plaintext into ciphertext, and thus we have a degree of data security.

Cryptographic algorithms, also known as *cryptosystems*, are sorted into two major categories: symmetric and asymmetric. ***Symmetric algorithms*** are ones in which the key to encrypt (e.g., to encode or apply encryption) and the key to decrypt (e.g., to decode or to remove encryption) are the same. This process of encrypting and decrypting is a fast one, so symmetric encryption is used most often within systems, such as encrypting a laptop or a database, as well as in network sessions once already established. Several major encryption algorithms are symmetric, such as Advanced Encryption Standard, the commonly used version of which is AES-256.

Now, there's a problem with symmetric encryption: both sides need the same key. How are we supposed to communicate that key securely when that key is supposed to provide us the security to communicate? For this reason, cryptographers in the twentieth century came up with ***asymmetric encryption***. These protocols work the following way: Both the sender and the recipient have two keys, a published public key and a secret private key. The sender uses the recipient's public key to encrypt their message before transmitting it, and the recipient uses their private key to decrypt it. This prevents anyone from intercepting the messages and reading them.

Asymmetric encryption has its own problem: between generating keys and encrypting messages, it's a bit slow. Thus, in transmission, these two types of algorithms are often paired: asymmetric encryption is used to establish a network session and send a key for symmetric encryption, which is then used to encrypt subsequent messages within that same session. Important asymmetric encryption algorithms are Rivest-Shamir-Adelman (RSA) and the Diffie-Hellman (DH) key exchange protocol.

In a recommended implementation, encryption is performed at multiple levels. For data at rest, the system is encrypted, specific databases are encrypted, and specific rows and columns are encrypted. For data in transit, the connection is encrypted (such as through a VPN), the sites use cryptographic protocols such as the most updated version of Transport Layer Security (TLS), and the data itself is encrypted. This layering of encryption is done so that, in case one is compromised, the others still work to protect the data.

Hashing

There are multiple topics related to cryptographic algorithms. One such topic is *hashing*. Hashing is the process of converting a string of characters, usually text, or a key into a fixed length of text and numbers for security purposes. Hashing uses an algorithm such as SHA-256 or MD5 to perform the conversion on a file or message. The output of this process is known as a hash. Unlike encryption, which is designed to be reversible with the correct key, a hash is intended to be a one-way function, like a one-way ticket on a plane or a train. The purpose of hashing is to prove the authenticity or integrity of a message. It differs from encryption, whose purpose is to protect the confidentiality of the data. While hashes are not reversible, with the right input information, a skilled threat actor may attempt to reverse engineer the hash. Encryption is recommended over hashing to protect the confidentiality of data.

Hashes, while not making data unreadable, ensure integrity. For example, when software files are shared online, a corresponding hash is often posted too. After downloading, a user can hash these files and compare the hash to the original one online. Matching hashes confirm that the files are unaltered and safe; differing hashes indicate potential tampering or corruption, signaling caution is needed.

Another use of hashing is in the storage of passwords. In a securely designed system, passwords are stored as hashes instead of the actual plaintext. Sometimes user IDs are hashed along with their respective passwords. Since hashes can be reverse engineered, systems are usually configured to "salt" their hashes—a term that refers to hashing a specific number alongside the information. Since this number is kept secret, an attacker might have the hashed passwords but be unable to reverse engineer and find the original.

Hashes are often used alongside encryption, such as in a digital signature, which is described in the following section.

Non-Repudiation

Another use for cryptographic algorithms is guaranteeing non-repudiation. The National Institute of Standards and Technology defines ***non-repudiation*** in SP 800-53 Rev. 5 as "[p]rotection against an individual who falsely denies having performed a certain action and provides the capability to determine whether an individual took a certain action, such as creating information, sending a message, approving information, or receiving a message." Essentially, non-repudiation is a way to have a person acknowledge something in a manner that they can't later deny.

One common example of non-repudiation in cybersecurity is a digital signature. A digital signature involves hashing the original message and encrypting that hash using the sender's private key. When the recipient decrypts the message using the sender's public key, they can be sure the sender really sent the message. This is particularly used in official documents, such as digitally signed contracts. Another use is digital timestamps, which provide proof of when certain actions happened, such as when a document was created or signed.

Like encryption, non-repudiation is used to provide certainty—here, the certainty of whether something truly did happen.

Authentication

Now, as we work through data security, let's take a moment and consider one of the major aspects of information security and an important technical safeguard: authentication. NIST FIPS Pub. 200 defines *authentication* as "[v]erifying the identity of a user, process, or device, often as a prerequisite to allowing access to resources in an information system." In simpler terms, authentication is checking identity before granting access.

Authentication relies upon several systems being in place: secure communication protocols, encryption, and access control lists. The essential workflow, with some variation depending on the type of system and its relative need for security, is the following: the user enters a login ID and a password, the system checks the hash (either just the password or both the login ID and password, depending on setup) against its records, and then the system proceeds to a next step, such as granting access or making a request for further verification. As part of this workflow, the system also checks the ID against an access control list.

The entering of ID and password is sometimes separately called *identification*. The process of granting access is sometimes separately referred to as *authorization*. Identification, authentication, and authorization are known as the three pillars of access control or information security, depending on the textbook, course, or professional publication.

Login IDs and passwords are the classic methods of authentication. But there are several more methods depending on system implementation:

- **Knowledge factors (something you know):** IDs, passwords, etc.

- **Inherence factors (something you are):** Fingerprints, face scans, retinal scans, etc.

- **Possession factors (something you have):** Badges, one-time password generators, etc.

- **Location factors (somewhere you are):** Being at a specific location, such as an office

- **Behavior factors (something you do):** A pattern, such as the way you type or draw (think of a pattern-drawing lock on a smartphone)

Because authentication is such an essential idea, the simplest way to understand its importance is to consider what would happen if it didn't exist, or wasn't adequately implemented, for a system. Without the verification of identity, there wouldn't be any safeguards to prevent anyone with an interest in sensitive data from accessing it. Authentication is thus an absolutely critical aspect of information security.

For this reason, many organizations no longer consider merely a login ID and a password as sufficient for secure authentication. Both login IDs and passwords can be stolen through various data exfiltration methods. Login IDs can be deduced based on organizational practices, such as the use of employee names, and passwords can be brute-forced through password generators or guessed through researching the user's social media. Additionally, many users don't follow password guidelines in the creation of passwords. Consequently, because of these risks, current industry best practices require using at least one authentication factor, such as a fingerprint, a facial scan, a specific location known to be secure, or a one-time password, in addition to a login ID and password. This practice is known as *multi-factor authentication (MFA)*.

One-Time Passwords

Because one-time passwords (OTPs) are currently so widely used, this topic deserves a bit of elaboration. Contrary to the name, OTPs are not traditional passwords. Instead, they function as possession factors, usually numeric codes, that prove a person has access to something they own (like a phone or token). Using two different passwords doesn't count as two-factor authentication because both are knowledge-based factors. OTPs, on the other hand, provide an additional layer of security by requiring something a person has, making them an effective tool against unauthorized access. They are often used along with a traditional password.

With the aid of complex math, algorithms are used to generate random numbers to use as OTPs. In an adequate implementation, these OTPs are generated using something the user already has, such as an authenticator app or a separate hardware device (e.g., a YubiKey). OTPs sent through text messages or email are not considered secure, because both methods transmit data in cleartext, which makes them at risk for compromise. In contrast, an authenticator app or YubiKey is more secure because it locally generates a random number. In all methods, OTPs expire after a certain amount of time, usually 15 or 30 seconds for apps and YubiKeys and 5 to 15 minutes for texts and emails.

Password Policy

As stated in the previous section, passwords are not considered sufficient for secure authentication implementation. Indeed, one current industry trend is toward passwordless authentication, in which passwords are entirely replaced by other authentication methods. However, many organizations still use passwords, in part due to cost limitations and in part due to the need for system compatibility and user education requirements. Consequently, organizations such as NIST and the PCI Council have released updated password requirements and guidelines.

Current industry best practices, some of which you may be familiar with, recommend the following for a *password policy*:

- At least eight characters, but the longer the better.

- At least one uppercase character, at least one lowercase character, at least one number, and at least one special character—although new NIST guidelines are actually de-emphasizing the value of such complexity, as users tend to use these characters in fairly predictable ways (how many times have you just added a special character and a number to the end of your passwords?).

- A maximum password age of 90 days—NIST guidelines suggest requiring a password change no more than once every 365 days, in order to encourage users to remember their passwords, but this has not yet caught on.

- Automatic monitoring of passwords to prevent passwords that are easily compromised from being used (think "P@ssword!"), as well as those that have recently appeared in password leaks.

- Eliminating password hints and disabling the "show password" option.

- Disallowing the sharing of passwords.

Because passwords are so critical to most systems, and because they rely so much on the memory of the user, it is important to analyze and understand how users create passwords, use them, and store them. When an organization's password policy makes it difficult for users to remember their passwords, such as requiring frequent changes, users make passwords of lesser quality or use facts about themselves that are easy to find on social media or through conversations with them (think names of family members and pets). Users may also resort to clicking "forgot my password" frequently, which may expose the account to further fraudulent activity as well as lead to more lower quality passwords.

The same need for analysis and understanding applies to password storage: one industry trend is to use password managers, but it is important to remember that these usually require setup, user education, and monitoring and that they, too, can be hacked. And, as a whole, policies that lead to a cure that is as bad as the curse need some thoughtful evaluation.

One final note before moving on: a password policy refers to two things: a technical configuration, as in cloud account settings and endpoint management for laptops and phones, and a clearly written document. Both are needed in an organization. The document sets expectations for users, and the technical configuration enforces them. If you're ever in a position to improve or audit a security program, see if you can make sure both of these are present.

Data Handling

Now that you know how data can be protected and transmitted, let's get to the data itself. ***Data handling*** covers an entirely separate section of data security—how data should be stored, processed, and transmitted based on its level of sensitivity—and has four major parts to it: classification, labeling, retention, and destruction. Although this might not sound as fascinating as encryption—and may seem more than a bit obvious—well-defined and well-implemented data handling processes and procedures help an organization with two things: conserving system resources for the data that actually does need to be protected, and preventing the sort of mistakes that lead to unauthorized disclosures and leaks. A discussion of the four major parts of data handling will help you better understand this domain, as well as link it back to the pillars of confidentiality and integrity we've already covered.

Data Classification

Data classification is based on a fairly simple idea: not all data is equal. The marketing copy for the public-facing website doesn't need the same protection as the algorithm that is the organization's proprietary "secret sauce" or the company's business strategy documents.

The authors usually see the following classifications, or some variation of them, used:

- **Public:** Information that is to be shared publicly and poses no risk of harm to the organization if leaked.

- **Confidential:** Information that may cause minimal or minor harm, including reputation harm, if leaked; most business documents are classified this way, like work products or policies.

- **Secret:** Information that may cause major harm if leaked; this may be protected information such as the personally identifiable information (PII) or protected health information (PHI) of employees or customers.

- **Top Secret:** Information that may cause catastrophic harm if leaked; this could be source code, business strategy documents, or undisclosed financial information—the sort of information that could sink the organization if released.

In the preceding list, did you note the risk assessment language used? Data classification categories depend on the organization's risk tolerance and vary widely from organization to organization. For example, a company that knows it doesn't have much personal data for employees and customers may choose to use a Secret classification for that data. A company that has very personal details and has a heavy data compliance burden may bump up the classification to Top Secret. Organizations may also choose to rename categories or consolidate them based on what makes sense from a risk perspective. Since each organization has different needs, one recommended practice is to inventory all of the organization's data and to update that inventory periodically so the organization has a clear idea of what to classify and how to do it.

The classifications in the preceding list are loosely based on those of the U.S. federal government, the guidance of which on data handling is widely followed and considered the industry standard. Again, the same terms don't appear in every organization. However, two terms that do are personally identifiable information (PII) and protected health information (PHI).

The acronyms PII and PHI are so universally used in cybersecurity that it is worth memorizing them. Both refer to, as the names suggest, types of personal information that are considered protected categories under U.S. federal law and receive similar levels of protection from other countries as well. These types of data, which include names, addresses, and demographics, as well as health records, require extra protection such as strong encryption and access control wherever they are stored or transmitted. Depending on the state and country, there may be fines for noncompliance, as well as the possibility for further legal action and major reputation harm.

Data Labeling

Okay, so we have data classification categories and maybe even an inventory of our organization's data. But how do we know which file deserves what level of protection? In the old days before digital records existed, files were labeled quite simply through their folders being stamped with the category or with watermarks. So how do we achieve the same level of clarity in digital records?

Watermarking, or rather its digital equivalent, is still a method for data labeling. Many companies mark files with text ("Confidential," for example), images, or numbers to indicate ownership or sensitivity. Additionally, companies often employ tagging strategies, incorporating classification levels directly into their file organization systems or cloud storage structures. Some organizations might also use file IDs that reflect the confidentiality level of the information. These approaches help in managing access and ensuring proper handling of data based on its sensitivity.

In addition to classification tags, an organization may also choose to mark certain files and folders as read-only, along with appropriate technical safeguards, to prevent anyone from editing them.

The process of performing data labeling includes the following steps: defining criteria, selecting tools to use for labeling, separating data based on established classifications, labeling the data, performing a quality check, monitoring to ensure data is used in accordance with its label, and repeating the process as part of a regular review cadence or when data must be labeled.

Data Retention

Moving right along, the next part of data handling is retention. Based on an organization's various requirements, including the need for financial reporting, legal obligations, or contractual commitments, the organization may need to retain certain data for certain periods of time. Or, to put it simply, an organization can't delete anything that it promised not to delete or was instructed not to delete by a government agency, a court of law, its customers and clients, or its own corporate leadership. So, how does an organization make sure it retains data that it is supposed to keep?

In the authors' experience, many organizations address this requirement by creating a schedule that lists all the types of data they possess and how long they are supposed to keep it, as demonstrated in the sample schedule presented in Table 8-2.

Table 8-2 Sample Schedule of Data Possession

Type of Information	Classification Level	Retention Period	Data Owner
Client contact information	Secret	7 years	Sales lead
Personal information of terminated employees	Secret	7 years	HR lead
Log data	Confidential	1 year	IT lead
Configuration baselines	Secret	1 year	IT lead
Marketing copy	Public	3 years	Marketing team

As you can see in this table, sensitive documents that might have legal or financial value are usually kept for 7 years. Technical documents may be kept for less time, such as 12 months or 1 year. Retention periods of other items, like marketing documents, depend on the needs of the organization.

To make their retention schedules effective, organizations need to periodically manually check their archives (whether in paper form, on physical servers, or on the cloud) to determine if it's time to delete data. Alternatively, they might be able to use a tagging system and automate scripts to purge data when its retention limit is reached. This method is particularly popular for cloud environments.

Some organizations approach data retention in a different way: instead of setting expiry dates, they simply retain all data until someone asks to have their data deleted. This method relies upon the cheapness of storage, particularly in cloud environments.

Data Destruction

Let's turn to the other side of retention: destruction. Just as keeping the right data is important, so is destroying the right data. There are two aspects to data destruction: physical disposal and digital disposal.

For physical disposal, such as the destruction of paper records, disks, or hard drives, the method used for the disposal is tied to the classification of the data involved— different procedures should be followed for Top Secret data versus Confidential data. These procedures include the following:

- **Wiping:** This is more than merely deleting the data and usually involves a specialized program to complete the task.

- **Overwriting:** This method renders the data nonsensical by inputting a stream of random 0's and 1's onto the drive or disk.

- **Degaussing:** This method uses a magnet to erase the data from the drive or disk.

- **Cutting:** Drives and disks may be cut to ensure they can never be reused; this is considered an especially secure method. For paper documents, the equivalent would be shredding, which normally involves a disposal bin that cuts the papers into long thin strips, or cross-cut shredding, which cuts the papers horizontally as well as vertically in order to prevent reconstruction.

- **Incinerating:** For drives, disks, and papers, burning the media may prove an effective mechanism to protect the confidentiality of the most sensitive data.

Keep in mind that these disposal methods are not meant to be done in your backyard. Many organizations hire certified disposal companies that perform disposals and provide certificates documenting and validating the disposal of the media. Because of the costs, more involved procedures like degaussing or incinerating might be reserved for more sensitive data.

By contrast, digital disposal, the disposal of files and records in a cloud environment, is much simpler. Many organizations use purge scripts, either manually or automatically executed, that delete individually tagged records, virtual machines, storage clusters, databases, or other cloud resources. These scripts are documented and are executed in accordance with retention schedules, business requirements, or customer requests.

Data Handling Policy

Data handling is reliant on the processes of data classification, labeling, retention, and destruction being repeatable and consistent. What good does it do anyone if no one can remember what the classification categories even are? Thus, this is an area in which it is particularly important for an organization to have a comprehensive policy document, with relevant and detailed specifics, covering the four parts of data handling discussed in the preceding sections. The authors have seen these areas usually divided into a data classification policy that includes labeling and a data retention and disposal policy with additional detail included in procedures. This forms the administrative safeguard, while the four parts of data handling are the technical safeguards (and physical as well, depending on the organization's systems).

Exam Preparation Tasks

As mentioned in the Introduction, you have a couple of choices for exam preparation: the exercises here, Chapter 13, "Final Preparation," and the exam simulation questions in the Pearson Test Prep Software Online.

Review All Key Topics

Review the most important topics in this chapter, noted with the Key Topics icon in the outer margin of the page. Table 8-3 lists a reference of these key topics and the page numbers on which each is found.

Table 8-3 Key Topics for Chapter 8

Key Topic Element	Description	Page Number
Paragraph	Describes encryption	143
Paragraph	Describes hashing	144
Paragraph	Define non-repudiation	145
Paragraph	Describes authentication	146
Section	Password Policy	147
Paragraph	Describes data handling	149

Define Key Terms

Define the following key terms from this chapter and check your answers in the glossary:

data security, encryption, symmetric algorithm, asymmetric encryption, hashing, non-repudiation, authentication, multi-factor authentication, password policy, data handling

Q&A

The answers to these questions appear in Appendix A. For more practice with exam format questions, use the Pearson Test Prep Software Online.

1. What is data security?

2. What is the difference between encryption and hashing?

3. What are the components of cryptographic algorithms, and what types of these algorithms exist?

4. What is non-repudiation?

5. What is authentication, and what are the three components to authentication?

6. What are the five authentication factors?

7. What is a password policy, and what are the currently recommended password requirements?

8. What is data handling, and what are the four parts to this domain?

9. What are PII and PHI?

References

NIST SP 800-53, Rev. 5, *Security and Privacy Controls for Information Systems and Organizations*: https://nvlpubs.nist.gov/nistpubs/SpecialPublications/NIST.SP.800-53r5.pdf

NIST FIPS Pub. 200, *Minimum Security Requirements for Federal Information and Information Systems* (Appendix A): https://nvlpubs.nist.gov/nistpubs/FIPS/NIST.FIPS.200.pdf

Soares, Luis. "Understanding Non-Repudiation: Ensuring Integrity and Accountability in Digital Communications." *Medium*, March 22, 2023: https://medium.com/@luishrsoares/understanding-non-repudiation-ensuring-integrity-and-accountability-in-digital-communications-d9608c3c9727

SumoLogic. "Authentication factor - definition & overview." 2024: https://www.sumologic.com/glossary/authentication-factor/

Vicente, Vice. "NIST Password Guidelines 2024." *Auditboard*, February 6, 2023: https://www.auditboard.com/blog/nist-password-guidelines/

Shide, Siddhesh. "Encryption vs Hashing: Which is Better for Your Data?" *Emeritus*, January 16, 2024: https://emeritus.org/blog/encryption-vs-hashing/

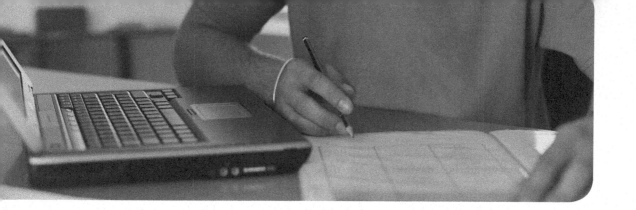

This chapter covers the following topics and corresponding proficiencies:

- **System hardening:** Describe the requirements and methods of configuring systems, including establishing baselines, to protect them from potential threats.

- **Logging and monitoring:** Describe the tools and processes that check the status of key components of an IT infrastructure.

- **Acceptable Use Policy:** Understand the purpose of this general policy and describe the concepts it communicates to users in an organization.

- **Bring Your Own Device Policy:** Understand the purpose of this general policy and describe the concepts it communicates to users in an organization.

- **Change Management Policy:** Understand the purpose of this general policy and describe the methods and processes it communicates to software developers and engineers in an organization.

- **Privacy Policy:** Understand the purpose of this general policy and describe the concepts it communicates to an organization's customers.

- **Security Awareness Training:** Describe the concept of educating users on their role in information security.

- **Social Engineering:** Describe a category of malicious activities that leverage human emotions and thinking processes to perpetrate attacks against organizations.

- **Password Protection:** Describe the concept of preventing password compromise through understanding user behavior and changes in technology.

CHAPTER 9

Security in the Life

Chapter 8, "Data and the System," covered the first half of security operations, with a lot of focus on the data and the way it's stored, processed, and transmitted securely from the systems that hold it. Now let's go behind the scenes a bit and discuss the systems themselves: how to configure them and how to monitor them. We will also discuss several more governance elements and the roles they play in setting up a robust information architecture and meeting the requirements of confidentiality, integrity, and availability. As in Chapter 8, as we go through each topic, we will further round out the picture of cybersecurity controls and the various interlocking processes performed every day to secure organizations. This chapter is called "Security in the Life" to represent the functions that must be performed every day to ensure the security of the organization.

The following Certified in Cybersecurity exam objectives are covered in this chapter:

- 5.1 Understand data security

  - 5.1c Logging and monitoring security events

- 5.2 Understand system hardening

  - 5.2a Configuration management (e.g., baselines, updates, patches)

- 5.3 Understand best practice security policies

  - 5.3c Acceptable Use Policy (AUP)

  - 5.3d Bring your own device (BYOD) policy

  - 5.3e Change management policy (e.g., documentation, approval, rollback)

  - 5.3f Privacy policy

- 5.4 Understand security awareness training

  - 5.4a Purpose/concepts (e.g., social engineering, password protection)

  - 5.4b Importance

"Do I Know This Already?" Quiz

The "Do I Know This Already?" quiz allows you to decide whether you need to read this entire chapter or skip to the "Exam Preparation Tasks" section. If you doubt your selection of answers to these questions or your own assessment of your knowledge of these topics, you may want to read the entire chapter. Table 9-1 lists the major headings in this chapter and their corresponding "Do I Know This Already?" Quiz questions. You can find the answers in Appendix A, "Answers to the 'Do I Know This Already?' Quizzes and Q&A Sections." Good luck!

Table 9-1 "Do I Know This Already?" Section-to-Question Mapping

Foundation Topics Section	Questions
System Hardening	1–4
Logging and Monitoring	5–7
Security Policies	8–12
Security Awareness Training	13–16

CAUTION The goal of self-assessment is to gauge your mastery of the topics in this chapter. If you do not know the answer to a question or are only partially sure of the answer, you should mark that question as wrong for purposes of the self-assessment. Giving yourself credit for an answer you correctly guess skews your self-assessment results and might provide you with a false sense of security.

1. What is system hardening?

    a. A process intended to eliminate a means of attack by patching vulnerabilities and turning off nonessential services

    b. Getting a baseline in place

    c. Blocking some ports and installing a few patches

    d. The implementation of controls to prevent the unauthorized access to and disclosure of data

2. What is a baseline?

    a. A framework such as NIST SP 800

    b. Technical and security specifications for implementing the system

    c. A way to build a server

    d. The idealized state at which security professionals strive to keep the system

3. What is patch management?

   a. A bandage for software

   b. A form of risk management

   c. The implementation of new systems when older ones reach the end of their lives

   d. The implementation of vendor fixes to remediate vulnerabilities and software issues

4. What are system updates and upgrades?

   a. Optimizing systems to run better and replacing them when the next version is available

   b. A grander version of patches

   c. Updates to specific vulnerabilities in a system

   d. None of these answers are correct.

   e. All of these answers are correct.

5. What is logging and monitoring?

   a. Tracking the day-to-day functioning and operations of a system

   b. Collecting information on a system's activities, including logins and file modification

   c. A key element of data security

   d. None of these answers are correct.

   e. All of these answers are correct.

6. What are logs?

   a. Implementation information for a system

   b. A system to forward records

   c. Records about the status of key components of an IT infrastructure

   d. Application code

7. Which of the following are monitoring tools?

   a. A Security Incident and Event Monitoring tool

   b. Cloud infrastructure monitoring tool

   c. Capacity monitoring tool

   d. None of these answers are correct.

   e. All of these answers are correct.

8. Which of the following does an Acceptable Use Policy usually *not* cover?

    a. What sort of smartphone to buy for personal use

    b. How to store documents

    c. Whether USBs can be used and how

    d. All the ways users might interact with technology

9. Which of the following does a bring your own device policy usually cover?

    a. How to use company-owned devices

    b. Step-by-step instructions for setting up corporate email

    c. What employees must to do to secure their personal devices

    d. Which pictures employees shouldn't delete

10. Which of the following are components of a change management policy?

    a. Design, testing, approval

    b. Rollback plans

    c. Documenting each part of a change request

    d. None of these answers are correct.

    e. All of these answers are correct.

11. Who is a privacy policy intended to be written for?

    a. The government

    b. Customers

    c. Employees

    d. Lawyers

12. Which of the following is a privacy policy intended to cover?

    a. The company's responsibilities to their customers.

    b. Every aspect of how an organization will use its users' data

    c. Only the basics of privacy regulation compliance

    d. Only how to request deletion of personal data

13. Which of the following is the purpose of security awareness training?

    a. Security compliance

    b. Cybersecurity risk mitigation

    c. User education

    d. Phishing tests

14. What areas can security awareness training cover?

    a. Possible attacks and best practices

    b. Secure development and coding

    c. Security policies

    d. None of these answers are correct.

    e. All of these answers are correct.

15. Which of the following are examples of social engineering attacks?

    a. Phishing emails, texts, and calls

    b. Impersonating employees

    c. Giving USBs with a malicious payload

    d. None of these answers are correct.

    e. All of these answers are correct.

16. How can passwords be protected?

    a. New password guidelines based on user behavior

    b. Implementation of automatic checks

    c. Multi-factor authentication

    d. None of these answers are correct.

    e. All of these answers are correct.

Foundation Topics

As mentioned in Chapter 8, the term *security operations* covers a number of cyber-security program areas and concerns the system itself and the data stored and pro-cessed on it. Since we've already covered the data, we will now discuss the system in greater depth: how we ensure its security and its resistance to exploitation, and how we monitor it and check that it is performing in the way we expect. Keep thinking of a castle layout if you need an analogy—what we discuss in this chapter is like ensur-ing we're following the proper protocols in building a castle and then verifying that it's actually working (please see Chapter 11 for additional details on this analogy). Now let's get started.

System Hardening

The National Institute of Standards and Technology (NIST) publication *A Profile for U.S. Federal Cryptographic Key Management Systems* (NIST SP 800-152) defines **system hardening** as "[a] process intended to eliminate a means of attack by patch-ing vulnerabilities and turning off nonessential services." This process uses a variety of tools, techniques, and best practices to find and reduce vulnerabilities in an orga-nization's technology stack. System hardening (also known as configuration man-agement) is an essential security practice that helps organizations maintain a secure computing environment and protect their assets from potential threats. We will discuss a few system hardening techniques next.

Baselines

Establishing a configuration baseline is one of the first steps in ensuring that an organization has the proper controls. This means understanding what the cur-rent environment looks like and what the minimum level of security needs to be to secure the system. Having this understanding helps the organization understand where deviations from this baseline are occurring and jump into action should an issue arise. Various frameworks provide guidance on what configurations should look like, such as the Center for Internet Security (CIS) Critical Security Controls, NIST Special Publication 800 series, International Organization for Standardiza-tion (ISO) 27000 series, or vendor-specific guidelines. Note that the ISO standard is international, while NIST is mainly used within the United States.

By implementing baselines, organizations can achieve the following:

- **Security:** Baselines help enforce secure configurations, reducing the attack surface and minimizing vulnerabilities.

- **Compliance:** Baselines help align configurations with industry regulations and best practices such as PCI DSS, HIPAA, or GDPR.

- **Consistency:** Baselines allow organizations to start from the same place when bringing new systems into the environment. They can reduce the time needed to get new systems up and running securely.

- **Efficiency:** Having a prebuilt baseline saves time and effort with configuring systems. This gives the teams more time to do other things within the organization to protect it.

Back in the day, those around the government might recall the U.S. Defense Information Systems Agency (DISA) Gold Disk and DISA Security Technical Implementation Guides (STIGs). The Gold Disk was software that allowed organizations to implement security configurations across their environment, including when new systems came online. This disk provided the baseline for a secure system. It wasn't the most fun way to implement security, but it did the job. DISA STIGs provided a great starting point for security configurations on devices such as routers, switches, firewalls, and other technology in organizations. Personnel would implement the various controls pertaining to their organization through a text file uploaded to each system. The other systems in our environment were updated via SCCM or some other tool. Over time, the use of the DISA Gold Disk was phased out and replaced with the Security Content Automation Protocol (SCAP) and other automated compliance tools.

Although the listed practices have largely fallen out of use, they have inspired more contemporary versions: in many cloud environments, configurations are managed through text-based files called *machine images* that specify virtual machine versions, sizes, memory, and software and can be executed to spin up new virtual machines, databases, storage clusters, containers, or other types of cloud resources. These practices are part of the body of newer technical implementation methods known as *infrastructure as code (IaC)*. Similarly, many organizations use endpoint management tools to create configurations for laptops, including which software to include, for when they set up workstations for new employees. Furthermore, many organizations monitor workstations, servers, and cloud environments to determine whether there are any deviations from the baseline.

Some best practices to consider when establishing configuration baselines include disabling services and ports that are not in use; applying regular updates provided by vendors; implementing strong password policies and multi-factor authentication (MFA); enabling firewalls and IDS/IPS; encrypting sensitive data; implementing connections for the monitoring and logging of system events; regularly backing up data; and conducting regular security checks.

Patch Management

Many vendors regularly announce a specific update to an issue within their technology that organizations should implement if they have that system. This is known as a *patch*, an update to a specific system, program, or product vulnerability. For example, Microsoft posts security patches on the second Tuesday of every month, unofficially known as Patch Tuesday. Patch management aims to ensure that organizations' systems have the latest security updates to protect against malicious actors. A proactive approach to patch management can help organizations minimize downtime, help with operating system performance, and promote productivity.

A patch management program should address the following key steps:

Step 1. **Asset inventory:** An organization cannot secure what it doesn't know it has. Creating an inventory of all assets in the organization can be done through network diagrams, spreadsheets, and/or software that tracks assets. The inventory allows an organization to identify which assets are the crown jewels for the organization, the most valuable assets that should receive priority in patch management.

Step 2. **Vulnerability assessment:** Conduct a vulnerability assessment to get an understanding of the vulnerabilities that exist in the environment. This will help the organization identify the solutions for vulnerabilities and prioritize remediation.

Step 3. **Testing of patches:** Patches should be tested in a nonproduction environment before being deployed to a system currently in production. Depending on the environment, patches may bring systems down.

Step 4. **Remediation and mitigation:** Once the patch is tested, it should be applied to the system or systems in question.

Step 5. **Validation and verification:** Verify that the patch was applied correctly and that the system is functioning as it should.

Step 6. **Reporting and monitoring:** Because patch management is a continuous process, reporting the success of the program to stakeholders is essential for continued program support. Organizations also should monitor their programs to correct issues or errors early.

Patch management may, among other priorities, seem unimportant. Why do we need to patch a system when we already have the system? In considering that question, we must remember that many patches are responses to known or newly discovered vulnerabilities—meaning that they are vulnerabilities malicious attackers have a high chance of exploiting.

For example, in 2017, the WannaCry ransomware was successfully deployed against organizations in Eastern Europe and around the world through the exploitation of unpatched instances of Microsoft Windows. Although Microsoft had already released patches, the organizations had not installed them, and this left their devices vulnerable to the attack. One of the lessons from the spate of incidents was the importance of regular and consistent patching.

That being said, though, many patches have a criticality attached to them, like vulnerabilities do, and should be prioritized accordingly.

Vulnerability Management

Vulnerability management is a big topic and quite beyond the scope of the Certified in Cybersecurity exam. But, since it's something you're likely to encounter as you enter the field of cybersecurity, let's cover it briefly.

The term *vulnerabilities* in this context refers to something slightly different than in risk management. Here, vulnerabilities are errors and issues in software and software implementation that create openings for attackers to exploit. Vulnerabilities can include out-of-date cryptographic protocols, the use of default admin passwords, and various code issues. Some vulnerabilities are easy to solve with a patch or a configuration adjustment, while others may require a system overhaul to remediate (such as the infamous log4j vulnerability first detected in the winter of 2021). Some vulnerabilities are rarely exploited by attackers, while others are often exploited. In order to detect vulnerabilities, many organizations employ vulnerability scanning tools that scan various aspects of their systems and applications for errors and issues.

Because there are thousands of potential vulnerabilities, multiple organizations rate the security risk of vulnerabilities as they are discovered, many vulnerability scanning tools automatically list the security risk, and many organizations create vulnerability remediation cycles based on risk prioritization to give some order to the chaos of it all. If you'd like to learn more, the authors recommend you start with researching CVE (https://cve.mitre.org/) and the CVSS scoring method (https://www.first.org/cvss/).

System Updates and Upgrades

Unlike patches, which address specific issues, system updates and upgrades have a broader scope and apply to an entire operating system (OS) rather than addressing a particular vulnerability. Updates encompass various aspects of the OS, including performance enhancements, bug fixes, and the introduction of new features.

On the other hand, system upgrades involve moving from one OS version to another. These upgrades often bring significant updates to both performance and security. For instance, when Microsoft transitioned from Windows 10 to Windows 11, it was considered a system upgrade. Upgrading a system requires more planning, as it involves updating the entire OS and may necessitate reconfiguring user preferences and settings. Often times, this upgrade is necessary because a vendor is phasing out an OS, after which it no longer provides patches for it. This phasing out is called End of Life (EOL). Many organizations monitor vendor communications for announcements regarding critical changes and coordinate transitions to implement compatibility for older applications and prevent mishaps and failures.

It is crucial to recognize that system updates and upgrades play distinct roles in maintaining the optimal functioning and security of a system. Staying up to date with system updates ensures that performance issues are addressed and new features are incorporated, while system upgrades encompass more extensive updates to both performance and security. Proper planning is necessary for system upgrades due to the comprehensive nature of the changes and the potential need for reconfiguring user settings. Applying updates and upgrades is similar to applying patches but with a little more coordination. The most important thing to remember is to have a plan and document the process.

Logging and Monitoring

The previous sections covered the setup of the system and checking for patches, updates, and upgrades. But that's the beginning of a system's life, so to speak, and all the milestones. What about in between, its day-to-day functioning and operations? How do we check that all the changes we're making as we go about the tasks of our organization don't knock the system offline? For that matter, how would we even know if someone *was* trying to attack it?

In a cybersecurity program, these questions are answered by *logging and monitoring*, the implementation of a set of tools that check the status of key components of an IT infrastructure, including applications, servers, databases, networks, cloud environments, and workstations. As those tools check on the status, they collect information about activities, such as successful login attempts, unsuccessful login attempts, accessing certain files, and making system changes. This information, known as *logs*, is then forwarded to an aggregator known as a Security Incident and Event Monitoring (SIEM) tool, which analyzes the information and alerts personnel if any anomalies are detected.

The preceding process is a general outline. There is such a wide variety of tools and services that every organization's implementation can look a little different. Some tools combine elements of logging and aggregating, while others log and monitor for multiple types of systems. Some ways of forwarding logs include using APIs and implementing agents on servers or virtual machines. Moreover, this domain is in great flux through the pioneering of new tools and methods to simplify and consolidate alerts analysis.

Logging and monitoring (cybersecurity professionals usually refer to them jointly in this order) is a key element of data security. Logging and monitoring allows us to verify and maintain the confidentiality and integrity by ensuring that we have records of everything that happens to the data and the system. In addition, through real-time alerts analysis, we can potentially detect an incident in its early stages.

Note that the previous paragraphs mentioned alerts a few times. In organizations with large security departments, alerts are analyzed by a dedicated security operations center (SOC) or network operations center (NOC). This analysis is often the first way in which an organization learns of a possible incident (more on this in Chapter 10).

The task of logging and monitoring is thus a key part of protecting the confidentiality and integrity of systems and data on both a daily basis and during incidents and emergencies.

Security Policies

To round out our discussion on security operations, let's cover several security policies that are considered industry best practice and are widely recommended for being documented in every organization.

Acceptable Use Policy

You've probably seen one of these before. An *Acceptable Use Policy (AUP)* is a staple in most organizations, from for-profit companies to universities, and for good reason: this document covers all the ways that users might interact with technology in an organization and tells them what they can and cannot do. A comprehensive AUP might include everything from using USBs and storing documents to surfing the Internet on company devices and posting on social media—thereby covering confidentiality and integrity. The management of this document, including having users read it upon hire and every year thereafter, is an important legal protection, and many compliance frameworks test whether an organization has an AUP. So read the next AUP you encounter a little more carefully before you sign it!

Bring Your Own Device Policy

Bring your own device (BYOD) policies span back to the early 2000s, paralleling the rapid advancement of personal technology devices like laptops, smartphones, and tablets. Initially spurred by individual employees seeking convenience and efficiency, BYOD gained momentum as organizations recognized the need to scale their operations such as by hiring contractors and expanding globally. This informal practice gradually prompted formal consideration from corporate IT departments and management, especially with the advent of cloud computing and mobile applications, which further facilitated the demand for seamless access to work-related data and applications across various devices and locations.

However, the widespread adoption of BYOD also brought forth significant security challenges. Organizations faced the task of securing sensitive corporate data on employee-owned devices, prompting the development of formal BYOD policies aimed at reconciling the benefits of device flexibility with the necessity of maintaining robust cybersecurity postures. These policies evolved to encompass comprehensive guidelines for device usage, security controls, data protection measures, and delineation of employee responsibilities, aiming to strike a delicate balance between enabling flexibility and ensuring security.

Over time, these BYOD policies continued to evolve in response to technological advancements, changes in workforce demographics, and emerging security threats. Modern BYOD policies are characterized by their adaptability to evolving technological landscapes, scalability to accommodate organizational growth, and integration with complementary measures such as AUPs, data classification policies, and incident response plans. Today, BYOD has become a standard practice in many organizations, supported by comprehensive policies, technical solutions, and regulatory compliance frameworks aimed at fostering a secure and productive work environment amidst the ever-changing digital landscape.

Change Management Policy

Change management is another important aspect of cybersecurity governance, particularly for the integrity of systems. Consider this: someone makes a tweak to a business-critical application or to the organization's infrastructure and never tells anyone, so the development team only finds out about the change when the application or the system crashes as customers are using it. You might be wincing. Whether the change is intentional or not, this is definitely a risk not to be easily dismissed.

In response to this sort of concern, many organizations implement a *change management policy* that requires all changes, or at least all major changes, for both systems and applications to be formally documented and tracked to the groans of software developers across the industry. This documentation usually involves the use of a ticketing system and incorporates a written design, the tests performed on the suggested code, and approvals from key personnel, such as team leads and quality assurance engineers. Depending on the sensitivity of the application, the organization might also require change risk assessments, rollback plans, and post-production reviews to be noted. Multiple approvals might be required. The organization might also require integration with code testing and management software to ensure the details in the ticket can't be easily tampered with. The ticket is then stored as a formal record of the change and used as reference for future changes or in case something goes wrong. Emergency changes and hotfixes usually follow an expedited version of this process.

Alongside the documentation and tracking process, a change management policy may also include specifics for a change control board (CCB) or a change advisory board (CAB). Whatever the name, these boards are usually comprised of managers and team leads and are required to discuss and approve changes, especially major changes and emergency changes, before they can be implemented. A change management policy might also specify the need for a change release calendar or mechanisms, such as email, by which changes are communicated to the organization and to external users such as clients and customers.

Though a change management policy does require a lot of documentation and paperwork, imagine how valuable the information might be in case of a major incident, turnover on the team, or an audit. That is why cybersecurity governance as a rule requires it.

Privacy Policy

Unlike the policies discussed so far in Chapter 8 and this one, a ***privacy policy*** is an external-facing document as much as, or more than, it is an internal one. Externally, a privacy policy helps users make informed decisions regarding how and what personal data is shared with an organization. Internally, it helps drive the protection of the data shared and how it should be handled. You've seen privacy policies before when downloading a new app or creating a new account; they're usually linked to the company's website or sign-in page. They are meant to cover every aspect of how the organization will use their users' personal data, including processing, storage, transmission, and potential sharing with third parties. These documents are intended not only to comply with applicable privacy laws, including disclosing possible data use and providing methods by which to request data to be deleted, but also to assure users of the steps the organization takes to protect their data from unauthorized disclosure. Many organizations are legally required to ask users to acknowledge their privacy policy before allowing them access to the company's services.

There's a lot to discuss regarding the particulars of privacy policies, along with their effectiveness and value to an organization. For the purposes of the Certified in Cybersecurity exam, understanding the basics of privacy policies and that they often require user acknowledgment should suffice.

Security Awareness Training

As you've read this book, you might have gathered that users are a critical part of an organization's level of information security. Many exploits and attacks begin with the user's malicious or ignorant actions, like inserting a USB, clicking a link, implementing a weak password, or simply leaving the door unlocked, and all the technical policies and implementations cannot prevent these vulnerabilities. Consequently, robust information security programs spend a lot of time and energy on security awareness training.

Security awareness training refers to educating users on their role in information security, on possible attacks and indicators of compromise, and on best practices to implement for themselves and for the organization, including network security at home, privacy screens on devices, and methods of social engineering and password protection (described in the sections that follow). This area is where security policies in general and an Acceptable Use Policy in particular might help with increasing user knowledge about security requirements and procedures. Historically, security awareness training was limited to PowerPoint presentations and boring videos that users just clicked through. Over time, organizations started to incorporate more engaging content such as skits, live sessions, and interactive videos to keep the interest of their employees and help the concepts stick.

One final note before we discuss a couple of specifics: certain roles in the organization merit additional training. It is industry best practice for software developers, especially leads, to receive training on secure development and coding, such as OWASP Top Ten, and for incident response team members to receive training on incident response procedures (more on this in the next chapter).

Social Engineering

Social engineering is a term that references a wide array of malicious activities that leverage human emotions and thinking processes to perpetrate attacks against organizations. These attacks include everything from phishing—emails, calls, or texts that attempt to have a user click a link, download a file, or respond—to more sophisticated acts of deception, such as impersonating an employee to enter a facility. These attacks range in scope from stealing a single file to infecting the network to complex acts of espionage and data exfiltration, and attackers very often use social engineering as merely the first step of a much larger plan. Thus, the initial vulnerability produced by a person who isn't paying attention can result in much greater disasters. For some examples, the authors recommend an online search for major incidents in the year 2023.

To address the risks posed by social engineering, many organizations require their personnel to complete courses in security awareness, such as through a learning management system, upon hire, and on an annual basis. Some organizations also periodically send phishing emails to test their personnel's ability to identify fraudulent emails. Some organizations may also put up posters or regularly discuss security topics in company newsletters.

Password Protection

Passwords are susceptible to compromise. Many users make very generic, easily cracked passwords, like Password1, or else vary their passwords in predictable ways, like changing only a number from one password renewal to the next. Others use their usernames in their passwords or reference their family members, pets, or birthdays—all of which can be found on social media and used to compromise an account. Still others reuse passwords from site to site. Yet the fact of the matter is that, even if a user does none of this, the vulnerabilities in the systems themselves may mean that passwords get leaked anyway and that new technologies could be used to crack passwords in ways we can't yet anticipate.

Referring to Chapter 8, the need to improve password protection is why the industry is in the middle of considering new password guidelines, such as longer passwords and less frequent password changes, as well as implementing automatic checks against lists of leaked and commonly used passwords. Additionally, increasingly more organizations supplement these measures through the use of multi-factor authentication, including one-time passwords and biometrics (e.g., facial recognition or fingerprint scans). These are additional approaches to password protection that provide additional security to passwords. Thus, technical controls are used to mitigate the chance of poor password hygiene. In essence, *password protection* means understanding user behavior and changes in technology in order to prevent password compromise.

Another mechanism for password protection is the use of a password manager or vault. These tools enable the user to create strong or complex passwords and store other authentication information as needed. These tools are accessible from a desktop, laptop, or other mobile device. These tools can also perform a security audit against currently used passwords and provide recommendations for making them stronger. Password managers ease the burden of having to remember hundreds of versions of a password.

If you're wondering why implementing the tools and techniques mentioned throughout is necessary, consider this: because of the complexity of modern attacks, security awareness must be something that every user has all the time. Since this sort of awareness is not natural to most people, one important aspect of security awareness is frequent reminders, but not so frequent that users will disregard them. It is a balance. When an organization implements the best practices listed, it has a greater chance of getting user support in protecting confidentiality, integrity, and availability of systems and data instead of user apathy.

Exam Preparation Tasks

As mentioned in the Introduction, you have a couple of choices for exam preparation: the exercises here, Chapter 13, "Final Preparation," and the exam simulation questions in the Pearson Test Prep Software Online.

Review All Key Topics

Review the most important topics in this chapter, noted with the Key Topics icon in the outer margin of the page. Table 9-2 lists a reference of these key topics and the page numbers on which each is found.

Table 9-2   Key Topics for Chapter 9

Key Topic Element	Description	Page Number
Paragraph	Describes system hardening	162
Paragraph	Describes logging and monitoring	166
Section	Acceptable Use Policy	167
Section	Bring Your Own Device Policy	167
Section	Change Management Policy	168
Section	Privacy Policy	169
Paragraph	Describes security awareness training	170
Section	Social Engineering	170
Section	Password Protection	171

Define Key Terms

Define the following key terms from this chapter and check your answers in the glossary:

system hardening, logging and monitoring, Acceptable Use Policy (AUP), bring your own device (BYOD) policy, change management policy, privacy policy, security awareness training, social engineering, password protection

Q&A

The answers to these questions appear in Appendix A. For more practice with exam format questions, use the Pearson Test Prep Software Online.

1. What is system hardening?

2. What is a system baseline, and what are the benefits of implementing a baseline?

3. What is the difference between a patch, an update, and an upgrade?

4. How is logging and monitoring implemented?

5. Who reviews logging and monitoring alerts in a large organization?

6. What are an Acceptable Use Policy, a bring your own device policy, a change management policy, and a privacy policy, and how are they different?

7. What is security awareness training intended to teach?

8. What are some types of attacks that can result from successful social engineering?

9. What are some user behaviors that can result in password compromise?

Reference

NIST SP 800-152, *A Profile for U.S. Federal Cryptographic Key Management Systems*: https://nvlpubs.nist.gov/nistpubs/SpecialPublications/NIST.SP.800-152.pdf

This chapter covers the following topics and corresponding proficiencies:

- **Incident response:** Describe the process used to address anomalies and security and availability events that may pose a threat to the organization.

- **Business continuity:** Describe the process used to prepare for organization-wide emergencies.

- **Disaster recovery:** Describe the process used to handle and recover from organization-wide emergencies.

- **Governance processes:** Understand the importance of governance documentation in establishing security controls.

- **Policies:** Differentiate between the various types of governance documents and understand the roles of policies in cybersecurity governance.

- **Standards:** Understand the roles of standards in cybersecurity governance.

- **Procedures:** Understand the roles of procedures in cybersecurity governance.

- **Regulations:** Describe the types of regulations that are relevant to cybersecurity.

CHAPTER 10

Security in Emergencies

Previous chapters have covered the various domains and processes of cybersecurity, from access control to network security to security operations. All of those areas, those controls, apply to the everyday functioning of systems in an organization. In this chapter, however, we will turn to security during emergencies, specifically incident response, business continuity, and disaster recovery, and take a deeper and broader look at security governance. Each of these elements helps ensure the confidentiality, integrity, and availability of systems and data. As we discuss each area, it is important to remember that, while these elements come to the fore during emergencies, preparation for them begins with actions taken every day.

The following Certified in Cybersecurity exam objectives are covered in this chapter:

- 1.5 Understand governance processes

  - 1.5a Policies

  - 1.5b Procedures

  - 1.5c Standards

  - 1.5d Regulations and laws

- 2.1 Understand business continuity (BC)

  - 2.1a Purpose

  - 2.1b Importance

  - 2.1c Components

- 2.2 Understand disaster recovery (DR)

  - 2.2a Purpose

  - 2.2b Importance

  - 2.2c Components

- 2.3 Understand incident response

    - 2.3a Purpose

    - 2.3b Importance

    - 2.3c Components

"Do I Know This Already?" Quiz

The "Do I Know This Already?" quiz allows you to decide whether you need to read this entire chapter or skip to the "Exam Preparation Tasks" section. If you doubt your selection of answers to these questions or your own assessment of your knowledge of these topics, you may want to read the entire chapter. Table 10-1 lists the major headings in this chapter and their corresponding "Do I Know This Already?" Quiz questions. You can find the answers in Appendix A, "Answers to the 'Do I Know This Already?' Quizzes and Q&A Sections." Good luck!

Table 10-1 "Do I Know This Already?" Section-to-Question Mapping

Foundation Topics Section	Questions
Incident Response	1–4
Business Continuity	5–9
Disaster Recovery	10–12
Governance Processes	13–16

CAUTION The goal of self-assessment is to gauge your mastery of the topics in this chapter. If you do not know the answer to a question or are only partially sure of the answer, you should mark that question as wrong for purposes of the self-assessment. Giving yourself credit for an answer you correctly guess skews your self-assessment results and might provide you with a false sense of security.

1. What is incident response?

    a. Helpdesk and customer service

    b. Putting out corporate fires

    c. Addressing anomalies and events in a timely fashion to minimize risk to the organization

    d. Remediating technical issues that pose a threat to the organization

2. What is an incident response plan?

   a. A document outlining how to respond to incidents

   b. Technical specifications for incident containment

   c. Another plan to seldom follow

   d. Training for incident response team members

3. What are the six steps of incident response?

   a. Detection, prioritization, isolation, response, recovery, reflection

   b. Monitoring, classification, containment, response, testing, reflection

   c. Analysis, classification, containment, response, recovery, lessons

   d. Detection, classification, containment, response, recovery, reflection

4. How are incident response plans tested?

   a. Actually responding to an incident

   b. Tabletop walkthroughs

   c. Simulations

   d. All of these answers are correct.

5. What is business continuity?

   a. Another name for incident response

   b. Plans and procedures for preparing systems for emergencies

   c. A list of people to call in an emergency

   d. Processes and procedures for the whole organization during emergencies

6. What is the purpose of a business impact analysis?

   a. Determining which systems and data are critical

   b. Conducting a secondary risk assessment

   c. Judging the impact of the business continuity plan on the organization

   d. Judging the risks to confidentiality, integrity, and availability if an emergency were to happen

7. An RTO refers to which of the following?

   a. The amount of money required to recover from an incident

   b. The latest time after an incident at which the system should be recovered and operational

     c. The amount of time required to recover from an incident

     d. The latest time after an incident at which the incident response plan should be completed

8. An RPO refers to which of the following?

     a. The most recent point before an incident to which the system can be recovered

     b. The amount of data lost during recovery from an incident

     c. The amount of time spent during recovery from an incident

     d. The last point at which the database was online

9. What are the four types of backups?

     a. Full, differential, incremental, real-time

     b. Full, real-time, cloud, differential

     c. Full, mirror, replicative, incremental

     d. Full, mirror, differential, incremental

10. What is disaster recovery?

     a. Processes for storing backups and resuming business operations

     b. Another name for incident response

     c. Processes for handling and recovering from disasters

     d. Practical plans for safeguarding systems and technology

11. What are the three types of backup sites?

     a. Hot, tepid, chilly

     b. Hot, warm, cold

     c. Hot, lukewarm, cold

     d. Boiling, hot, warm

12. What is failover testing?

     a. Testing backup restoration

     b. Switching over to alternate sites or redundant cloud setups

     c. A disaster recovery plan test

     d. All of these answers are correct.

13. For what purpose can governance documents be used?

    a. To fulfill the requirements of audits and vendor questionnaires

    b. To meet the requirements of regulations and laws

    c. To provide reference points during emergencies, staff changes, and training

    d. All of these answers are correct.

14. What is the hierarchy of governance documents?

    a. General statements, manuals, plans, guidelines

    b. Policies, standards, procedures, plans

    c. Policies, standards, procedures, guidelines

    d. Policies, manuals, plans, regulations

15. What are the two primary sources of regulations in the cybersecurity industry?

    a. Government agencies and industry groups

    b. Legislatures and government agencies

    c. International organizations and cybersecurity associations

    d. Government agencies and international organizations

16. Which of the following lists four laws and regulations that could apply to an organization?

    a. HIPAA, SOX, PCI DSS, GDPR

    b. HIPAA, SOC, CFAA, GDPR

    c. PCI DSS, HiTRUST, FedRAMP, FCPA

    d. PCI DSS, ISO 27001, SOX, HIPAA

Foundation Topics

Data and systems are critical to almost every part of modern organizations. Almost every organization stores and processes some specific data for its products and services, has email and a website (or most do!), and has a method for handling money. So, what happens when systems crash and are no longer available to customers, clients, and employees? A modern IT infrastructure is built on hundreds, if not thousands, of components, and many of them, like fiber-optic cables and power lines, aren't within an organization's control. A myriad of threats also complicate issues, from malware on Internet sites to general phishing emails to more targeted attacks. With all of this complexity and all of these sources of risk, emergencies aren't merely a possibility but a probability. Then, add into the mix an event such as a weather emergency or a pandemic. Now we have the distinct likelihood of something bad happening to our systems. So how do we control the situation and prepare?

Incident Response

The importance of *incident response* (IR), the process of addressing anomalies and events in a timely fashion to minimize risk to the organization, goes without saying, considering all of the incidents and breaches that make the news. Every organization, no matter how small or large, secure or insecure, prepared or not, is at risk of being hacked. All the controls we've discussed in previous chapters may deflect most attacks and mitigate most mistakes, but not all of them, even when perfectly implemented. When, not if, organizations are attacked, they need to follow certain steps, the purpose of which—the purpose of incident response—is to mitigate the risks and protect as much of the systems and the data from compromise and from loss of availability.

Keep in mind that incident response is an area requiring specialized training. To actually respond to an incident is a daunting endeavor, as it means having to stay cool and perform complex tasks under immense pressure. Thus, many incident response teams (IRTs) practice responding to incidents during periods in which there are no incidents (more on this later). Furthermore, in addition to training, an effective IRT must have wider company participation, such as from IT, legal, and executive management, who also participate in training and testing. This enables the IRT to make important, time-bound decisions and have access to any necessary resources. It is valuable to note here that not all IRT members are dedicated to that function or to security as a whole: many IRT members are crossovers from other departments, and some organizations outsource incident response to other organizations.

There are multiple incident response models. In the authors' experience, however, most of them can be condensed to these six steps: detect, classify, contain, respond, recover, and post mortem. In a well-designed information security program, all of these steps, with details specific to the organization, are documented into an incident response plan (IRP).

Detection

How do we know if we're facing an incident? Answering this question is crucial, because we can't respond to an incident if we haven't detected it.

Recall the discussion on logging and monitoring from Chapter 9. The detection of many incidents begins with anomalies reported by logging and monitoring tools and analyzed by security or network operations center analysts. Additionally, an employee or a client might report a suspicious error or anomaly—which many organizations encourage through providing internal and external incident reporting mechanisms. Another common practice is for security personnel to read publications by security industry groups and government agencies to learn about possible vulnerabilities and emerging threats, and then scan their organization's environment to find any related indicators of compromise. In all of these cases, proactive detection is at play, and that is excellent. The last thing anyone wants is to find out from the attackers, such as through a ransom message or a public posting of stolen data, that an attack has occurred. Proactivity is critical because it safeguards both the organization's assets and its reputation.

Classification

Similar to the classification of risks in risk management, classification is crucial to incident response. Picture this: you are a Security Operations Center (SOC) analyst responsible for analyzing and triaging hundreds of alerts, most of which are spam, or clients are submitting incident tickets for minor application errors and bugs. Most of these don't require mustering the entire incident response team. So, how do we tell the difference?

The National Institute of Standards and Technology (NIST) publication *Minimum Security Requirements for Federal Information and Information Systems* (FIPS Pub. 200) defines an incident as "an occurrence that actually or potentially jeopardizes the confidentiality, integrity, or availability of an information system or the information the system processes, stores or transmits or that constitutes a violation of imminent threat of violation of security policies, security, procedures, or acceptable use policies." For our purposes, an incident is an event that threatens the security of an information system.

Each organization has its own ranking of incidents, but, for the most part, there are five categories documented in IRPs:

- **P4:** Catastrophic risk to the organization; examples: sensitive data posted publicly, an employee disclosing data in response to a phishing email, ransomware on the system

- **P3:** High risk to the organization; examples: virtual machines on the cloud being accessible from the Internet, a distributed denial-of-service (DDoS) attack

- **P2:** Medium risk to the organization; examples: application components going offline, a use of USBs on workstations

- **P1:** Low risk to the organization; examples: system slowdowns, a blocked download of unauthorized software

- **P0:** No risk to the organization; examples: random spam, resetting passwords

Notice that these examples include incidents impacting availability as well as security. Many organizations differentiate between security incidents and availability incidents and handle them through different processes. Further note that organizations classify incidents differently based on their needs, their existing security controls, and the types of data they possess. Not every organization considers a system slowdown as posing a low risk, and not every organization considers a ransomware attack as posing a catastrophic risk.

Based on the incident classification, the organization will decide what resources to allocate. This includes the team members who need to be involved and what kind of system resources, such as laptops and virtual machines, those members need.

As part of calling up team members, many IRPs include an escalation tree or chart, which lists the personnel and level of management who should be contacted depending on the severity of the incident.

Containment

The third step of the incident response process is containment. Once classification and resource allocation are established, the IRT works to isolate points of intrusion and infection or to pinpoint the source of the issue. For example, if malware is detected on a laptop, the team might remove the infected laptop from the network and disable the user's access. In an availability incident, for example, the team might run tests to determine why the company's application isn't loading. Sometimes, in a major incident, containment may require taking the organization's entire infrastructure offline.

The precise methods used for containment depend on the incident. But be aware of one fundamental: don't just unplug an infected device! See the final step.

Response

After or at the same time as containment, the IRT will work to respond to the incident. Continuing the previous examples, the IRT might remove malware or roll back the application to a previous version. The goal here is to prevent the incident from spreading further and to address the root cause of whatever happened. Sometimes, this may require implementing the organization's disaster recovery plan.

At this time, an organization may need to consider informing all personnel or external parties. In some parts of the world, laws and regulations require communication with law enforcement agencies and with clients when major incidents occur. If the incident is large enough and involves sensitive data, the response phase may need to include such notifications.

Recovery

After or at the same time as containment and response, the IRT will work to return the system to normal operations and salvage as much of the affected sections as possible. Depending on the scale of the incident, this may be an extended process and may include other personnel not on the IRT. The IRT may need to request changes, system maintenance, or even modifications of large sections of the IT infrastructure. Additionally, depending on the scale and impact of the incident, communications may need to continue with external parties such as the government and the company's clients.

Reflection

In the final step, once the incident has been resolved, the IRT should document what happened. Ideally, this documentation, especially of the incident's root cause, timeline, and resolution, should be interactively completed during the incident, but that may not always be possible when there is a huge amount of pressure to restore normal operations. But whether during or after an incident, the IRT should take time to reflect, review their performance and any lessons learned, and update the incident response plan if necessary.

Testing

Before we move on to the next section, let's take a moment to consider what an organization should do if it hasn't experienced any incidents. Just because it hasn't experienced any incidents, whether in the past year or ever, that doesn't mean an incident can't happen, and, like any sort of training, people can forget what they're supposed to do if they haven't had to recall the information in a long while. For this reason, many organizations perform annual testing of their IRP. The IRT gathers, either talks through a scenario in what is called a *tabletop test* or actually simulates an incident, and evaluates whether the team can respond effectively and whether the technology used for actions like backup and recovery actually functions (more on backup and recovery in the sections that follow).

Business Continuity

Business continuity (BC) refers to the actions to take to ensure an organization is operational during and following a disaster or emergency.

Unlike an incident response plan, however, a BCP doesn't solely cover a single event or just the IT and security departments. The BCP lays out processes and procedures for the whole organization during large, extraordinary events, such as a pandemic, as well as more singular incidents, such as a major power outage. For these emergencies, the BCP lays out which systems are critical and which data must be secured first. Furthermore, the BCP addresses the grim realities of events like key organizational leaders leaving, being terminated, or passing away.

The BCP also states which personnel should contact which in an emergency (also known as a call tree) and which systems should be used for contact in case primary methods like corporate email or messaging are unavailable. These primary methods are called *in-band communications*, and alternate methods, like texting or calling personal phones, are called *out-of-band* communication. Both should be listed in the BCP.

Business Impact Analysis

The previous section mentioned that the BCP states which systems and data are critical. Those determinations come from a process that should be completed before the BCP is drafted, a *business impact analysis (BIA)*. A BIA is much like a risk assessment, but instead of focusing on specific risks, it focuses on rating the company's IT assets based on how susceptible they are to risk. One method of making these determinations is to judge the risk that a loss of the asset would pose to confidentiality, integrity, and availability, as recommended by NIST FIPS Pub. 200, *Minimum Security Requirements for Federal Information and Information Systems*. Table 10-2 shows a sample BIA.

Table 10-2 Sample Business Impact Analysis

Asset	Risk to Confidentiality if Compromised	Risk to Integrity if Compromised	Risk to Availability if Compromised	Security Category
Cloud instances containing key application components	High	High	High	High
External informational web pages	Low	Low	Medium	Medium
Endpoint management software	High	High	Medium	High
Corporate network	High	Medium	High	High
Corporate email	Medium	Medium	High	High
Marketing material	Low	Low	Low	Low

As you can see in this example, the highest rating the system has for confidentiality, integrity, and availability is the system's rating. These determinations should be used to calculate the values in the sections that follow.

In addition to conducting a BIA, a risk assessment should be conducted to evaluate and understand the impact specific risks have on specific systems an organization owns. The risk assessment and BIA work together: the BIA provides the potential impact of a disruption to business operations, while the risk assessment quantifies the likelihood and impact of security risks. With these documents, organizations can prioritize mitigation strategies and allocate resources effectively.

Testing

Like an IRP, a BCP should be tested at least annually. These tests, like those in incident response, often take the form of tabletop scenarios, in which relevant personnel from across the organization (not just IT) discuss what they would do in a specified scenario. This exercise includes testing out the call tree by having personnel attempt to contact each other and by discussing how they would escalate issues if someone in the call tree is unavailable or if in-band communication is unavailable.

Backup and Recovery

Before we move on to disaster recovery, let's briefly discuss the role of backup and recovery in business continuity. A *backup*, as the name suggests, is a copy of the data in a system stored in a format that can be easily loaded and used for recovery. An example is the backup file generated when you use the backup utility on your smartphone or laptop. You can easily use that file to restore your system. There are a few more details about backup and recovery to consider, though.

The four major types of backups are as follows:

- **Full:** A complete copy of the system at a specific time. This backup takes up the most space on the backup system or medium. A full backup takes the longest time to complete, from hours to days depending on the amount of data on the system, but is the fastest to use to recover as all the data from the system is in one place.

- **Incremental:** A copy of the data that's changed since the last full backup. So, after a full backup, the first incremental backup would include the changes since that full backup. Then, after that first incremental backup, the second incremental backup would include changes between the first and the second incremental backups. Then, after the second incremental backup, the third incremental backup would include changes between the second and the third incremental backups. And so on. An incremental backup takes up less space than a differential backup (and the least space overall). This backup takes the shortest amount of time to complete but is the slowest recovery time due to having to use all the previous incremental backups to return to normal operation.

- **Differential:** A copy of the data that's changed since the last full backup. That means that, on the first, second, third, and more backups, this backup will keep referring to the last full backup instead of simply to the last backup. Backups will increase in size as each differential run as complete copy of changes is backed up. If a full backup was run on Monday, the backup run Tuesday would capture changes from Monday. If another backup was run on Wednesday, it would capture changes from Monday and Tuesday. Differential backups take a moderate amount of time to complete but are faster than incremental to restore.

- **Mirror:** A copy of system data with the exception that all files, including deleted files, are compressed into a few files. Only the latest version files are stored so there is no version history. The space needed to store the backup is like that of a full backup. When a mirror backup is run, it captures the changes since the last mirror backup.

Table 10-3 provides a high-level look at the differences between the various backup types.

Table 10-3 Backup Types

Backup Type	Time to Complete	Time to Restore	Characteristics	Amount of Space Used	Ideal Use Case	Security Considerations	Files Needed for Restoration
Full	Longest	Fastest	Copies all data Requires most storage Complete data snapshot	Most space needed	Comprehensive backups where time and space are not constraints	Secure storage critical due to comprehensive data coverage	The latest full backup
Incremental	Shortest	Slowest	Only changes since last backup Minimizes storage needs	Least space initially, grows with changes	Frequent backups, minimizing storage space and time	Incremental changes must be securely linked to prevent tampering	The last full backup plus all subsequent incremental backups
Differential	Moderate	Faster than Incremental	Changes since last full backup Larger than incremental over time	More than incremental, less than full	Balancing between comprehensive coverage and efficient storage use	Secure storage important; differential backups grow in size and sensitivity	The last full backup plus the last differential backup
Mirror	Moderate to Long	Fast	Exact copy of source No historical versions	Similar to full, reflects current state only	Real-time/ near-real time data mirroring with immediate recovery needs	Mirrored data must be protected in real-time; risks of immediate data deletion	The latest mirror backup

In many organizations, whether using cloud or on-premises infrastructure, multiple types of backups are required. For example, an organization could do a full backup on a weekly basis and do incremental backups on a daily basis. Or, an organization could do a full backup every month and differential backups every week. The choice of configurations depends on the system and the amount of data loss the organization is willing to risk.

In previous decades, it was common to create backups manually on tapes, and although the terminology "tape backup" is still often used, the use of tapes is uncommon now (although you may encounter tapes used to back up systems containing particularly sensitive data). The more common practice now is to create digital backups on high-capacity drives or using cloud resources. Keep in mind that, although data storage is becoming increasingly cheaper, modern systems tend to be quite large in terms of file size. Storage and capacity management is an increasingly critical part of IT and cloud storage because of the possibility of either losing track and ending up with a huge bill or not having enough memory and storage at the wrong moment.

Let's end this section with a brief mention of testing backups. It does no good to conduct backups only to discover later that the backups don't work. There are a number of tools for automation, testing whether the backup was successful, and restoring from the backup when necessary. Thus, many organizations test their backups, either through automated tools or by actually restoring from them. This type of full restoration may be part of failover testing, which is covered in the upcoming "Failover Testing" section.

Disaster Recovery

Disaster recovery (DR) refers to the step-by-step processes of handling and recovering from disasters. While many organizations use BC and DR interchangeably, they are slightly different. The DR plan is a subcomponent of the larger BC plan, and the BC and DR processes are sometimes collectively referred to as BC/DR.

Incident response and business continuity have plans, but usually disaster recovery has procedures instead of a plan (but we can abbreviate it as DRP just the same). This is because disaster recovery is more focused on the specifics of what exactly is required to recover from a disaster. For example, how exactly does IT restore from backups and set up the environment again? If the electricity goes out or there is a hurricane, what has to be done to protect the organization's people (always the highest priority) and, if it doesn't risk their lives, secure critical system components? Where are the backups stored, and what needs to be salvaged first? What should the organization do to resume business operations? The disaster recovery procedures (or plan) cover the practicalities of safeguarding the organization, the people foremost and the technology second, and returning to normal as soon as possible.

Various metrics are used in disaster recovery planning, as depicted in Figure 10-1 and discussed next.

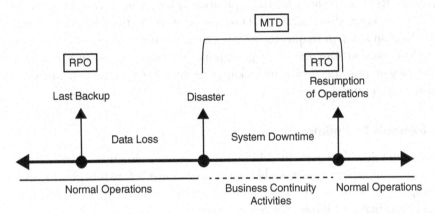

RPO = Recovery Point Objective
RTO = Recovery Time Objective
MTD = Maximum Tolerable Downtime

Figure 10-1   Disaster Recovery Metrics

Recovery Time Objective

A *recovery time objective (RTO)* specifies the latest time after an incident at which the system should be fully recovered and functional. In other words, an RTO is the deadline for a system's recovery. Based on the BIA, each system should have its own RTO if possible. In calculating RTOs, it should be noted that cost is inverse to time. The faster a system must be recovered, the greater the amount of resources and cost required to recover it. For example, if recovery of a critical application must take place within an hour, a large number of teams might need to be scrambled to initiate backup recovery, examine the software code, communicate with external parties, scan the infrastructure, and so on. Near-instantaneous recovery is almost always impossible because it would take a massive amount of personnel, energy, time, and infrastructure to achieve.

Recovery Point Objective

A *recovery point objective (RPO)* specifies the most recent point before an incident to which a system can be recovered. In other words, it's the latest backup. Because systems are not backed up continuously, any changes made to the system between the latest backup and the incident will be lost after the system is restored.

How do we decide where we can accept data loss? As with RTOs, each system should have its own RPO. Establishing an RPO for a system determines how frequently it should be backed up. For example, suppose a company has an application that is its primary product and is essential to its operations. The company has designated an RPO of one hour for the application. That means it would need to be backed up every hour. Also similar to RTOs, cost is inverse to the time frame of an RPO. Backing up a system frequently is more expensive. If the company has to have a backup from only an hour ago at any given point in time, we would need to spend a lot of money on near-instantaneous backups that mirror the production environment at any given time.

Maximum Tolerable Downtime

The maximum tolerable downtime (MTD) is the maximum amount of time a system, service, or process is unavailable or nonoperational before it begins to significantly impact the business. This is the limit beyond which the impact of downtime becomes unacceptable or intolerable to the organization.

Granted, hosting resources on the cloud does address some of the cost concerns associated with RTO or RPO; however, keep in mind that using system resources on the cloud does have a cost. More frequent backups and creating additional replicas of key applications require more resources, and each additional use raises the amount requested on cloud-hosting provider invoices. Like many things in life and in security, a balance is needed.

Replication, Hot Sites, Warm Sites, and Cold Sites

Because part of disaster recovery is returning systems to normal, many organizations replicate their systems.

Replication is a concept related to backups. But where a backup creates a copy of a system's data, replication creates a duplicate of the entire production environment. Replication can be done through several mechanisms, such as copying over configurations on premises or creating redundant resources in other zones and regions on the cloud.

The concept of replication comes into play when setting up an alternate site for an organization. Alternate sites come in three forms:

- **Hot site:** A perfect mirror of the organization's primary location, fully furnished, with equipment ready and available and a replica of all applications and systems active and functioning. The organization could immediately shift there and start working.

- **Warm site:** A periodically updated version of the organization's primary location, with some furnishings and some replication of some, but not all, systems already conducted. Some effort would be required for the organization to get up and running here.

■ **Cold site:** A location that has some basic setup, like electrical cables and an Internet connection and perhaps a couple of pieces of furniture, but would require effort and time to become fully functional and replace the primary site.

Remember here that alternate sites are considered in disaster recovery planning in case a disaster requires actually switching offices, including giving people places to work, not just moving the technology.

You might say the obvious choice is the hot site, where becoming fully functional won't require much time. However, the reason an organization might choose a warm site or a cold site is, as usual, cost.

The cost factor applies to using the cloud as well. Although it is much easier and much cheaper to replicate an environment in the cloud and to run parallel processing in multiple zones and regions, this still takes up system resources and has a price tag. And, as some companies have experienced over the last few years, even a fully remote workforce still requires disaster recovery preparation, in case an emergency impacts employees' ability to work at all or, more importantly, their safety.

Failover Testing

Now that we've gone over replication and alternate sites, we need to address an important question: How do we know whether our replicated environment can actually handle the strain of becoming the primary? For this, we need to conduct *failover testing* (also known as a *DRP test*), in which we test whether the environment actually fails over as required. For physical locations, this might mean something resembling a fire drill, where organizational operations are entirely or partially switched over to the alternate site (depending on what scope is approved for the drill). For a cloud environment, it might mean bringing up the redundant instances and transferring all traffic and processing to them.

Additionally, as a part of DRP testing, an organization may also test backup restoration for emergencies in which a full failover may not be possible. This would require loading backup drives or restoring from cloud snapshots. The goal here would be to complete the restoration as efficiently as possible while meeting the RPO and render the environment fully functional within the RTO. Such testing may also be done in conjunction with the BCP test in certain organizations.

Governance Processes

In Chapter 2, "Risk Management," we introduced cybersecurity governance through the discussion of security controls. Now that we've actually encountered these safeguards, the physical, the technical, and some of the administrative, let's wrap things up with a deeper dive into the administrative controls. Recall that *governance processes* are documents and methods used to oversee a cybersecurity program and ensure risks are being properly addressed and all controls are being implemented as specified.

While governance documents such as policies, guidelines, and procedures are used to establish critical processes and controls, usually they are not referenced on a day-to-day basis. Security team members, software developers, HR personnel, and other employees know their roles, and, once they've completed initial training, they typically don't continuously refer to governance documents. It's like driving a car: once you know how to drive, you just drive for the most part. However, in scenarios that deviate from the everyday grind, policies, procedures, and standards are valuable, such as when the senior team member who used to manage a whole domain by themselves leaves, when rapid turnover occurs, when someone new is onboarded, and when emergencies and disasters strike. This is key to ensuring confidentiality, integrity, and availability are protected as they are meant to be.

It is worth noting here that governance documents are a major requirement for audits and vendor questionnaires, as well as for meeting the requirements of regulations and laws. However, external checkups are not the only reason for spending the time, energy, and money to write governance documents in the first place and then to annually review and update them and have them formally approved. Accurate policies aligned with what the organization is currently doing and currently needs ensure that there is a reference point in case of an emergency, a place to look when, for example, no one remembers which encryption setting they were supposed to use.

There are four types of governance documents: policies, standards, procedures, and guidelines, as covered in the sections that follow. Figure 10-2 shows the hierarchy of these documents.

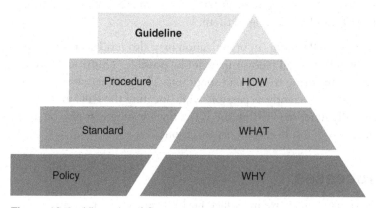

Figure 10-2 Hierarchy of Governance Documents

Policies

A *policy* is a set of general guidelines, expectations, and approaches that an organization creates to maintain confidentiality, integrity, and availability of data. Policies may be created based on frameworks such as NIST 800-53 or the CIS Benchmarks. Policies are the "why" something should be done. Policies can exist in two forms: either they are the only documents in the organization, which hold all sorts of large and small details, or they are large, generalized documents that set out brief directions for what needs to happen in each domain (think each chapter, heading, and subheading between Chapters 2 through 10 in this book), including authorizing the creation of procedures, standards, and guidelines. This second definition is the more formal definition, but the authors have seen both used in practice.

As a further complexity to the preceding statements, policies such as the AUP, the BYOD policy, the password policy, and the privacy policy are nearly always called "policy" even when they may not fit the definition of a policy exactly. (Chapters 8 and 9 delve into the specifics of these policies.)

In addition to detail or direction, policies should define roles and responsibilities for each domain—which position, such as the director of engineering, is responsible for what—and should include exception-handling clauses in case there are situations requiring actions that go against policy.

Finally, there is no point to a policy if it doesn't actually describe what's going on in the organization. So, if you ever find yourself writing a policy, make sure it's accurate.

Standards

Following the idea that policies provide brief, general direction, standards are the next level of granularity. *Standards* describe "what" should be done to adhere to a policy. Standards contain actual specifics, like the names of the logging and monitoring tools that should be used, and are usually lengthy and full of detail—almost like the discussions in this book but tailored to your organization. Standards are the first place you should look when your car's dashboard starts flashing strange lights. Standards are typically cross-referenced in a policy so that readers know where to go to get more clarity on what needs to be done.

Procedures

As indicated in the hierarchical structure shown in Figure 10-2, *procedures* identify "how" standards are implemented, the step-by-step guide. Procedures contain instructions on how to implement certain processes, such as how to conduct a failover test. The IRP, BCP, and DRP could all be considered as procedures, even if they're called plans, because they are intended to contain very specific detail and show how to respond to incidents, maintain business operations, and fail over during emergencies at a granular level.

The value of governance documents is also most readily apparent in emergency situations: Having an existing BCP or DRP to reference helps responders focus their energy on addressing the situation rather than on making up new processes on the spot, which is challenging even in nonemergency situations.

Keep in mind that some organizations conflate standards and procedures or have procedures instead of standards. Also remember that this talk of detail can be a bit subjective and that some organizations have more detail to include than others.

Guidelines

Finally, *guidelines* are recommendations, not requirements like the other three types of documents, and might include items like how to best set up your laptop, how to use corporate email signatures, how to deploy a cloud resource, or how to code a type of application component. Guidelines, like procedures, should be very thorough, with annotated screenshots and diagrams if necessary. These documents aren't always present in organizations and are not used for critical security controls, but we describe them here in case you come across them or are asked to write them.

Regulations and Laws

We've come again to the topic of regulations and laws, our final topic for this chapter and our almost-final topic for this book. *Regulations and laws* impose requirements on security programs to ensure data is appropriately protected and kept private.

When considering regulations and their impact on an organization, be aware of this difference: a regulation could refer to a rule enacted by a government entity or one from an industry body. The former is as legally binding as a law, and a violation can be a criminal offense; the latter is not legally binding but may need to be adhered to in order to maintain good standing in the industry. Also note that every country has its own regulations and laws, and a transnational organization (one that operates outside its own country's borders) may be obligated to uphold other countries' laws as well as the laws of the country in which it is based. When these obligations conflict...well, this is where the cybersecurity team needs some support from the legal department.

The following are some examples of important regulations and laws relevant to cybersecurity (at the time of writing; the legal and regulatory landscape is in great flux):

- U.S. Computer Fraud and Abuse Act (1986)

- U.S. Health Insurance Portability and Accountability Act (HIPAA) (1996)

- U.S. Sarbanes-Oxley Act (SOX) (2002)

- California-specific California Consumer Privacy Act (CCPA) (2018)

- European Union General Data Protection Regulation (GDPR) (2016)

Important governmental regulations include requirements from the Federal Trade Commission (FTC), the Securities and Exchange Commission (SEC), and those related to HIPAA.

Important industry regulations include FedRAMP (compliance with which is required for U.S. federal government contractors) and Payment Card Industry Data Security Standard (PCI DSS) (compliance with which is required by payment card companies for any organization handling payment card data).

Important frameworks—not regulations but used as a point of reference by many— include NIST SP 800-53, HiTRUST (related to healthcare and HIPAA), ISO 27001 (international standard), and American Institute of Certified Public Accountants (AICPA)'s System and Organization Controls (SOC).

Knowledge of specific regulations and laws is beyond the scope of the Certified in Cybersecurity exam but is important for cybersecurity professionals, so you should consider researching each of these laws, rules, and regulations as best suits your interests, opportunities, and roles.

Exam Preparation Tasks

As mentioned in the Introduction, you have a couple of choices for exam preparation: the exercises here, Chapter 13, "Final Preparation," and the exam simulation questions in the Pearson Test Prep Software Online.

Review All Key Topics

Review the most important topics in this chapter, noted with the Key Topics icon in the outer margin of the page. Table 10-4 lists a reference of these key topics and the page numbers on which each is found.

Table 10-4   Key Topics for Chapter 10

Key Topic Element	Description	Page Number
Paragraph	Describes incident response	180
Paragraph	Describes business continuity	184
Paragraph	Describes backups	185
Paragraph	Describes disaster recovery	188
Paragraph	Describes recovery time objective	189
Paragraph	Describes recovery point objective	189
Paragraph	Describes failover testing	191
Paragraph	Describes governance processes	191
Paragraph	Describes policies	193
Paragraph	Describes standards	193
Paragraph	Describes procedures	193
Paragraph	Describes guidelines	194
Paragraph	Describes regulations and laws	194

Define Key Terms

Define the following key terms from this chapter and check your answers in the glossary:

incident response, business continuity (BC), backup, disaster recovery (DR), recovery time objective (RTO), recovery point objective (RPO), failover testing, governance processes, policies, standards, procedures, guidelines, regulations and laws

Q&A

The answers to these questions appear in Appendix A. For more practice with exam format questions, use the Pearson Test Prep Software Online.

1. What is incident response?

2. What is business continuity?

3. What are RTO and RPO?

4. What are backups?

5. What is disaster recovery?

6. What is failover testing?

7. What are the different types of governance documents?

8. What types of laws and regulations are relevant to cybersecurity programs?

References

NIST FIPS Pub. 200, *Minimum Security Requirements for Federal Information and Information Systems*: https://csrc.nist.gov/pubs/fips/200/final

Kirvan, Paul. "RPO vs. RTO: Key differences explained with examples, tips." *TechTarget*, Mar. 1, 2024: https://www.techtarget.com/searchstorage/feature/What-is-the-difference-between-RPO-and-RTO-from-a-backup-perspective

Fellows, Russ and Paul Crocetti. "Types of backup explained: Full, incremental, differential, etc." *TechTarget*, Dec. 14, 2022: https://www.techtarget.com/searchdatabackup/feature/Full-incremental-or-differential-How-to-choose-the-correct-backup-type

Fisher, Tim. "What Are Mirror Image Backups?" *Lifewire*, Sep. 7, 2022: What Is a Mirror Image Backup? (lifewire.com)

CHAPTER 11

Tying It All Together

This chapter does not cover a specific element of the Certified in Cybersecurity objectives. It is intended as an overview chapter that connects the pieces of cybersecurity into a whole. Therefore, reading this chapter is entirely up to your discretion.

As you conclude your studies in cybersecurity, let's take a moment to talk about the big picture of cybersecurity and put together all the pieces you've learned into a cohesive whole. Let's make it make sense.

Security as a Whole

Cybersecurity is comprised of many domains. There are many areas of interest and work beneath the cybersecurity umbrella, as this book's chapters show, and learning all the intricacies of just one domain could constitute a career. Yet there is a caveat here: when we study cybersecurity domain by domain and focus on the one that interests us most, we start to think that one domain is the most important, the linchpin without which everything will come crashing down, the be-all and end-all of the entire cybersecurity industry. That leads to overreliance on a single set of controls. And that is a major problem in a world full of ever-shifting and ever-adapting threats. The far more prudent and secure approach is to realize that every piece of cybersecurity relies on every other piece and together they form an interconnected, interlocking whole that protects confidentiality, integrity, and availability in service of the mission of the organization.

Defense-in-Depth

As you learned in Chapter 7, "Network Security Infrastructure," the term for that interlocking whole is *defense-in-depth*. To understand the concept better, picture the following scenarios that lack full defense-in-depth:

- A complete networking setup, with default deny-all on the external firewalls and segmentation on the inside, but no encryption or access control. How would this network stop any unauthorized users from getting to whatever resources they want?

- A database implemented with redundancy and encryption (your choice if it's on the cloud or on-premises!), but lacking any documentation to tell us which patches need to be implemented when, and what we should do when we need to replicate our assets as we need more.

As you can see, every part counts.

The domains of cybersecurity, when well implemented, form layers. Each layer supports the others and provides redundancy and fallbacks so that if one layer is compromised, the others still stand strong. For example, if the firewall fails, the antivirus on individual devices might still discover malware and contain its spread. Each domain has a role to play in defending, monitoring, or governing—each domain provides administrative, technical, and physical safeguards to keep the whole organization safe. Thus, whatever you learn in cybersecurity should be integrated into the concept of defense-in-depth.

The Castle Analogy

Drawing upon our previous references to castles, the authors here present you with a new castle. A giant flying castle, like an airship, that drifts upon the clouds (pun entirely intended).

Are you picturing it yet? Or looking it up online? (We would give you an image, but the ones we're thinking of require licensing! But if you want to follow our train of thought here, imagine the really popular ones! Or a giant spaceship!)

In our flying castle of cybersecurity, we have a number of forces, departments, and offices to consider. The castle has to be able to stay in the air, which means it needs to keep moving, it needs to trade for fuel, and it absolutely cannot have system failure. The machinery required to keep it aloft and functioning is really complex, so the castle needs to address every threat proactively.

Let's explore from the outside in. The perimeters, the outer sections of the castle, are very closely monitored by guards, and a lookout is stationed on the tallest tower and is carefully examining the sky as far as she can see for rivals, pirates, and dragons. The walls keep out the cold temperatures and smaller mythical beasts. These are our network perimeter, firewalls, intrusion detection and prevention systems, and threat intelligence analysts. Confidentiality, integrity, and availability are the spells cast here.

The castle is moving above the clouds, so the engines and the propulsion systems must work efficiently and smoothly, with plenty of backup sections in case one part ceases to function. This is our infrastructure, including the network perimeter, and we have a team dedicated to monitoring it. That team has all sorts of cool dials and buttons on their dashboards and the tablets they carry, which let them keep an eye on fuel levels and engine function, as well as wear and tear on the walls. They also store all this information in the castle archives (they're digital, on wisps of cloud, aren't they?) and send it to other teams as well. This is our logging and monitoring portion of our security operations domain. Integrity and availability are the spells cast here.

Based on the information collected by the infrastructure team, another team uses high-impact steel and titanium to patch any holes in the walls and replace any worn components in the engines. They also repair consoles and walkways around the castle whenever they break so that the castle staff can work, and they print new equipment with their 3D printer based on existing schematics as necessary. This is system hardening as part of security operations. Integrity and availability are the spells cast here.

There are certain secure areas in our castle, and the castle itself needs to be secure. We don't want any pirates or rogue elves stealing our secrets. For this reason, the guards on the gate question and demand identification from everyone who tries to dock at our external docking stations. More guards patrol the more sensitive areas of the castles, near the treasury, the engine chambers, and the bridge (where the castle leaders hold court), as well as other important places. These guards also ask questions and demand identification at certain checkpoints, since staff members and even castle leaders are not supposed to have access to everything (just in case there is a changeling or spy among us!). This is our access control domain. Integrity is the spell cast here.

Our castle also has communication systems. There are intercom systems and message relay networks comprised of couriers, chutes along the walls, and enchantments. The infrastructure team and the maintenance team need to take care of these, too, as our giant castle requires a lot of coordination to keep it in the sky. We also need to transmit messages to other castles since we need to trade for more fuel and more 3D printing material—we use small drones and enchanted birds to do this. Moreover, a lot of these messages are in code, since we don't want anyone to intercept them, so we have special equipment that is built to properly encrypt our messages before sending them off. This is our networking domain. Availability is the spell cast here.

As we explore, we realize that all of these teams are only a portion of the staff. Most of the staff are busy crafting new products, with some actively making and maintaining the machinery the rest are using. The products and the machinery both require a lot of specialized material, and the castle carefully guards the secrets of how they're made and what sort of material is used. Every tweak, especially to the machinery, has to be recorded. That's software development and change management for you. Confidentiality and integrity are the spells cast here.

Along with the secrets of the products and the machinery are the names of the staff, which we need to protect from all the pirates and rogue elves out there. These scrolls and digital tablets are kept in guarded archives and only accessed with express permission from the castle leaders. The scrolls and tablets can only be destroyed using special methods like incineration prior to casting into the sea of clouds, and express permission is required for this as well. This is data handling as a part of security operations. Confidentiality is the spell cast here.

We've seen everything else, so it's time to seek out the castle leaders. This group, often found in the bridge, carries around airtight cases of scrolls, which they reference as they decide how much 3D printing material to use, what to repair, which products to make, and who gets special access to secrets. Based on the castle's needs, they predict as many threats as they can and instruct the teams on the tasks they need to accomplish to proactively secure the castle and keep it secured. The results of implementing those instructions are used to update the scrolls and design better instructions. The castle leaders also gather together a number of staff members and prepare for attacks—especially from pirates and dragons—and make plans for emergencies, including evacuations and relocations (because the lives of the staff are most important). This is security governance, risk management, incident response, business continuity, and disaster recovery. All three spells, confidentiality, integrity, and availability, are cast here.

Finally, the castle staff is often reminded by their leaders and each other to adhere to codes of castle staff ethics.

The Whole of Information Assurance

The preceding castle analogy, while entertaining and hopefully easy to remember, simplifies all sorts of elements. But the key point here is that everything in cybersecurity fits together and that it is all meant to defend confidentiality, integrity, and availability for the sake of the mission of the organization. Keep in mind as you piece it all together that cybersecurity protects and enables the organization to operate; undervaluing cybersecurity compromises the organization, yes, but overvaluing it can stifle the organization's capability to perform necessary functions. Cybersecurity is an industry of service. It's important to remember that.

Summary

The domains of cybersecurity are many, but they are meant to fit together into a cohesive whole, not remain as scattered pieces, in the pursuit of ensuring confidentiality, integrity, and availability. A well-architected cybersecurity program, implemented with neither excess nor deficiency, makes sense, and, though no system is perfect, such a program might just be able to defend the organization against most threats. The critical point of cybersecurity is defense and protection of data and the lives connected to that data.

You have made it to the end of the substantive cybersecurity material. The next two chapters are related to the Certified in Cybersecurity exam and certification.

Welcome to the world of cybersecurity!

CHAPTER 12

After the Certification

Entering the dynamic world of cybersecurity with a newly acquired ISC2 Certified in Cybersecurity certification is an accomplishment worth celebrating. Now that you have successfully completed the exam, it's time to strategically plan your next steps for a rewarding and impactful cybersecurity career. Let's delve into what to do after achieving this certification.

Take a Breather and Reflect

Before diving into the next phase of your career, take a moment to rest and rejuvenate. Preparing for a cybersecurity certification can be intense, and your brain needs a short break after the exam. This pause allows you to reflect on your achievement, reassess your goals, and approach the next steps with a clear mind.

Update Your Professional Profiles

Once you've taken a well-deserved break, the first practical step is to update your professional profiles. Platforms like LinkedIn, work profiles, and your resume should prominently reflect your newly obtained certification. Highlight key skills, the certification itself, and any notable achievements. Remember, your professional presence is the gateway to networking opportunities and career advancement.

Actively engaging with the cybersecurity community is pivotal. Connect with at least three professionals daily on LinkedIn or professional forums. Target individuals in roles or organizations aligned with your career interests. Comment on their posts or invite a virtual coffee. Visibility within the community is key to opening doors to new opportunities.

Showcase Your Passion and Knowledge

Use platforms like Medium or GitHub to share your passion and knowledge with the broader community. Consider contributing or volunteering with relevant cybersecurity groups such as ISC2 or the Women's Society of

Cyberjutsu (WSC). These platforms and groups provide avenues to give back, share insights, and build your reputation within the cybersecurity community.

Participate in Capture-The-Flag (CTF) competitions on Hack The Box and TryHackMe. These competitions offer hands-on experience, allowing you to apply theoretical knowledge to practical scenarios and enhance problem-solving skills.

Seek Mentorship and Sponsorship

In the cybersecurity field, mentorship is invaluable. Seek out mentors at various career stages to provide guidance. Additionally, identify sponsors who are invested in your career advancement and can provide access to opportunities you might not have on your own. Further insights on mentorship and sponsorship can be found in the LinkedIn Learning course, "Land Your First Cybersecurity Job."

Stay Informed About Emerging Threats and Technologies

Remaining informed about emerging threats and technologies is paramount in cybersecurity. Subscribe to cybersecurity news sources such as SANS Reading Room, Dark Reading, and the Cybersecurity and Infrastructure Security Agency (CISA). Platforms like Reddit's r/cybersecurity and threat briefs from cybersecurity vendors like FireEye and Palo Alto offer additional insights into the evolving threat landscape.

As your cybersecurity career progresses, the need for specialized training becomes evident. Use platforms like Pearson or Udemy to acquire deeper knowledge tailored to your job role and career path.

Contribute to the Community Through Thought Leadership

Beyond showcasing your skills, consider establishing yourself as a thought leader in the cybersecurity space. Write in-depth articles or whitepapers on platforms like LinkedIn or cybersecurity-focused blogs. This demonstrates your expertise and contributes valuable insights to the community.

Engage in webinars and conferences to stay current with industry trends and connect with professionals. Conferences such as Black Hat, DEF CON, Cyberjutsu Con, or local cybersecurity events offer excellent opportunities for networking and learning.

Get involved in open-source projects related to cybersecurity. Contributing to projects on platforms like GitHub adds practical experience to your portfolio and allows you to collaborate with experts in the field.

Explore Further Education Opportunities

Consider pursuing advanced degrees or specialized certifications to deepen your expertise. Institutions like the SANS Institute and universities offer advanced programs in cybersecurity. These programs provide a structured curriculum, hands-on experience, and networking opportunities that can significantly contribute to your career growth.

Cybersecurity is multifaceted, and diversifying your skill set can enhance your career prospects. Explore areas such as penetration testing, incident response, and cloud security. Online platforms like Cybrary and Offensive Security provide specialized training courses to help you acquire new skills.

Evaluate Career Progress and Set New Goals

Periodically assess your career progress and set new goals. Are you achieving the milestones you envisioned? Are there areas where you can improve? Setting clear, measurable goals ensures you stay on track and continue to advance in your cybersecurity career.

Explore advanced certifications such as the ISC2 Certified Information Systems Security Professional (CISSP) to further solidify your expertise and open doors to higher-level roles in cybersecurity.

Summary

Achieving the ISC2 Certified in Cybersecurity certification is a significant milestone, but it is just the beginning. By strategically updating your profiles, actively engaging with the community, participating in practical experiences, seeking mentorship, staying informed, investing in continuous learning, contributing to thought leadership, expanding your network, exploring further education opportunities, diversifying your skill set, and evaluating your career progress, you position yourself for a successful and fulfilling career in cybersecurity.

CHAPTER 13

Final Preparation

The first 12 chapters of this book cover the technologies, protocols, design concepts, and considerations required for your preparation in passing the ISC2 Certified in Cybersecurity (CC) exam. This chapter covers the information that is necessary to pass the exam. However, most people need more preparation than simply reading the first 12 chapters of this book. This chapter, along with the Introduction of the book, suggests a study plan that will help you complete your preparation for the exam.

Suggested Plan for Final Review and Study

This section lists a suggested study plan from the point at which you finish reading this book through Chapter 12 until you take the ISC2 Certified in Cybersecurity (CC) exam. You can ignore this five-step plan, use it as is, or modify it to better meet your needs.

Step 1. **Review key topics:** You can easily locate the key topics either by consulting the Key Topics table at the end of each chapter or by flipping through the pages looking for the Key Topic icons in the outer margin of the pages.

Step 2. **Review key terms:** Each chapter lists a set of key terms that you should be familiar with. The glossary lists the definitions of all terms for your study prep.

Step 3. **Review testable content:** ISC2 maintains a list of testable content. Review it and make sure you are familiar with every item that is listed. You can download a copy at https://www.isc2.org/certifications/cc/cc-certification-exam-outline.

Step 4. **Study "Q&A" sections:** Go through the review questions at the end of each chapter to identify areas in which you need more study.

Step 5. **Use the Pearson Test Prep software to practice:** The Pearson Test Prep software provides a bank of unique exam-realistic questions available only with this book.

The Introduction of this book contains the detailed instructions on how to access the Pearson Test Prep Software. This database of questions was created specifically for this book and is available to you either online or as an offline Windows application. As covered in the Introduction, you can choose to take the exams in one of three modes: Study Mode, Practice Exam Mode, or Flash Card Mode.

Summary

The tools and suggestions listed in this chapter have been designed with one goal in mind: to help you develop the skills required to pass the ISC2 Certified in Cybersecurity (CC) exam and gain the skills needed to begin your cybersecurity career. This book has been developed from the beginning both to present you with a collection of facts and to help you learn how to apply those facts. Regardless of your experience level before reading this book, it is our hope that the broad range of preparation tools, and even the structure of the book, will help you pass the exam with ease. We wish you success in your exam and hope that our paths cross again as you continue to grow in your cybersecurity career.

Answers to the "Do I Know This Already?" Quizzes and Q&A

Chapter 1

"Do I Know This Already?" Quiz

1. b
2. c
3. d
4. d
5. d
6. b
7. a

Q&A

1. Information assurance is designed to provide a guarantee of data, and this is important because the value of our applications and systems is the data they contain

2. The three pillars are confidentiality, integrity, and availability, also known as the CIA triad. Confidentiality is about the secrecy of the data, integrity is about the data staying intact, and availability is about the data being accessible at the right time.

3. Privacy is proof that sensitive data is secret. While confidentiality is about technical secrecy, privacy is about how the secrecy of the data impacts human beings.

4. The ISC2 Code of Ethics is a set of principles concerning protection, honor, and service that those who take the Certified in Cybersecurity exam promise to adhere to.

Chapter 2

"Do I Know This Already?" Quiz

1. d
2. b
3. c
4. d
5. a
6. c
7. d
8. d
9. d
10. a
11. b
12. d
13. d
14. a
15. b
16. c
17. b

Q&A

1. Threats are the sources of danger, vulnerabilities are weaknesses that threats can take advantage of, and risks are the level of danger posed by threats and are assessed based on likelihood and impact. Risks, threats, and vulnerabilities are evaluated in risk assessments.

2. Risk management is a fundamental part of cybersecurity and concerns planning for future emergencies and engaging in activities to lessen the impact of, or even prevent, those emergencies.

3. A risk assessment's scope can be a specific system, a set of systems, or the entire organization.

4. Once risks are identified, personnel prioritize, evaluate, and assign responses to risks during a risk assessment. This is followed by risk treatment.

5. There are four options: reduction/mitigation, transference, acceptance, and avoidance.

6. There are three types: administrative, technical, and physical.

7. Security controls, whether directly decided upon through a risk assessment or not, are intended to address some sort of risk.

8. Governance documentation comprises administrative safeguards.

9. Many security controls are based on legal and regulatory requirements, whether those requirements come from governments in which the organization operates or from public and private industry groups.

Chapter 3

"Do I Know This Already?" Quiz

1. c

2. b

3. b

4. d

5. d

6. a

7. c

8. c

9. b

10. c

11. c

12. b

13. d

Q&A

1. Threat intelligence sharing is vital in cybersecurity for enhancing security posture and mitigating cyber threats.

2. The effectiveness of ransomware lies in its encryption capabilities, time-limited ransom demands, and ability to spread across networks, exploiting vulnerabilities.

3. A DDoS is a malicious and coordinated effort by a threat actor to overwhelm a system's resources. This is achieved by flooding the system with a high volume of traffic involving a high number of systems.

4. A next-generation firewall (NGFW) combines the power of detection and prevention with behavior analytics and machine learning to offer enhanced security.

5. A pentest includes the additional step of exploiting the vulnerabilities discovered during the vulnerability scan.

Chapter 4

"Do I Know This Already?" Quiz

1. c
2. a
3. c
4. c
5. c
6. d
7. c
8. d
9. a
10. a

Q&A

1. Three types of badge system include proximity, smart, and biometric.

2. When an organization wants to move a camera, they should consider using a pan, tilt, zoom camera.

3. Gates help create a single point of entry to a facility.

4. CCTV systems are monitored and controlled by video management software (VMS).

5. Security guards act as a first line of defense and visual deterrent. Alarms alert the team to an issue in real time. Logs help security teams identify the series of events before and after an incident. CCTV captures activity in real time via cameras around the facility.

Chapter 5

"Do I Know This Already?" Quiz

1. b
2. b
3. b
4. a
5. b
6. d
7. a
8. d

Q&A

1. The three permissions used in DAC are -r: read, -w: write, and -x: execute.
2. RBAC include the following elements: role assignment, role authorization, and permission authorization.
3. The Bell-LaPadula model focuses on the confidentiality of information using security levels such as confidential or top secret.
4. Automation helps organizations with access control by granting or revoking permissions, updating passwords, and identifying information.

Chapter 6

"Do I Know This Already?" Quiz

1. c
2. d
3. b
4. a
5. c
6. c
7. a
8. b
9. b
10. a

11. a

12. d

13. d

Q&A

1. The following devices are typically seen in a LAN: switches, network interface cards, wireless access points, servers, modems, and cables.

2. IP addresses fall into one of three buckets: well-known ports (0–1023), registered ports (1024–49151), and dynamic ports (49151–65535).

3. The OSI model contains the following seven layers: application, presentation, session, transport, network, data link, and physical.

4. ARP is a Layer 2 protocol that maps MAC addresses to IP addresses.

Chapter 7

"Do I Know This Already?" Quiz

1. B

2. A

3. B

4. C

5. C

6. A

7. C

8. D

9. A

10. C

11. C

12. D

Q&A

1. The four types of fire suppression systems include sprinkler, gas, foam, and wet/dry chemical.

2. Three types of virtual private networks (VPNs) include remote access, site to site, and mobile VPN.

3. The following six elements should be included in an MOU: Purpose of partnership, goals, duties of each party, timeline, confidentiality clause, and a process for resolving disputes.

4. Four types of cloud deployment models include public, private, community, and hybrid.

5. IaaS, PaaS, and SaaS represent three cloud service models.

Chapter 8

"Do I Know This Already?" Quiz

1. b
2. b
3. d
4. d
5. c
6. a
7. b
8. c
9. d
10. b
11. a
12. a
13. a

Q&A

1. Data security refers to a set of controls used to protect data from being altered or disclosed in an unauthorized way or by an unauthorized user. These controls include encryption and data handling.

2. Encryption is reversible, while hashing is not. However, it is possible to reverse engineer a hash with the right input of data, whereas it is not possible to easily reverse engineer encryption because of the random numbers involved in generating encrypted text.

3. The components of cryptographic algorithms are the key, the ciphertext, and the key generator. Algorithms are either symmetric, where the key used to encrypt and the key used to decrypt are the same, or asymmetric, where the key used to encrypt and the key used to decrypt are different.

4. Non-repudiation refers to technical configurations that ensure a person acknowledges something in a manner they can't later disavow. Examples include digital signatures and digital timestamps.

5. Authentication refers to verifying identity before granting access. The first part, identification, is presenting a login ID and password. The second, authentication, is checking the hashed password against a list of hashes and the ID against an access control list. The third, authorization, is granting access.

6. The five factors are the following: knowledge, such as passwords; inherence, such as fingerprints; possession, such as one-time password generators; location, such as being at the office; and behavior, such as drawing a pattern.

7. A password policy refers to both technical configurations and a clearly written document. Currently recommended password requirements include at least eight characters; complexity through at least one uppercase character, one lowercase character, one special character, and one number; a max password age of 90 days or more; automatic monitoring to prevent the use of easily compromised or already leaked passwords; eliminating password hints and disabling the "show password" option; and disallowing the sharing of passwords. While these requirements are important, many organizations are moving to passwordless authentication or multi-factor authentication.

8. Data handling refers to how data should be stored, processed, and transmitted based on its level of sensitivity. Data handling is comprised of classification (creating categories based on sensitivity); labeling (marking files with the classifications); retention (preventing data that isn't supposed to be deleted from being deleted); and destruction (deleting data that should be deleted in a manner appropriate to its sensitivity).

9. PII stands for personally identifiable information, a legally protected category of information that includes names, addresses, and demographics. PHI stands for protected health information, a legally protected category of information that includes health records alongside the items covered by PII. Both categories must be protected through strong encryption and access control for legal and compliance reasons and are often placed in the highest data classification an organization has.

Chapter 9

"Do I Know This Already?" Quiz

1. a

2. b

3. d

4. a

5. e

6. c

7. e

8. a

9. c

10. e

11. b

12. b

13. c

14. e

15. e

16. e

Q&A

1. System hardening is a set of cybersecurity practices for reducing the system vulnerabilities in our technology by applying patches and locking down system configurations. Implementing system hardening helps an organization maintain a secure computing environment and protect its assets from potential threats.

2. A system baseline captures what an organization deems to be the basics for a secure system configuration. There are four benefits to implementing baselines: security, compliance, consistency, and efficiency.

3. A patch is an update to vendor technology in response to a specific vulnerability. An update applies to the entire operating system and includes performance enhancements, bug fixes, and the introduction of new features. An upgrade refers to changing from one operating system version to a newer version.

4. A set of specialized software tools check the status of key components of an IT infrastructure. Those tools collect information about the system's activities, and that information, known as logs, is forwarded to aggregators, which analyze the information and alert personnel if any anomalies are detected.

5. These alerts are analyzed by a security operations center (SOC) or network operations center (NOC), depending on which is present in an organization.

6. An AUP is a general internal-facing policy that covers all the ways a user might interact with technology in an organization and everything that the user can and cannot do. A BYOD policy is a general internal-facing policy that informs employees of what they cannot do with organizational data and what they

are required to do to secure their devices. A change management policy is an internal-facing policy specifically intended for development teams and related personnel that requires all changes for both systems and applications in an organization to be formally documented and tracked, from initial design to approval. A privacy policy is an external-facing policy for customers that covers every aspect of how the organization will use their personal data, including processing, storage, transmission, and third-party sharing, as well as how the organization will secure it.

7. Security awareness training is intended to teach users about their role in information security, about possible attacks and indicators of compromise, and about best practices to implement for themselves and their organization, including ways to protect themselves from social engineering and safeguard their passwords. In the context of application development, security awareness training is intended to teach developers about secure development practices.

8. Attacks that begin with social engineering, whether through phishing emails, employee impersonation, or other methods, may result in the theft of a single file, infection of a network, or complex acts of espionage and data exfiltration.

9. User behaviors that can result in password compromise include the use of very generic, easily cracked passwords, predictable variation in passwords, the use of basic facts about the user to create passwords (such as family member names), and the reuse of passwords from site to site.

Chapter 10

"Do I Know This Already?" Quiz

1. c
2. a
3. d
4. d
5. d
6. a
7. b
8. a
9. d
10. c
11. b
12. d

13. d

14. c

15. a

16. a

Q&A

1. Incident response refers to the established process of addressing anomalies and events in a timely fashion to minimize risk to the organization.

2. Business continuity refers to the processes and procedures established to protect the whole organization during large, extraordinary events.

3. The recovery time objective (RTO) and recovery point objective (RPO) are metrics used for business continuity planning. The RTO is the latest time after an incident at which the system should be fully recovered and functional. The RPO is the most recent point before an incident to which a system can be recovered.

4. Backups are copies of the data in a system stored in a format that can be easily loaded and used for recovery. There are four options for creating backups: full, mirror, differential, and incremental.

5. Disaster recovery refers to the step-by-step processes of handling and recovering from disasters.

6. Failover testing refers to evaluating whether the disaster recovery plan functions as designed, such as through switching to alternate sites or redundant cloud instances or by restoring backups.

7. There are four types: policies, standards, procedures, and guidelines. Policies are either general, brief directions for other documents or the primary documents and full of many large and small details. Standards contain the next level of granularity and are full of detail. Procedures are step-by-step procedures on how to implement certain processes. Guidelines contain recommendations for implementing processes that are not critical security controls. Depending on the organization, policies, standards, or procedures might be used to refer to all the organization's documents or these four types of documents might be hierarchically arranged.

8. Alongside governmental laws, regulations can come from either government agencies or industry groups. Regulations are separate from frameworks that organizations choose to follow. Both laws and regulations impose requirements on security programs to ensure data is appropriately protected and kept private.

CC Certified in Cybersecurity Cert Guide Exam Updates

Over time, reader feedback allows Pearson to gauge which topics give our readers the most problems when taking the exams. To assist readers with those topics, the authors create new materials clarifying and expanding on those troublesome exam topics. As mentioned in the Introduction, the additional content about the exam is contained in a PDF on this book's companion website, at https://www.pearsonitcertification.com/title/9780138200381.

This appendix is intended to provide you with updated information if ISC2 makes minor modifications to the Certified in Cybersecurity exam upon which this book is based. When ISC2 releases an entirely new exam, the changes are usually too extensive to provide in a simple update appendix. In those cases, you might need to consult the new edition of this book for the updated content. This appendix attempts to fill the void that occurs with any print book. In particular, this appendix does the following:

- Mentions technical items that might not have been mentioned elsewhere in the book

- Covers new topics if ISC2 adds new content to the exam over time

- Provides a way to get up-to-the-minute current information about content for the exam

Always Get the Latest at the Book's Product Page

You are reading the version of this appendix that was available when your book was printed. However, given that the main purpose of this appendix is to be a living, changing document, it is important that you look for the latest version online at the book's companion website. To do so, follow these steps:

Step 1. Browse to www.pearsonitcertification.com/title/9780138200381.

Step 2. Click the Updates tab.

Step 3. If there is a new Appendix B document on the page, download the latest Appendix B document.

> **NOTE**   The downloaded document has a version number. Comparing the version of the print Appendix B (Version 1.0) with the latest online version of this appendix, you should do the following:
>
> - **Same version:** Ignore the PDF that you downloaded from the companion website.
> - **Website has a later version:** Ignore this Appendix B in your book and read only the latest version that you downloaded from the companion website.

Technical Content

The current Version 1.0 of this appendix does not contain additional technical coverage.

Glossary of Key Terms

A

Acceptable Use Policy (AUP)   A general policy that covers all the ways that users might interact with technology in an organization and tells them what they can and cannot do.

access point (AP)   Component of a wireless network that serves as a central hub that connects wireless devices to the network. It broadcasts the wireless signal and allows devices to communicate with each other and access resources. Users must know the AP's service set identifier (SSID) to connect.

advanced persistent threat (APT)   A highly sophisticated and targeted attack conducted by skilled threat actors, typically state-sponsored groups, looking to gain access to sensitive data or cause a disruption in operations.

alarm system   Provides an additional layer of physical security should someone try to gain access to areas they are not authorized to access. Alarms are triggered when someone enters an area without permission.

application layer   Topmost OSI layer (Layer 7) that ensures end users can exchange data with other applications on different devices and networks.

asymmetric encryption   With this protocol, both the sender and the recipient have two keys, a published public key and a secret private one. The sender uses the recipient's public key to encrypt their message before transmitting it, and the recipient uses their private key to decrypt it.

authentication   The process by which identity is checked before granting access.

availability   Ensuring that the data is accessible when and how it's needed.

B

backup   A copy of the data in a system stored in a format that can be easily loaded and used for recovery.

badging system   Enables an organization to control access to its facilities, secure areas, computer systems, and other places only authorized employees can access.

Bell-LaPadula Model   A mandatory access control (MAC) model that emphasizes confidentiality. It uses the concept of security levels (such as Top Secret, Secret, and Confidential) to control access and prevent information from being leaked to unauthorized users.

Biba Model   A mandatory access control (MAC) model that emphasizes integrity. It prevents subjects with lower integrity levels from modifying or corrupting objects with higher integrity levels.

biometric IDs   A badging system that combines the power of biometric identification with smart card technology. Biometric IDs can store fingerprint data, retina data, and other types of information that relates to someone's identity.

bollards   Beams or poles that control the flow and safety of pedestrian and vehicle traffic around a facility.

bring your own device (BYOD) policy   A policy to regulate BYOD programs by informing employees of what they cannot do with organizational data, even when it's on their own devices, and by informing them of what they are required to do to secure their devices.

business continuity (BC)   Actions to take to ensure an organization is operational during and following a disaster or emergency.

C

change management policy   A policy that requires all changes for both systems and applications in an organization to be formally documented and tracked.

Clark-Wilson Model   A mandatory access control (MAC) model that aims to ensure data integrity and consistency. It achieves this by enforcing specific procedures and rules for subject access and modification of objects, promoting controlled and authorized changes.

classless inter-domain routing (CIDR)   An IP addressing scheme that allows for a more flexible allocation of IP addresses with various subnet sizes without the constraints of class boundaries.

closed-circuit television (CCTV)   A network of cameras strategically placed to monitor and record activities in and outside a facility.

cloud deployment models   Refer to where the cloud infrastructure is hosted and who manages said infrastructure and cloud resources. Where data is stored and how it is accessed determines which model works best for an organization.

community cloud deployment model   Brings together organizations with similar interests to share and collaborate on cloud resources. Multiple organizations, such as government agencies, educational institutions, or healthcare providers, unite to pool their resources and share a tailored cloud infrastructure.

confidentiality   Preserving authorized restrictions on information access and disclosure, including means for protecting personal privacy and proprietary information.

D

data center   Provides a controlled and secure environment for housing physical devices such as routers, switches, servers, and other network devices.

data closet   Serves a similar purpose to a data center but on a much smaller scale. Typically, this is a room or empty space in an office building that can be secured with lockable doors, restricted access, and environmental monitoring systems.

data handling   Protocols regarding how data should be stored, processed, and transmitted based on its level of sensitivity; this domain has four major parts to it: classification, labeling, retention, and destruction.

data link layer   OSI layer (Layer 2) that is responsible for node-to-node delivery of information, error free.

data security   Methods used to protect data from being altered or disclosed in an unauthorized way or by an unauthorized user.

defense-in-depth (DiD)   A robust security strategy that goes beyond mere network segmentation. It involves implementing multiple layers of security measures to provide comprehensive data protection by impeding threat actors and allowing security teams sufficient time to respond.

demilitarized zone (DMZ)   A segregated network segment between an organization's internal network and the external, untrusted network, typically the Internet.

disaster recovery (DR)   The step-by-step processes of handling and recovering from disasters.

discretionary access control (DAC)   A security model that grants or restricts access to objects based on the discretion of the data owner. DAC models are discretionary because the object owner can transfer access to other subjects without consulting an administrator.

distributed denial-of-service (DDoS)   A malicious and coordinated effort by a threat actor to overwhelm a system's resources, achieved by flooding the system with a high volume of traffic.

E–F–G

embedded systems   Specialized computer systems, composed of both hardware and software, that are designed to perform specific tasks or functions at specific times. Typically integrated into larger mechanical or electrical systems to carry out their designated tasks.

encryption   A method by which to ensure that the data itself is protected by rendering it unreadable except by those who have the key.

encryption algorithm, asymmetric   An encryption algorithm in which both the sender and the recipient have two keys, a published public key and a secret private key.

encryption algorithm, symmetric   An encryption algorithm in which the key to encrypt (e.g., to encode or apply encryption) and the key to decrypt (e.g., to decode or to remove encryption) are the same.

environmental controls   Controls that safeguard IT equipment and facilities from physical environmental factors such as temperature, humidity, and water damage. Fire suppression systems are great examples of controls in place to protect against environmental damage from fire.

failover testing   Testing whether the disaster recovery plan functions as designed.

fire suppression systems   Environmental control systems that help reduce and eliminate building and data center fires by using extinguishing agents such as water, foam, or other chemical compounds.

firewall   A network security device that sits at the edge of a network, monitoring incoming and outgoing traffic to identify and block potential cyber threats based on predetermined security policies.

governance processes   Documents and methods used to oversee a cybersecurity program and ensure risks are being properly addressed and all controls are being implemented as specified.

guidelines   Documents containing recommendations for implementing processes that are not critical security controls.

H

hashing   The process of converting a string of characters, usually text or a key, into a fixed length of text and numbers for security purposes.

header   Part of a packet that contains information about the packet, the source and destination information, sequence numbers, and other control information to help deliver the packet to the correct destination

heating, ventilation, and air conditioning   Heat, cool, and circulate air throughout a facility. Maintaining proper temperature and humidity levels is crucial to prevent damage to sensitive equipment.

high availability (HA)   Maintaining network accessibility and functionality with minimal interruptions.

host-based intrusion detection system (HIDS)   Type of IDS that is positioned directly on the host system or endpoint and monitors the traffic for that specific host (versus traffic for the entire network).

hybrid cloud deployment model   A mix of public and private cloud environments that provides organizations with flexibility and control over their data and applications.

Hypertext Transport Protocol (HTTP) flood   A distributed denial-of-service (DDoS) attack that targets web servers by sending HTTP Get and Post requests to the systems to exhaust their resources.

I

incident   An event occurrence that actually or potentially jeopardizes the confidentiality, integrity, or availability of an information system or the information the system processes, stores, or transmits or that constitutes a violation of imminent threat of violation of security policies, security, procedures, or acceptable use policies.

incident response   Responding to anomalies and events in a timely fashion to minimize risk to the organization.

information assurance   Ensuring that data is where it is supposed to be, in the form it is supposed to be, and accessible only to the intended people to whom it is supposed to be accessible.

Infrastructure as a Service (IaaS)   Cloud service model in which the cloud service provider (CSP) leases/rents virtualized resources and services that an organization can access over the Internet and thereby avoid purchasing expensive hardware for its data center needs.

Integrity   Ensuring the data isn't changed or deleted without authorization and being able to prove that.

Internet Protocol (IP)   The most common connectionless protocol that provides "best effort delivery" and is used at the network layer. IP logical addresses are either IP version 4 or IP version 6. They determine the network and device to which a packet should be routed.

Internet Protocol version 4   Version of IP created with IP addresses, which are 32-bit dotted-decimal notation addresses that identify the network and host to which a packet is transferred.

Internet Protocol version 6   Version of IP created to account for the rising number of devices on the Internet and address security concerns with IPv4. These addresses are 128-bit, broken into eight groups separated by colons, known as hexadecimal notation. This means the address space available for use is enormous. IPv6 addresses are assigned to interfaces instead of nodes, allowing multiple interfaces on a device to have an IP address.

intrusion detection system (IDS)   Monitors computer network traffic and sends alerts on malicious activity or unauthorized access to systems as data enters and exits the network.

intrusion prevention system (IPS)   Monitors computer network traffic and blocks suspicious activity as data enters and exits the network.

ISC2 Code of Ethics   Very general guidance from ISC2 intended to give direction on professional cybersecurity ethics while also not becoming a replacement for ethical judgment.

L–M

local-area network (LAN)   A network in a single physical location, such as an office building, school, or home. LANs are the most common type of network and can vary in size from small to large. They enable users to connect to internal networks for purposes of printing, file sharing, accessing shared applications and databases, and accessing other resources necessary for business operations.

logging and monitoring   The implementation of a set of tools that check the status of key components of an IT infrastructure, including applications, servers, databases, networks, cloud environments, and workstations.

Logical Link Control (LLC)   Sublayer of the data link layer (Layer 2) of the OSI reference model that is responsible for sending each frame to the next destination along its journey, known as flow control. This sublayer handles the communication between the network layer and the MAC sublayer.

malware   Programs designed specifically to disrupt, damage, or gain unauthorized access to a computer system.

man-in-the-middle (MITM) attack   A threat actor gains access to data between communicating parties and intercepts or alters the data, tricking victims into thinking they are communicating with each other.

managed service providers (MSPs)   Outsourced services delivered to customers to support their IT needs. The employees of an MSP monitor each customer's environment for issues and concerns and report any relevant information to the customer.

mandatory access control (MAC)   A security model that enforces access control based on classification levels and security labels. A classification level indicates the relative importance of classified information for national security and determines the specific security requirements for that information.

maximum tolerable downtime   The maximum amount of time a system, service, or process is unavailable or nonoperational before it begins to significantly impact the business.

Media Access Control (MAC)   Sublayer of the data link layer (Layer 2) of the OSI reference model that connects the LLC sublayer to the physical layer. This is where the hardware address lives. The MAC address is hardcoded and burned on all NICs by the manufacturer and is unique to every device. Data encapsulation and error control are handled by the MAC sublayer as well.

memorandum of understanding/agreement (MOU/MOA)   A nonbinding written agreement that outlines two or more parties' intended actions and responsibilities. It is a foundational document that promotes effective collaboration and minimizes the likelihood of misunderstandings or disputes.

metropolitan-area network (MAN)   A network that connects multiple LANs across a city, providence, or large geographical area to provide access to shared resources and data. A MAN is larger than a LAN but smaller than a WAN. Cable networks and telephone systems are examples of a MAN. Modems and cables (such as fiber optic) are typically used to connect LANs in a MAN.

microsegmentation   A network security technique that provides enhanced protection by implementing security controls between workloads within a network, significantly reducing the risk of lateral movement. With microsegmentation, each segment is isolated, and access between is closely monitored and controlled, making it harder for attackers to propagate or expand their reach in the event of a breach.

mobile VPN   VPN that is integrated as a service into mobile device management systems or provided through dedicated applications.

multi-factor authentication   Requires users to provide at least one authentication factor, such as a fingerprint, a facial scan, a specific location known to be secure, or a one-time password, in addition to a login ID and password.

N

need to know   Logical access control concept that users only need to know or have access to certain information to complete their job functions and shouldn't have access to any other information.

Network Access Control (NAC)   A comprehensive security solution that combines authentication, endpoint security checking, and access controls to tightly control access to corporate or private networks.

network address translation (NAT)   A technique to conserve IPv4 address space by enabling an organization to connect its internal network to the Internet using private IP addresses by assigning a single public IP address to a device within its network.

network intrusion detection system (NIDS)   Type of IDS that analyzes network traffic, log files, and other data sources to detect suspicious activity associated with known threats.

network layer   OSI layer (Layer 3) that takes segments sent from the transport layer and determines the best path to route the segments based on their Internet Protocol (IP) address.

next-generation firewall (NGFW)   Firewall type that takes detection and protection a step further by introducing machine learning (ML) and behavior analytics to allow or deny traffic. These devices conduct deep packet inspection (DPI) to determine if the packet should be allowed or denied.

non-repudiation   A method by which to have a person acknowledge something in a manner that they can't later deny.

O–P

Open Source Interconnection (OSI) model   Model created by the International Organization for Standardization (ISO) in the 1970s as a vendor-neutral, conceptual model used to visualize and describe the logical communication between network devices.

packet   A unit of data, a small piece of a larger message sent across the network.

packet filtering firewall   Firewall type that inspects data packets as they traverse the network based on a predefined set of rules; inspects the surface-level data, such as source and destination IP addresses and ports, to decide whether to allow or drop a packet.

password policy   Both a technical configuration, as in cloud account settings and endpoint management for laptops and phones, and a clearly written document.

password protection   Prevention of password compromise through understanding user behavior and changes in technology.

payload   Part of a packet that is the data that is being transmitted, such as an email or data from or to a website.

penetration test   A way for organizations to test their technology and safeguards currently in place by attempting to exploit vulnerabilities found during a vulnerability scan.

personal-area network (PAN)   A network of devices connected within an individual's workspace. It typically includes devices like smartphones, computers, tablets, and other mobile devices. The range of a PAN is usually limited to a few centimeters to a few meters, and devices are often connected wirelessly or via Bluetooth, such as headphones or other peripheral devices.

physical layer   OSI layer (Layer 1) that is responsible for transmitting and receiving raw data bits over the physical medium, such as copper wires, optical fibers, or wireless radio waves. The physical layer is concerned with the electrical, mechanical, and timing aspects of data transmission. It defines the physical characteristics of the network, including the physical connectors, signaling, voltage levels, and data transmission rates. The primary function of the physical layer is to establish and maintain the physical link between network devices, ensuring reliable and efficient data transfer.

Platform as a Service (PaaS)   Cloud service model in which the cloud service provider (CSP) provides organizations with a complete cloud solution for their business needs, accessible via the Internet from any location. The CSP manages the maintenance and updating of the infrastructure, allowing the organization to focus on building and testing its custom applications and tools.

policies   A set of general guidelines, expectations, and approaches that an organization creates to maintain confidentiality, integrity, and availability of data. These are documents establishing governance processes by either containing brief directions for other documents or containing all sorts of large and small details.

ports   The starting and ending points for network communications between computer devices. Ports identify where the data should go. 65,535 ports are available.

power sources   Systems that bring power to the facility.

presentation layer   OSI layer (Layer 6) that translates data to be presented in the correct format for the recipient. This allows communication with both the application layer (Layer 7) and the lower layers.

principle of least privilege (POLP)   Implementing the correct access controls to take action on information resources. Once access levels are determined, role-based access controls are implemented that grant the least amount of permissions necessary to complete their job function. This is the principle of least privilege (POLP).

privacy   Proof that sensitive data is secret, will remain so, and won't be accessed without permission.

privacy policy   An external-facing policy that covers every aspect of how the organization will use and secure its users' personal data, including processing, storage, transmission, and sharing with third parties; this policy should comply with legal requirements.

private cloud deployment model   Similar to the public cloud deployment model, with servers, networking, storage, and all the functionality of the cloud, but each deployment is for a specific organization.

procedures   Documents containing step-by-step procedures on how to implement certain processes.

protocol   Provides a framework for reliable and efficient communication between devices on a network. It defines the syntax, formatting, and semantics of the message being sent. The protocol also outlines the actions that should be taken during communication, such as error handling and data validation.

proximity cards   Use radio frequency identification (RFID) technology to communicate with card readers and allow access based on proximity to the reader.

proxy, application-aware firewall   Firewall type that operates at the application layer of the OSI model. These devices monitor application traffic between a client and server for malicious activity based on the content or payload of the packet in addition to the source and destination IP information.

public cloud deployment model   IT services and resources such as storage, servers, and networking are accessible to anyone via the Internet or a virtual private network (VPN). This is the most commonly used deployment model.

R

ransomware   Malicious software that encrypts data or systems to block access and demands some form of payment in exchange to regain access and decrypt that information.

recovery point objective (RPO)   The most recent point before an incident to which a system can be recovered. This is usually based on the last backup that was completed. Any data not backed up between the incident and the last backup will be lost.

recovery time objective (RTO)   The latest time after an incident at which the system should be fully recovered and functional.

redundancy   Provides multiple paths, duplicate components, or backup systems in a network.

regulations and laws   In the context of cybersecurity, the imposition of requirements on security programs by governments and industry groups to ensure that data is appropriately protected and kept private.

remote access VPN   VPN type that allows users to connect securely to a private network or a third-party server, enabling access to files and data.

risk   The level of danger something poses, as assessed by its impact and likelihood.

risk assessment   The second step of a risk assessment, in which risks are prioritized, evaluated, and assigned one of four response options.

risk identification   The first step of a risk assessment, in which risks, including technological and business risks, that an organization realistically faces are analyzed based on likelihood and impact.

risk management   Planning for future emergencies and engaging in activities to lessen the impact of, or even prevent, those emergencies.

risk prioritization   Risks assigned qualitative or quantitative ratings based on likelihood and impact to determine which need to be addressed first or require more resources.

risk tolerance   An organization's appetite for risk.

risk treatment   The third step of a risk assessment, in which concrete steps are designed to implement risk responses.

role-based access control   A security model that grants or restricts access to objects based on the user's assigned role. The permissions are defined by the job functions and responsibilities rather than individual user accounts, simplifying access management and reducing overhead.

router   Component of a wireless network that connects the wireless network to the Internet. It routes data packets between the local network and the Internet, enabling devices to access online resources.

S

scanning   The process of using a set of tools to conduct vulnerability scans across a network of systems. These scans check for holes in the environment that should be fixed for optimal security. Scanning an organization's environment helps the organization understand what assets they have, any associated vulnerabilities, and ways to remediate and mitigate those vulnerabilities.

security awareness training   The education of users on their role in information security.

security controls   The variety of documents, configurations, and actions used to defend an organization.

security guards   Patrol and monitor the premises for any signs of unauthorized access, suspicious activity, or security breaches. Guards are essentially the first line of defense when it comes to physical security and serve as a physical deterrent.

segregation of duties (SOD)   Dividing critical tasks and responsibilities among multiple individuals to ensure that one person doesn't have complete control over a process. This concept helps to reduce error and fraud.

service-level agreement (SLA)   A written contract between a provider and its customers outlining the terms and conditions of the services provided.

session layer   OSI model layer (Layer 5) that establishes, manages, and terminates sessions with applications on different systems. This layer connects the upper and lower layers, preparing the data and connection for secure transmission.

side-channel attack   Exploits information leaked unintentionally by a system's physical implementation rather than a vulnerability in software or an algorithm.

site-to-site VPN   VPN type that is widely used in large organizations with multiple networks distributed across different locations.

smart cards   Identity cards that have an embedded microchip containing data for identification and authentication. This data typically includes a password, PIN, private key, and other access information that is needed.

social engineering   Malicious activities that leverage human emotions and thinking processes to perpetrate attacks against organizations.

Software as a Service (SaaS)   Cloud service model in which the cloud service provider (CSP) is responsible for all platform aspects, from the infrastructure to the application, while the organization is only responsible for how the application will be used and who needs access.

standards   Documents containing specifics that are usually lengthy and full of detail.

synchronization (SYN) flood   A distributed denial-of-service (DDoS) attack that occurs when SYN requests are sent to a system but not responded to, creating half-open connections.

system hardening   The requirements and methods of configuring systems to protect them from potential threats using baselines, patches, updates, and upgrades; another name for configuration management.

symmetric encryption   Algorithms in which the key to encrypt (e.g., to encode or apply encryption) and the key to decrypt (e.g., to decode or to remove encryption) are the same.

T

tactics, techniques, and procedures (TTPs)   Behaviors used by attackers to design and execute attacks on enterprise networks.

TCP/IP model   A suite of protocols used to facilitate communication between networked devices. This is the foundation of the Internet we use today. Contains four layers: application, transport, Internet, and network access (or physical).

threat   The source of a danger; the source of risk.

trailer   Optional part of a packet that contains error detection and parity checks.

transport layer   OSI layer (Layer 4) that is responsible for data delivery between networks. Once the data is packaged, the transport layer determines which delivery method is best for it. Error checking also occurs here to ensure that data is correctly transmitted or fixed for retransmission.

Trojan   Malicious program or software disguised as a harmless, useful tool to trick users into downloading it, after which it exfiltrates data from the system on which it is installed. Additionally, Trojans are stealthy, can be executed without permission or the user's knowledge, and serve a specific purpose such as data theft, remote control, facilitating other attacks, or persistence in the system.

turnstiles   Electronic barriers that are typically used to control pedestrian traffic as they allow entry of only one person at a time into a facility.

U–V

User Datagram Protocol (UDP) flood   A distributed denial-of-service (DDoS) attack that is similar to a SYN flood but uses UDP packets to flood a system and exhaust the resources. UDP is a connectionless protocol.

virtual local area network (VLAN)   Provides a logical division within a physical network, resulting in multiple isolated virtual networks.

virtual private networks (VPNs)   Provide users with a secure way to access networks, ensuring privacy and data protection. By utilizing encryption, VPNs safeguard network connections on public networks, preventing eavesdropping and interception.

virus   Code that runs on computer systems without the user's knowledge. If the user or system executes a compromised file, the virus can spread copies of itself throughout the network. Viruses are not self-replicating and need assistance from a user to spread.

vulnerability   A weakness that a threat can take advantage of; the weakness that lets a risk become reality.

W–Z

web-application filtering firewall (WAF)   Firewall type that is similar to proxy firewalls but specific to protecting against web-based server attacks such as SQL injection and cross-site scripting (XSS).

wide-area network (WAN)   A network that contains multiple LANs and MANs connected via radio waves or telephone lines. WANs provide connectivity to a large number of systems and shared resources to business offices located further away from each other, connecting a large number of computers over a large area.

Wi-Fi   Technology of wireless networks that operates based on the IEEE 802.11 standards, which define the protocols and specifications for wireless communication. These standards enable devices to communicate with each other within a LAN or connect to the Internet.

wireless local-area network (WLAN)   A network similar to a LAN that provides local wireless connectivity. Devices can connect to a WLAN network using Wi-Fi-enabled devices. WLANs are commonly found in settings like cafes, airports, and public spaces where users can access the Internet wirelessly.

wireless network interface card (WNIC)   Component of a wireless network that is installed on individual computer systems to enable connection to a network. These cards aid in communication between devices. A WNIC allows for communication with wireless-enabled devices.

worm   Standalone, self-replicating malware that is typically spread through the Internet or a local area network (LAN).

Index

Numerics

5 nines, 133

A

access control, 62
  discretionary, 76–77
  hierarchical, 80
  list. *See* ACL (access control list)
  logical
    need to know, 74
    privilege levels, 74–75
    SOD (segregation of duties),
      75–76
  mandatory, 77–78
  natural, 62
  network, 123–124
  role-based, 74, 79–80
  server room, 29
ACL (access control list), 76–77
administrative controls, 29
administrator, 74
AES (Advanced Encryption
    Standard), 144
AI (artificial intelligence), 125
alarm system, 65, 225
algorithm
  cryptographic, 143–144
    asymmetric, 144
    hashing, 144–145
    non-repudiation, 145–146
    symmetric, 144
  hashing, 144–145

antivirus, 20
  next-generation, 44
  signature-based, 44
AP (access point), 104, 225
API (application programming
    interface), 131
application layer, 95–96, 225
APT (advanced persistent threat), 23,
    43, 225
ARP (Address Resolution Protocol), 103
ARPANET (Advanced Research Projects
    Agency Network), 85, 125
asymmetric encryption, 144, 225
attack/s, 18
  DDoS (distributed denial-of-service),
    23, 43–44
  detection tools, 45
    firewall, 46–48
    IDS (intrusion detection system), 45
    IPS (intrusion prevention
      system), 45
  network, 43
    MITM (man-in-the-middle), 44
    side-channel, 44
  password, 147
  social engineering, 170–171
AUP (Acceptable Use Policy), 167, 225
authentication, 146, 225. *See also*
    password
  behavior factors, 146
  biometric, 62
  inherence factors, 146

knowledge factors, 146
multi-factor, 81, 147, 163
possession factors, 146
authorization, 8, 80, 146
authorized versus unauthorized
        personnel, 66
availability, 8, 132, 133, 225

B
backup and recovery, 185–188. *See also*
        DR (disaster recovery)
    differential backup, 186
    full backup, 186
    incremental backup, 186
    mirror backup, 186
    tape backup, 188
    testing backups, 188
badge systems, 56–59
bands, wireless network, 104
barrier gates, 60–61
baselines, 162–163
BCP (business continuity plan), 184, 226
Bell-LaPadula model, 78, 226
BIA (business impact analysis), 184–185
Biba model, 78, 226
biometric authentication, 62
biometric ID, 58, 226
bollards, 60–61, 226
breach, security, 38
business
    continuity plan, 184
    impact analysis, 184–185
    results, 133
    risks, 24
    secrets, 7
BYOD (bring your own device), 123,
        167–168, 226

C
cables, 90
calculating, risk, 19
CCTV, 59, 63, 64–65, 226

change management policy, 168–169, 226
CIA triad
    availability, 8
    confidentiality, 7, 9
    integrity, 8
CIDR (classless inter-domain routing),
        99, 226
CISA (U.S. Cybersecurity and
        Infrastructure Security Agency), 38
Clark-Wilson model, 78, 226
classful IP addressing, 99
classification
    data, 149–150
    incident response, 181–182
cloud, 125
    challenges, 134
    community, 127–128
    deployment models, 125, 226
    digital disposal, 152
    governance, 134
    hybrid, 128–129
    MSP (managed service provider),
        133–134
    private, 126–127
    public, 125–126
    service model, 129–130
        IaaS (infrastructure as a service), 130
        PaaS (platform as a service), 130–131
        SaaS (software as a service), 131–132
code
    infrastructure as, 163
    malicious, 39
cold site, 191
collaboration, MOU/MOA, 117–118
Colonial Pipeline incident, 42
community cloud, 127–128, 226
compensating control, 29
compliance
    data protection, 150
    regulatory, 162
confidentiality, 10, 167, 227. *See also* privacy
    business secrets, 7

PHI (protected health information), 7
  privacy and, 9
configuration, machine image, 163
constrained model, 80
containment, 182–183
control/s, 7, 24–25. *See also* access control
  access, 62
    discretionary, 76–77
    logical, 74–76
    mandatory, 78
    role-based, 79–80
  administrative, 29
  compensating, 29
  corrective, 29
  detective, 29
  deterrent, 29
  environmental, 62–63, 115–116
  owner, 28
  physical security, 56
    badge systems, 56–59
    gates, 59–61
    monitoring, 63–66
  preventive, 29
  security, 18, 28–29
  technical, 29
core model, 79
corrective control, 29
CPTED (Crime Prevention Through
    Environmental Design), 62–63
cryptography, 143
  algorithm, 143–144
    asymmetric, 144
    symmetric, 144
  hashing, 144–145
  non-repudiation, 145–146
customer SLA, 132
cybersecurity, 6. *See also* security
  advanced degrees, 207
  castle analogy, 200–202
  leadership opportunities, 206–207
  regulation, 30
  threat intelligence, 38–39

D
DAC (discretionary access control),
    76–77, 227
data
  availability, 8
  center, 115, 227
  classification, 149–150
  closet, 115, 227
  destruction, 152
  encryption. *See* encryption
  fragmentation, 95
  handling, 149, 153, 202, 227
  information assurance, 6
  labeling, 150–151
  retention, 65, 151–152
  security, 143
  sharing, 39
data link layer, 102–103, 227
DDoS (distributed denial-of-service)
    attack, 23, 43–44, 227
decapsulation, 94
decryption, 144
degaussing, 152
detection
  incident response, 181
  motion, 65
  network attack, 45
    firewall, 46–48
    IDS (intrusion detection system), 45
    IPS (intrusion prevention system), 45
detective control, 29
deterrent control, 29
DH (Diffie-Hellman) key exchange
    protocol, 144
DiD (defense-in-depth), 119–120,
    199–200, 227
differential backup, 186
digital signature, 145
DISA (U.S. Defense Information Systems
    Agency), 163
DMZ (demilitarized zone), 121, 227
documentation, 65–66

downtime, maximum tolerable, 190, 231.
    See also availability
DPI (deep packet inspection), 47–48
DR (disaster recovery), 188–189, 227
    failover testing, 191
    metrics
        MTD maximum tolerable
            downtime), 190
        RPO (recovery point objective), 189
        RTO (recovery time objective), 189
    replication, 190–191
DRP (disaster recovery plan), 133
dynamic ports, 93
dynamic separation of duties, 80

E

EDR (endpoint detection and
        response), 45
email, phishing, 40, 41
embedded systems, 124, 228
encapsulation, 94
encryption, 143, 228
    asymmetric, 144
    symmetric, 144
    wireless network, 105
environmental controls, 62–63,
        115–116, 228
EOL (End of Life), 165–166
error rate, 132

F

failover testing, 228
fault tolerance, 117
fire suppression systems, 116–117, 228
firewall, 46, 228
    next-generation, 47–48
    packet filtering, 46–47
    proxy, application-aware, 47
    rules, 47
    web application, 47
Fix, Bernd Robert, 44
foam-based fire suppression, 116

fraud, risk, 24
full backup, 186

G

gas-based fire suppression, 116
gates, 59
    barrier, 60–61
    bollards, 60–61
GitHub, 205–206
Gold Disk, 163
governance, 29, 191–192, 228
    cloud, 134
    guidelines, 194
    policies, 193
    procedures, 193–194
    regulations and laws, 194–195
    standards, 193
guidelines, 194, 228

H

HA (high availability), 117, 229
hashing, 144–145, 228
header, 228
hexadecimal notation, 100
HIDS (host-based intrusion detection
        system), 45, 229
hierarchical access control, 80
HIPAA (U.S. Health Insurance
        Portability and Accountability
        Act), 7
host-based firewall, 46
hot site, 190
HTTP flood, 44, 229
HVAC (heating, ventilation, and air
        conditioning), 116, 229
hybrid cloud, 128–129, 229

I

IaaS (infrastructure as a service), 130, 229
IAM (identity and access management), 81
ICMP (Internet Control Message
        Protocol), 98

identification, 146
identity, 146–147
IDS (intrusion detection system), 45, 120, 230
IGMP (Internet Group Management Protocol), 98
impact, 19, 25. *See also* BIA (business impact analysis)
incident response, 65, 180–181, 229
 classification, 181–182
 containment, 182–183
 detection, 181
 incident ranking, 182
 recovery, 183
 reflection, 183
 response, 183
 team, 180
 testing, 183–184
incremental backup, 186
information assurance, 6, 202, 229
 CIA triad
  availability, 8
  confidentiality, 7
  integrity, 8
 privacy, 9
infrastructure
 cloud, 125. *See also* cloud
 as code, 163
 network
  embedded systems, 124
  environmental controls, 115–116
  fire suppression systems, 116–117
  redundancy and high availability, 117
 as a service, 130
integrity, 8, 229
internal SLA, 132
Internet, 98
inverted tree model, 80
IoT (Internet of Things), 124, 131
IP (Internet Protocol), 98, 229, 230
 CIDR (classless inter-domain routing), 99

classful addressing, 99
header, 99–100
NAT (Network Address Translation), 100
octet, 99
IPS (intrusion prevention system), 45, 120, 230
IPsec, 98
IPv6, 100–101
ISAC (Information Sharing and Analysis Center), 38
ISC₂
 CC exam
  final preparation, 209–210
  planning your next steps after certification, 205–207
  updates, 223–224
 Code of Ethics, 9–10, 230

J-K-L
KPI (key performance indicator), 133

LAN (local-area network), 90, 230
lattice/hybrid model, 80
laws, 194–195
leadership, 206–207
likelihood, 25
LLC (Logical Link Control), 230
logical access control
 need to know, 74
 SOD (segregation of duties), 75–76
  dynamic, 80
  static, 80
logs, 65–66, 166–167, 230. *See also* monitoring

M
MAC (mandatory access control), 77–78, 231
MAC (Media Access Control), 231
machine image, 163
maintenance, 62

malicious insider, 23, 24
malware, 20, 23, 39, 230
  ransomware, 20, 23, 41
    Colonial Pipeline incident, 42
    WannaCry, 41, 165
  Trojan, 41
  virus, 39–40
  worm, 40
MAN (metropolitan-area network),
  91, 231
maximum tolerable downtime, 231
McCarthy, John, 125
Melissa virus, 40
mentorship, 206
metrics
  DR (disaster recovery)
    MTD maximum tolerable
    downtime), 190
    RPO (recovery point objective), 189
    RTO (recovery time objective), 189
  SLA (service-level agreement),
    132–133
MFA (multi-factor authentication), 81,
  147, 163, 231
microsegmentation, 120–121, 231
mirror backup, 186
mitigation, risk, 25
MITM (man-in-the-middle) attack,
  44, 230
ML (machine learning), 44–45
MOA (memorandum of agreement),
  117–118, 231
mobile VPN, 123
model/s
  cloud deployment, 125
    community, 127–128
    hybrid, 128–129
    private, 126–127
    public, 125–126
  cloud service, 129–130
  core, 79
  OSI (Open Source Interconnection), 94

application layer, 95–96
data link layer, 102–104
network layer, 98
physical layer, 106
presentation layer, 96
session layer, 96
transport layer, 97
security, 76
  DAC (discretionary access control),
    76–77
  MAC (mandatory access control),
    77–78
  RBAC (role-based access control),
    79–80
TCP/IP, 106–107
modem, 90
monitoring
  physical security, 63
    alarm systems, 65
    authorized versus unauthorized
    personnel, 66
    CCTV, 64–65
    logs and documentation, 65–66
    security guard, 63
  SLA (service-level agreement), 8
  system, 166–167
MOU (memorandum of understanding),
  117–118, 231
MSP (managed service provider),
  133–134, 231
MTD maximum tolerable downtime), 190
MTU (maximum transmission unit), 95
multilevel SLA, 132

N

NAC (network access control),
  123–124, 232
NAT (Network Address Translation), 232
natural access control, 62
natural surveillance, 62
need to know, 74, 232

network layer (OSI model), 98, 232
network/s, 85
  attacks, 43. *See also* attack/s
    DDoS (distributed denial-of-service), 43
    detection tools, 45–48
    HTTP flood, 44
    MITM (man-in-the-middle), 44
    side-channel, 44
    SYN flood, 43
    UDP flood, 44
  DiD (defense-in-depth), 119–120
  fault tolerance, 117
  firewall, 46
    next-generation, 47–48
    packet filtering, 46–47
    proxy, application-aware, 47
    rules, 47
    web application, 47
  infrastructure
    DMZ (demilitarized zone), 121
    embedded systems, 124
    environmental controls, 115–116
    fire suppression systems, 116–117
    redundancy and high availability, 117
  local-area, 90
  metropolitan-area, 91
  personal-area, 89
  segmentation, 118–119
  type comparison, 93
  virtual local area. *See* VLAN (virtual local area network)
  virtual private, 120, 122–123
  VMS (video management system), 64
  wide-area, 91–92
  wireless, 104
    encryption, 105
    local-area, 91
    standards, 104–105
    WEP (Wired Equivalent Privacy), 105
NGAV (next-generation antivirus), 44

NGFW (next-generation firewall), 47–48, 232
NIC (network interface card), 90, 104
NIDS (network intrusion detection system), 45, 232
NIST (National Institute of Standards and Technology)
  Minimum Security Requirements for Federal Information and Information Systems (FIPS Pub. 200), 7, 8, 146, 181, 184
  A Profile for U.S. Federal Cryptographic Key Management Systems (SP 800–152), 153
  Risk Management Framework for Information Systems and Organizations (SP 800–37, Revision 2), 18–19, 22
  Security and Privacy Controls for Information Systems and Organizations (SP 800–53), 28–29, 145
  SP 800–83, 39
  SP 1800–15, 38
non-repudiation, 145–146, 232

O

object, 76
octet, 99
organizations, 21–22
  DAC (discretionary access control), 76–77
  physical security controls, 56
    access control, 62
    authorized versus unauthorized personnel, 66
    badge systems, 56–59
    environmental controls, 62–63
    gates, 59–61
    monitoring, 63–66
  risk assessment, 19–22, 24–26

security awareness training, 170
threats, 23
OSI (Open Source Interconnection)
    model, 94, 95, 232
    application layer, 95–96
    data link layer, 102–103
    network layer, 98
    physical layer, 106
    presentation layer, 96
    session layer, 96
    transport layer, 97
OTP (one-time password), 147
overwriting, 152

P

PaaS (platform as a service), 130–131, 233
packet, 95, 232
    filtering firewall, 46–47
    trailer, 237
PAN (personal-area network), 89, 233
partnership, MOU/MOA, 117–118
password, 147
    attacks, 147
    hashing, 145
    manager, 171
    one-time, 147
    policy, 147–149, 232
    protection, 171–172, 233
    security, 134
patching/patch management, 45, 164–165
payload, 233
penetration test, 48, 233
permissions, 80
PHI (protected health information), 7,
    150
phishing, 40, 41
physical layer, 106, 233
physical security controls, 56
    access control, 62
    badge systems, 56–59
    environmental design, 62–63

gates, 59
    barrier, 60–61
    bollards, 60–61
    turnstiles, 59–60
monitoring, 63
    alarm systems, 65
    authorized versus unauthorized
        personnel, 66
    CCTV, 64–65
    logs and documentation, 65–66
    security guard, 63
SPOE (single point of entry), 63
PII (personally identifiable
    information), 150
POC (proof of concept), 134
policy, 193, 233
    Acceptable Use, 167
    BYOD (bring your own device), 123,
        167–168
    change management, 168–169
    data handling, 153
    password, 147–149
    password protection, 171–172
    privacy, 169, 234
    security, 120
    zero-trust, 77
POLP (principle of least privilege), 58,
    74–75, 233
port/s, 93, 233
    dynamic, 93
    registered, 93
    well-known, 93
post-admission NAC, 123
power, sources, 115, 233
PPP (Point-to-Point Protocol), 103
pre-admission NAC, 123
on-premises network infrastructure. *See*
    infrastructure
presentation layer, 96, 233
preventive control, 29
prioritization, risk, 20

privacy, 7, 169, 234
private cloud, 126–127, 234
privilege levels, 74–75
procedures, 193–194, 234
A Profile for U.S. Federal Cryptographic Key Management Systems (NIST SP 800–152), 153
protocol/s, 94, 234. *See also* IP (Internet Protocol)
   application layer, 96
   data link layer, 103–104
   network layer, 98
   presentation layer, 96
   transport layer, 97
proximity card, 57, 234
proxy, application-aware firewall, 47, 234
public cloud, 125–126, 234

R

ransomware, 20, 23, 41, 234
   Colonial Pipeline incident, 42
   WannaCry, 41, 165
RBAC (role-based access control), 74, 79–80, 235
redundancy, 117, 235
registered ports, 93
regulations, 194–195
   cybersecurity, 30
   risk, 24
remote access VPN, 122, 235
replication, 190–191
reputation, 24
residual risk, 28
review, risk management, 28
RFID (radio frequency identification), proximity card, 57
risk, 21, 235
   acceptance, 26
   assessment, 21–22, 24–26, 56, 185
   avoidance, 26
   business, 24

   calculating, 19
   definition, 18–19
   fraud, 24
   identification, 23–24, 235
   malicious insider, 24
   management, 18, 235
      review process, 28
      risk assessment, 24–26
      risk identification, 23–24
      risk treatment, 26–28
      scope, 21–22
   matrix, 19–20, 24–25, 26, 27
   priority, 20, 235
   rating, 20–21, 25
   reduction/mitigation, 25
   regulation, 24
   remediation, 20
   reputation, 24
   residual, 28
   tolerance, 25, 235
   transference, 25
   treatment, 235
Risk Management Framework for Information Systems and Organizations (NIST SP 800–37, Revision 2),18–19, 22
router, 104, 235
RPO (recovery point objective), 189, 234
RSA (Rivest-Shamir-Adelman) key exchange, 144
RTO (recovery time objective), 189, 234
rules, firewall, 47

S

SaaS (software as a service), 131–132, 236
scanning, 48, 235
SCAP (Security Content Automation Protocol), 163
scope, risk management, 21–22
SDLC (Synchronous Data Link Control Protocol), 103–104

security. *See also* access control; attack/s;
    authentication; control/s;
    encryption
  awareness training, 170, 236
  breach, 38
  clearance, 58, 77
  controls, 18, 28–29
  data, 143
  DiD (defense-in-depth), 119–120,
    199–200
  guard, 63, 65, 236
  logical
    need to know, 74
    POLP (principle of least privilege),
      74–75
    SOD (segregation of duties), 75–76
  metric, 133
  models, 76
  network infrastructure
    environmental controls, 115–116
    fire suppression systems, 116–117
    microsegmentation, 118–119
    redundancy and high
      availability, 117
  password, 134
  physical, 56. *See also* physical security
    controls
    access control, 62
    badge systems, 56–59
    environmental design, 62–63
    gates, 59–61
    monitoring. *See* monitoring, physical
      security
  policy, 120
  POLP (principle of least privilege), 58
  threat/s, 19. *See also* threat/s
    advanced persistent, 43
    definition, 38
    malware, 39
    to an organization, 23
  vulnerability, 19, 165

Security and Privacy Controls for
    Information Systems and
    Organizations (NIST SP
    800–53),28–29, 145
  segmentation
    micro, 120–121
    network, 118–119, 121
  sensor, XDR, 45
  server room, access, 29
  service
    infrastructure as a, 130
    platform as a, 130–131
    software as a, 131–132
  session layer, 96, 236
  side-channel attack, 44, 236
  SIEM (security incident and event
    management), 48, 166
  signature-based antivirus, 44
  site-to-site VPN, 123, 236
  SLA (service-level agreement), 8,
    132–133
  smart card, 58, 236
  SOAR (security orchestration,
    automation, and remediation), 81
  SOC (security operations center), 133,
    167, 181
  social engineering, 170–171, 236
  SOD (segregation of duties), 75–76, 236
    dynamic, 80
    static, 80
  software
    antivirus, 20
    Gold Disk, 163
    as a service, 131–132
  SOP (standard operating procedure), 65
  spear phishing, 40
  SPOE (single point of entry), 59, 63
  sprinkler systems, 116
  SSO (single sign-on), 81
  standards, 104–105, 193, 236
  stateful packet filtering firewall, 47

stateless packet filtering firewall, 47
static separation of duties, 80
Stuxnet, 40
subject, 76
surveillance, natural, 62
switch, 90
symmetric encryption, 144, 237
SYN flood, 43, 236
system, 21–22
  hardening, 162, 236
    baselines, 162–163
    logging and monitoring, 166–167
    patch management, 164–165
    system updates and upgrades,
      165–166
    vulnerability management, 165
  risk assessment, 19–22

T

tabletop test, 183–184
tailgating, 59
tape backup, 188
TCP (Transmission Control Protocol),
  85, 97
TCP/IP model, 85, 106–107, 237
team, incident response, 180
technical controls, 29
technological obsolescence, 23
territorial reinforcement, 62
test/ing
  backups, 188
  business continuity plan, 185
  failover, 191
  penetration, 48, 233
  tabletop, 183–184
threat/s, 19, 237
  advanced persistent, 43
  definition, 38
  intelligence, 38–39
  malware, 39. *See also* malware
    ransomware, 41–42
    Trojan, 41

  virus, 39–40
    worm, 40
  to an organization, 23
time-sharing system, 125
tools
  logging and monitoring, 166–167
  SIEM (security incident and event
    management), 48
trailer, 237
training, 206
  security awareness, 170
  security guard, 63
transport layer, 97, 237
tree model, 80
Trojan, 41, 237
turnstiles, 59–60, 237

U

UDP (User Datagram Protocol), 97, 237
UDP flood, 44
updates, 45
  ISC_2 CC exam, 223–224
  professional profile, 205
  system, 165–166
upgrades, system, 165–166
UPS (uninterruptible power supply), 115
uptime, 132

V

vendor
  patching, 45, 164–165
  SLA (service-level agreement), 132–133
Vienna virus, 44
virus, 39–40, 44, 237
VLAN (virtual local area network),
  121–122, 237
VMS (video management system), 64
VPN (virtual private network), 120,
  122–123, 231, 237
vulnerability/ies, 19, 24–25, 238
  management, 165
  scan, 48, 165

W

WAF (web application firewall), 47, 238
WAN (wide-area network), 91–92, 238
WannaCry, 41, 165
WAP (wireless access point), 90
warm site, 190
well-known ports, 93
WEP (Wired Equivalent Privacy), 105
wet and dry chemical fire suppression
    systems, 116
Wi-Fi, 104, 238. *See also* network/s,
    wireless
wiping, 152
wireless network
  AP (access point), 104

bands, 104
encryption, 105
standards, 104–105
WEP (Wired Equivalent Privacy), 105
WLAN (wireless local-area network),
    91, 238
WNIC (wireless network interface
    card), 238
worm, 40, 238

X-Y-Z

XDR (extended detection and response), 45

zero-trust, 77
Zeus, 41